The Politics of Place and the Limits to Redistribution

Rogers joins a growing group of scholars applying the lens of political geography to the study of inequality and fiscal redistribution. In this book, she offers a new set of mechanisms connecting political institutions to redistribution levels, demonstrating through multiple channels the costs of territorially focused political institutions for income inequality.

Bonnie M. Meguid, *University of Rochester, USA*

This book makes an important contribution to better understanding one of the most important social problems. By highlighting the relevance of political geography, it offers a fresh explanation for how and why institutions shape the representation of the poor and the politics of inequality.

Margit Tavits, *Washington University in St. Louis, USA*

Numerous scholars have noticed that certain political institutions, including federalism, majoritarian electoral systems, and presidentialism, are linked to lower levels of income redistribution. This book offers a political geography explanation for those observed patterns. Each of these institutions is strongly shaped by geography and provides incentives for politicians to target their appeals and government resources to localities. Territorialized institutions also shape citizens' preferences in ways that can undermine the national coalition in favor of redistribution. Moreover, territorial institutions increase the number of veto points in which anti-redistributive actors can constrain reform efforts. These theoretical connections between the politics of place and redistributive outcomes are explored in theory, empirical analysis, and case studies of Argentina, Germany, and the USA.

Melissa Ziegler Rogers is Assistant Professor of Political Science at Claremont Graduate University. She specialises in comparative political institutions, political economy, political geography, and Latin American politics.

Routledge advances in international relations and global politics

1 **Foreign Policy and Discourse Analysis**
France, Britain and Europe
Henrik Larsen

2 **Agency, Structure and International Politics**
From ontology to empirical enquiry
Gil Friedman and Harvey Starr

3 **The Political Economy of Regional Co-operation in the Middle East**
Ali Carkoglu, Mine Eder, and Kemal Kirisci

4 **Peace Maintenance**
The evolution of international political authority
Jarat Chopra

5 **International Relations and Historical Sociology**
Breaking down boundaries
Stephen Hobden

6 **Equivalence in Comparative Politics**
Edited by Jan W. van Deth

7 **The Politics of Central Banks**
Robert Elgie and Helen Thompson

8 **Politics and Globalisation**
Knowledge, ethics and agency
Martin Shaw

9 **History and International Relations**
Thomas W. Smith

10 **Idealism and Realism in International Relations**
Robert M. A. Crawford

11 **National and International Conflicts, 1945–1995**
New empirical and theoretical approaches
Frank Pfetsch and Christoph Rohloff

12 **Party Systems and Voter Alignments Revisited**
Edited by Lauri Karvonen and Stein Kuhnle

13 **Ethics, Justice & International Relations**
Constructing an international community
Peter Sutch

14 **Capturing Globalization**
Edited by James H. Mittelman and Norani Othman

15 **Uncertain Europe**
Building a new European security order?
Edited by Martin A. Smith and Graham Timmins

16 **Power, Postcolonialism and International Relations**
Reading race, gender and class
Edited by Geeta Chowdhry and Sheila Nair

17 **Constituting Human Rights**
Global civil society and the society of democratic states
Mervyn Frost

18 **US Economic Statecraft for Survival 1933–1991**
Of sanctions, embargoes and economic warfare
Alan P. Dobson

19 **The EU and NATO Enlargement**
Richard McAllister and Roland Dannreuther

20 **Spatializing International Politics**
Analysing activism on the internet
Jayne Rodgers

21 **Ethnonationalism in the Contemporary World**
Walker Connor and the study of Nationalism
Edited by Daniele Conversi

22 **Meaning and International Relations**
Edited by Peter Mandaville and Andrew Williams

23 **Political Loyalty and the Nation-State**
Edited by Michael Waller and Andrew Linklater

24 **Russian Foreign Policy and the CIS**
Theories, debates and actions
Nicole J. Jackson

25 **Asia and Europe**
Development and different dimensions of ASEM
Yeo Lay Hwee

26 **Global Instability and Strategic Crisis**
Neville Brown

27 **Africa in International Politics**
External involvement on the continent
Edited by Ian Taylor and Paul Williams

28 **Global Governmentality**
Governing international spaces
Edited by Wendy Larner and William Walters

29 **Political Learning and Citizenship Education Under Conflict**
The political socialization of Israeli and Palestinian youngsters
Orit Ichilov

30 **Gender and Civil Society**
Transcending boundaries
Edited by Jude Howell and Diane Mulligan

31 **State Crises, Globalisation and National Movements in North-East Africa**
The horn's dilemma
Edited by Asafa Jalata

32 **Diplomacy and Developing Nations**
Post-cold war foreign policy-making structures and processes
Edited by Justin Robertson and Maurice A. East

33 **Autonomy, Self-governance and Conflict Resolution**
Innovative approaches to institutional design in divided societies
Edited by Marc Weller and Stefan Wolff

34 **Mediating International Crises**
Jonathan Wilkenfeld, Kathleen J. Young, David M. Quinn and Victor Asal

35 **Postcolonial Politics, the Internet and Everyday Life: Pacific Traversals Online**
M. I. Franklin

36 **Reconstituting the Global Liberal Order**
Legitimacy and regulation
Kanishka Jayasuriya

37 **International Relations, Security and Jeremy Bentham**
Gunhild Hoogensen

38 **Interregionalism and International Relations**
Edited by Heiner Hänggi, Ralf Roloff and Jürgen Rüland

39 **The International Criminal Court**
A global civil society achievement
Marlies Glasius

40 **A Human Security Doctrine for Europe**
Project, principles, practicalities
Edited by Marlies Glasius and Mary Kaldor

41 **The History and Politics of UN Security Council Reform**
Dimitris Bourantonis

42 **Russia and NATO Since 1991**
From cold war through cold peace to partnership?
Martin A. Smith

43 **The Politics of Protection**
Sites of insecurity and political agency
Edited by Jef Huysmans, Andrew Dobson and Raia Prokhovnik

44 **International Relations in Europe**
Traditions, perspectives and destinations
Edited by Knud Erik Jørgensen and Tonny Brems Knudsen

45 **The Empire of Security and the Safety of the People**
Edited by William Bain

46 **Globalization and Religious Nationalism in India**
The search for ontological security
Catrina Kinnvall

47 **Culture and International Relations**
Narratives, natives and tourists
Julie Reeves

48 **Global Civil Society**
Contested futures
Edited by Gideon Baker and David Chandler

49 **Rethinking Ethical Foreign Policy**
Pitfalls, possibilities and paradoxes
Edited by David Chandler and Volker Heins

50 **International Cooperation and Arctic Governance**
Regime effectiveness and northern region building
Edited by Olav Schram Stokke and Geir Hønneland

51 **Human Security**
Concepts and implications
Shahrbanou Tadjbakhsh and Anuradha Chenoy

52 **International Relations and Security in the Digital Age**
Edited by Johan Eriksson and Giampiero Giacomello

53 **State-Building**
Theory and practice
Edited by Aidan Hehir and Neil Robinson

54 **Violence and Non-Violence in Africa**
Edited by Pal Ahluwalia, Louise Bethlehem and Ruth Ginio

55 **Developing Countries and Global Trade Negotiations**
Edited by Larry Crump and S. Javed Maswood

56 **Civil Society, Religion and Global Governance**
Paradigms of power and persuasion
Edited by Helen James

57 **War, Peace and Hegemony in a Globalized World**
The changing balance of power in the 21st Century
Edited by Chandra Chari

58 **Economic Globalisation as Religious War**
Tragic convergence
Michael McKinley

59 **Globalization, Prostitution and Sex-trafficking**
Corporeal politics
Elina Penttinen

60 **Peacebuilding**
Women in international perspective
Elisabeth Porter

61 **Ethics, Liberalism and Realism in International Relations**
Mark D. Gismondi

62 **Law and Legalization in Transnational Relations**
Edited by Christian Brütsch and Dirk Lehmkuhl

63 **Fighting Terrorism and Drugs**
Europe and international police cooperation
Jörg Friedrichs

64 **Identity Politics in the Age of Genocide**
The Holocaust and historical representation
David B. MacDonald

65 **Globalisation, Public Opinion and the State**
Western Europe and East and Southeast Asia
Edited by Takashi Inoguchi and Ian Marsh

66 **Urbicide**
The politics of urban destruction
Martin Coward

67 **Transnational Activism in the UN and the EU**
A comparative study
Jutta Joachim and Birgit Locher

68 **Gender Inclusive**
Essays on violence, men and feminist international relations
Adam Jones

69 **Capitalism, Democracy and the Prevention of War and Poverty**
Edited by Peter Graeff and Guido Mehlkop

70 **Environmental Change and Foreign Policy**
Theory and practice
Edited by Paul G. Harris

71 **Climate Change and Foreign Policy**
Case studies from East to West
Edited by Paul G. Harris

72 **Securitizations of Citizenship**
Edited by Peter Nyers

73 **The Power of Ideology**
From the Roman Empire to Al-Qaeda
Alex Roberto Hybel

74 **The Securitization of Humanitarian Migration**
Digging moats and sinking boats
Scott D. Watson

75 **Mediation in the Asia-Pacific Region**
Transforming conflicts and building peace
Edited by Dale Bagshaw and Elisabeth Porter

76 **United Nations Reform**
Heading North or South?
Spencer Zifcak

77 **New Norms and Knowledge in World Politics**
Protecting people, intellectual property and the environment
Preslava Stoeva

78 **Power, Resistance and Conflict in the Contemporary World**
Social movements, networks and hierarchies
Athina Karatzogianni and Andrew Robinson

79 **World-Regional Social Policy and Global Governance**
New research and policy agendas in Africa, Asia, Europe and Latin America
Edited by Bob Deacon, Maria Cristina Macovei, Luk Van Langenhove and Nicola Yeates

80 **International Relations Theory and Philosophy**
Interpretive dialogues
Edited by Cerwyn Moore and Chris Farrands

81 **Superpower Rivalry and Conflict**
The long shadow of the Cold War on the Twenty-first Century
Edited by Chandra Chari

82 **Coping and Conformity in World Politics**
Hugh C. Dyer

83 **Defining and Defying Organized Crime**
Discourse, perception and reality
Edited by Felia Allum, Francesca Longo, Daniela Irrera and Panos A. Kostakos

84 **Federalism in Asia**
India, Pakistan and Malaysia
Harihar Bhattacharyya

85 **The World Bank and HIV/AIDS**
Setting a global agenda
Sophie Harman

86 **The "War on Terror" and the Growth of Executive Power?**
A comparative analysis
Edited by John E. Owens and Riccardo Pelizzo

87 **The Contested Politics of Mobility**
Borderzones and irregularity
Edited by Vicki Squires

88 **Human Security, Law and the Prevention of Terrorism**
Andrej Zwitter

89 **Multilayered Migration Governance**
The promise of partnership
Edited by Rahel Kunz, Sandra Lavenex and Marion Panizzon

90 **Role Theory in International Relations**
Approaches and analyses
Edited by Sebastian Harnisch, Cornelia Frank and Hanns W. Maull

91 **Issue Salience in International Relations**
Edited by Kai Oppermann and Henrike Viehrig

92 **Corporate Risk and National Security Redefined**
Karen Lund Petersen

93 **Interrogating Democracy in World Politics**
Edited by Joe Hoover, Meera Sabaratnam and Laust Schouenborg

94 **Globalizing Resistance against War**
Theories of resistance and the new Anti-War Movement
Tiina Seppälä

95 **The Politics of Self-Determination**
Beyond the decolonisation process
Kristina Roepstorff

96 **Sovereignty and the Responsibility to Protect**
The power of norms and the norms of the powerful
Theresa Reinold

97 **Anglo-American Relations**
Contemporary perspectives
Edited by Alan P. Dobson and Steve Marsh

98 **The Emerging Politics of Antarctica**
Edited by Anne-Marie Brady

99 **Genocide, Ethnonationalism, and the United Nations**
Exploring the causes of mass killing since 1945
Hannibal Travis

100 **Caribbean Sovereignty, Development and Democracy in an Age of Globalization**
Edited by Linden Lewis

101 **Rethinking Foreign Policy**
Edited by Fredrik Bynander and Stefano Guzzini

102 **The Promise and Perils of Transnationalization**
NGO activism and the socialization of women's human rights in Egypt and Iran
Benjamin Stachursky

103 **Peacebuilding and International Administration**
The cases of Bosnia and Herzegovina and Kosovo
Niels van Willigen

104 **The Politics of the Globalization of Law**
Getting from rights to justice
Edited by Alison Brysk

105 **The Arctic in International Politics**
Coming in from the cold
Peter Hough

106 **Understanding Transatlantic Relations**
Whither the West?
Serena Simoni

107 **India in South Asia**
Domestic identity politics and foreign policy from Nehru to the BJP
Sinderpal Singh

108 **A Strategic Understanding of UN Economic Sanctions**
International relations, law and development
Golnoosh Hakimdavar

109 **Politics and the Bomb**
The role of experts in the creation of cooperative Nuclear Non-Proliferation Agreements
Sara Z. Kutchesfahani

110 **Interpreting Global Security**
Mark Bevir, Oliver Daddow and Ian Hall

111 **Foreign Policy, Domestic Politics and International Relations**
The case of Italy
Elisabetta Brighi

112 **The Scourge of Genocide**
Essays and reflections
Adam Jones

113 **Authority, Ascendancy, and Supremacy**
China, Russia, and the United States' pursuit of relevancy and power
Gregory O. Hall

114 **The Politics of Arctic Sovereignty**
Oil, ice and Inuit governance
Jessica M. Shadian

115 **Small States and International Security**
Europe and beyond
Edited by Clive Archer, Alyson J. K. Bailes and Anders Wivel

116 **Networked Governance and Transatlantic Relations**
Building bridges through science diplomacy
Gabriella Paár-Jákli

117 **The Role, Position and Agency of Cusp States in International Relations**
Edited by Marc Herzog and Philip Robins

118 **The Politics of Conflict Economies**
Miners, merchants and warriors in the African borderland
Morten Bøås

119 **Exercising Human Rights**
Gender, agency, and practice
Robin Redhead

120 **State Responses to International Law**
Who complies?
Kendall Stiles

121 **Regional Integration and Democratic Conditionality**
How democracy clauses help democratic consolidation and deepening
Gaspare M. Genna and Taeko Hiroi

122 **Profits, Security and Human Rights in Developing Countries**
Global lessons from Canada's extractive sector in Colombia
Edited by James Rochlin

123 **The Politics of Place and the Limits to Redistribution**
Melissa Ziegler Rogers

The Politics of Place and the Limits to Redistribution

Melissa Ziegler Rogers

Routledge
Taylor & Francis Group
NEW YORK AND LONDON

First published 2016
by Routledge
605 Third Avenue, New York, NY 10017

and by Routledge
2 Park Square, Milton Park, Abingdon, Oxon OX14 4RN

First issued in paperback 2021

Routledge is an imprint of the Taylor & Francis Group, an informa business

Publisher's Note
The publisher has gone to great lengths to ensure the quality of this reprint but points out that some imperfections in the original copies may be apparent.

Library of Congress Cataloging in Publication Data
Rogers, Melissa Ziegler.
The politics of place and the limits to redistribution / Melissa Ziegler Rogers.
pages cm. – (Routledge advances in international relations and global politics ; 123)
Includes bibliographical references and index.
1. Distribution (Economic theory)–Political aspects. 2. Income distribution–Political aspects. 3. Distributive justice. 4. Democracy–Economic aspects. 5. Representative government and representation. I. Title.
HC79.I5R647 2015
330.1–dc23 2015017713

ISBN 13: 978-1-03-224266-8 (pbk)
ISBN 13: 978-0-415-82432-3 (hbk)

DOI: 10.4324/9780203545294

Typeset in Times New Roman
by Wearset Ltd, Boldon, Tyne and Wear

Contents

Figures

Tables

Acknowledgments

Thank you to Lisa Piergallini, Dong-wook Lee, and Alma Bezares-Calderon for wonderful research assistance throughout the project. I am grateful for funding from the Fletcher Jones Foundation at Claremont Graduate University for support for the data collection.

1 Territorial Institutions, Inequality, and Redistribution

Introduction and Overview

If Harold Lasswell's (1950) definition of politics—who gets what, when and how—is correct, then inequality and distribution are central concerns of political science. This book uses the lens of political institutions to evaluate the role of income inequality in national politics. The central question of the book is: how do political institutions structure government responses to inequality? My answer is that political institutions influence what notions of inequality (interpersonal or interregional) are salient in the political system through the electoral incentives they provide to politicians. These incentives shape how political parties address inequality and whether national constituencies interested in redistribution are able to organize effectively to pass legislation against opposition.

Political institutions have long had a place in explanations of redistributive policy outcomes around the world. These works have demonstrated variance across political institutions on whether the majority of poor individuals are able to use their numerical advantage to advance redistribution. In this book, I consider whether the region, in addition to the individual, is an appropriate unit for evaluating political interests and constituencies. My primary contribution is the inclusion of political geography in both the theory and measurement of distributive pressures, institutional effects, and distributive policy outcomes in national politics. To add to Lasswell's quote, I examine who gets what, when, how, and *where*.

Previous research has shown that certain institutions (especially federalism, majoritarian elections and presidentialism) appear to work against fiscal redistribution and other proactive government responses to income inequality. Among the variety of reasons this may be is that each of these institutions privileges geographic regions in the political distributive game. Three primary mechanisms that link region-centered institutions to lower levels of redistribution are central to my analysis. First, geographically designed political constituencies incentivize politicians to deliver local public goods above social goods targeted to low income individuals. Second, political institutions structured around geography tend to separate power and protect minority interests. Institutions that divide power have the effect of fragmenting the majority and empowering minorities, especially rich individuals and rich regions opposed to redistribution. Third, the two previous mechanisms, regional constituencies and separation of power, contribute to decentralizing and fragmenting party cohesion and organization.

As parties coalesce across regions and pull together heterogeneous coalitions, majority preferences for fiscal distribution become diluted. Each mechanism will be addressed for the three institutions that structure the following chapters.

The premise of the book is that the politics of inequality is a distributive game not just between individuals and social classes but also across and within geographic districts (Beramendi 2007). Institutions of government influence the extent to which national or local interests are paramount to politicians and constituents, based on reelection incentives, party discipline, and fiscal and administrative structures. The relevance of the different forms of inequality to government distribution depends on how politicians are elected and how constituents view quality representation. For politicians in geographically oriented systems, distribution across and within districts may be critical. In countries with a national orientation in which social groups dominate representation, politicians will likely be attentive to distributive claims made by individuals and their social constituencies. This straightforward observation has important consequences for how distributive conflict is waged within a nation, and how inequality is addressed by the governing system through redistribution.

The central theoretical point of the book is that political institutions shape political expression and policies to affect income inequality through their effects on representation. In particular, institutions structure the nature and political power of constituencies and construct identities for political purposes. In strongly territorial systems, therefore, individuals may think of themselves not only as belonging to a particular economic class, race, ethnicity, religion, or linguistic group, but also as a resident of a specific place. Localized identities and geographic distributions of political goods increase the relevance of spatial distributive conflict. Furthermore, political institutions layered upon these constituencies influence the activation of territorial representation. Centralizing, "demos enabling" institutions such as parliamentarism, closed-list proportional representation (PR), and unitary government dilute territorial effects (Stepan 2004). Under these circumstances, distributive conflict will exist primarily among national (non-territorial) groups.

This approach takes a step back from the conceptualization of inequality predominant in all fields of social science—that of the individual-level income distribution, typically aggregated to one national level value. In this view of inequality, hereafter labeled interpersonal inequality, what is most important is how income is distributed across all individuals in the nation. I also address an alternate concept of inequality based on the spatial distribution of income whereby income is aggregated into politically relevant units, such as voting or administrative districts, called interregional inequality. This notion of inequality should be relevant in political systems with strong geographic features, such as territorial constituency structures, localized electoral systems (and party systems), and federalism. Throughout the book, I consider which type of inequality (or both or neither) may be most important in the minds of politicians evaluating policy choices in the national arena.

This book takes seriously the variation in representation and institutions that structure the contestation to determine government redistribution. My ultimate goal is to contribute to our understanding of how inequality interacts with representative structures to influence political outcomes, in particular fiscal redistribution. Accordingly, the theoretical development of the book and considerations of measurement of inequality will be structured to evaluate differences in distributive outcomes across and within nations.

Why is Inequality Important?

Inequality is a primary concern of the social sciences, including political science, economics, sociology, psychology, anthropology and history. Again, if politics is about distribution, as Lasswell claims, then inequality structures politics in all nations. Inequality is a natural by-product of capitalism, but governments play a central role in addressing the extent of inequality within nations (Lindert 2004). Inequality is known to increase conflict in society as the poor look to expropriate from the rich and the rich seek to retain their wealth (Acemoglu and Robinson 2006; Boix 2003). Moreover, inequality is the central organizing cleavage around which democratic politics and party systems are structured, through the left–right dimension (Bobbio 1996). The role of inequality in political structures and political outcomes is critical to understanding the origins, functioning, and fate of democracy.

The primary focus of this book is the effects of political institutions on government responses to income inequality. The relationship between inequality and government policies is never simple or direct, but is always filtered through the institutional structures of a nation. The level of inequality influences the extent of conflict over government size and distribution. Both inequality and political institutions influence the preferences of voters, the behavior of politicians, and the tools and resources of constituencies and accordingly political parties. Inequality, therefore, is central to the crux of democratic politics: government accountability and representation.

The concern with inequality has its origins in political theory, political behavior, and political economy. Income is known to structure preferences for government allocation and redistribution (Romer 1975; Melter and Richard 1981). From a political behavior perspective, inequality can affect voters' resources to press for quality representation and hold politicians accountable for policy choices. Income and wealth affect the likelihood of voters showing up at the polls, the time and attention that can be devoted to political activities, and the conditions to engage in collective action (Rosenstone and Hansen 2002; Benabou 2000). Importantly, the political economy of inequality perspective also stresses the relevance of non-voting resources to modern politics, especially campaign finance, that might weight political outcomes toward the interests of the rich (Bartels 2009b). Moreover, the undeniably strong role of economic factors in politicians' fates gives business interests, primarily advocated by the well-off, a sway in politics that outweighs their smaller voting numbers (Lindblom 1982).

The scholarly interest in inequality concerns both its effects and its origins (Boix 2010). Inequality not only influences government policy, but government policy also drives changes in the distribution of wealth within and across nations.

Inequality can only be reasonably examined as being subject to a feedback mechanism whereby inequality influences both the input and output of government policy.

Given the centrality of political institutions to my account of the effects of inequality on government outputs, I address not only the feedback of government policy on inequality, but also the endogeneity of political institutions. For example, class conflict influenced the design of electoral institutions in Western Europe (Boix 1999; Iversen et al. 2006; Lipset and Rokkan 1967). That is, the choice of electoral rules and constitutional structures may depend on the nature of income inequality in a nation and on the conflict and common interests among relatively rich and poor groups. Interregional and intraregional inequality were also likely motivators for the design of federal representative and fiscal structures (Beramendi and Wibbels 2010; Beramendi et al. 2015b). If institutions are designed with regional economies in mind, it is important to understand what this means for national politics. This idea is addressed in each subsequent chapter and in a substantial portion of the conclusion chapter.

Types and Measurement of Inequality

In most political science and economics research, inequality has been examined using one particular lens. The overwhelmingly predominant concept of inequality has been the distribution of income among individuals or households in a nation. More specifically, inequality has been measured as the distribution across income deciles. With these indicators, higher inequality represents a greater concentration of income in the richest 10 percent (or 1 percent or 0.1 percent) (Stiglitz 2012; Piketty and Saez 2006). Such measures assume ontological individualism and thus suggest that the most appropriate unit of analysis in politics is one person or household. All of the most common indicators of inequality, including the Gini coefficient and other income ratios, are based on an interpersonal concept of income inequality.[1]

Interpersonal inequality measures are also most often aggregated to the level of the nation. This aggregation has a methodological and theoretical origin. Methodologically, scholars use it to capture inequality within the entire nation in cross-national regressions or time series analyses. Theoretically, this aggregation matches a national referendum, as exemplified by Romer's (1975) and Meltzer and Richard's (1981) seminal model of distributive politics in a progressive tax system (hereafter the RMR model). They argue that increased inequality will lower the wage of the decisive median voter (relative to the mean), who will press for more redistribution.

Yet, political institutions almost never resemble a referendum (Milanovic 2000). All political systems have some deviation from purely national constituencies and all have some degree of separation of powers. These divisions of power attenuate the role of the national median voter and of national majority coalitions. By allocating representation on the basis of geographic jurisdictions, for example, *regional* medians compete for political influence and must coordinate across districts to persuade voters and influence policy outcomes (Kang and Powell Jr. 2010).[2] As policy authority is distributed across institutions—such as legislatures, presidents, sub-national governments, supra-national governments, and courts—distinct medians emerge from these different constituencies. The aggregation of interests in a nation is accordingly affected, and its precise character will differ depending on institutional arrangements. RMR also cannot account for the fact that increased inequality not only heightens demand for redistribution but also the incentives to constrain it (Aysan 2005). Because redistribution favors one income group (the poor) against another, wealthy constituents have strong incentives to block such initiatives, and they may have the tools to do so under certain institutional conditions.

Where representation is geographically partitioned, the interests of localities become relevant to politicians and constituents alike. Politicians evaluate voters in terms of the likelihood of gaining their support in elections (Bueno de Mesquita et al. 2003). In districted politics, a politician's universe of voters is geographically bound as well as shaped by ideological and socio-demographic factors. Politicians cannot win elections by appealing to voters outside of their districts. Accordingly, they must target their appeals to that geographic zone, which may differ in important ways from the nation as a whole. This limits politicians' incentives to deliver policies to a national median.

Constituents, for their part, evaluate the performance of politicians as acting for or against their interests. One important way constituents evaluate the promotion of interests is in local terms, i.e., as to whether politicians effectively represent the people and economy of their home. This geographic frame is particularly apparent where one politician is the sole delegate of a single district. The theoretical justification for conceptualizing politics according to the politically decisive national median is attenuated in such a setting.

Empirical measures of inequality aggregated to the national level can also be called into question where politics is divided across districts or institutions. The distribution of incomes at the top 10 and bottom 90 percent of the entire nation may not represent the distributive pressures present in the political system unless those same inequalities are relatively consistent across constituencies. On the contrary, every nation has varied population patterns, which are influenced by the economic structure, cost of living, and job opportunities that are directly related to the wealth and income distribution of the various regions that comprise that nation (Beramendi 2012). This demographic and economic diversity shapes political preferences across jurisdictions, and this renders a simple aggregation of national income a very rough measure of the likely political effects of inequality.

Theoretical and empirical models using nationally aggregated income inequality have not succeeded in explaining redistributive policy in comparative politics (Lupu and Pontusson 2011; Korpi and Palme 1998; Alesina and Glaeser 2004). One important reason for this may be the lack of attention given to territorial political representation in theory and measurement. Whether redistributive policy is likely to be enacted depends on the effectiveness of the political voice of groups that would benefit from these policies and the on the tools available for opponents to block reform. Accordingly, we must be able to identify how and whether groups at different income levels are represented in the political system by measuring inequality with an eye toward political representation. Specifically, this entails knowing how inequality is spread (across individuals and districts), and how that distribution corresponds to voting constituencies and their representation within political institutions.

Puzzles in the Literature

Comparative politics research over the last 30 years has thoroughly critiqued the RMR model based on its stark assumptions about the nature of representation, the complexity of political decision-making, and the preferences of voters. Specifically, representation is not an automated process whereby all citizens vote in their short-term economic interests. Voting rates are strongly correlated with income, meaning that poor citizens vote less than rich ones. Voters do not express preferences in a single referendum process, but are typically separated into voting districts, and always organized by political parties that aggregate a range of preferences along multiple dimensions (Roemer 1998). Political institutions include multiple veto points whereby those opposed to redistribution may weaken or block legislation (Bartels 2009a; Hacker and Pierson 2010). Moreover, voters may not have predictable distributive preferences; the rich may be more amenable to redistribution and the poor less favorable than often assumed (Ansell and Samuels 2010; Haggard et al. 2013; Dion and Birchfield 2010). In short, despite its intuitive logic, many scholars have dismissed the RMR model as not only too minimal to represent reality, but also misleading in its predictions about political processes.

This research on the politics of inequality has fundamentally transformed our understanding of the representative process, political coalitions, and political economy. However, this literature too has largely ignored an important strand of institutional research focused on the local nature of representation and the politics of the personal vote (Cain et al. 1987; Carey and Shugart 1995). That politicians and voters alike may think of representation in territorial terms has been seen as a mostly orthogonal issue to the politics of inequality. Accordingly, differences in interregional distribution of income have rarely been addressed in this body of research (Beramendi 2007, 2012).

Failure to examine the politics of place in the politics of inequality has contributed to several continuing challenges, both theoretical and empirical. First, the unit of representation, and the construct of identity more generally, have focused almost exclusively on individuals and social groups. While this may be the most important facet of identity for many voters in many political systems, it is not the only basis for identity for many or most voters. Where territorial politics is important, place becomes a relevant part of "compounded identity" in addition to other socioeconomic features (Tuschhoff 1999). In short, voters may evaluate politicians for what they do for their geographic community as well as what they do for their socio-cultural community and their nation. The place-based notion of identity may become increasingly salient as territorial inequalities diverge (Jeffery 1999).

Related to this, research on local politics coming in particular from the case of the USA, has recognized that different electoral structures motivate distinct patterns of distributive allocation. Specifically, those systems that encourage local politics tend to encourage geographically targeted public goods (also known as pork) and transfers to regions in their national budget (Weingast et al. 1981; Cain et al. 1987). Research on "centripetal" and nationalized political systems shows that they allocate more toward (ostensibly redistributive) social spending (see Gerring et al. 2005; Iversen and Soskice 2006).[3] It stands to reason that in a zero-sum budget process, those systems that predominantly encourage the distribution of pork will skimp on social spending. Thus "nationalized" political systems will appear more redistributive.

It is certainly possible and plausible that nationalized systems are more redistributive. Political institutions that encourage nationalized politics are regularly shown to be associated with higher levels of redistribution (Bradley et al. 2003). The theoretical justification for this has almost always been coalitional—where politics are nationalized, the low-income coalition in favor of redistribution faces fewer barriers to national policy reform (Rodden 2009; Pierson 1995). In localized systems, the preferences of constituencies and their organizational strategies diverge, leaving the national collective welfare system underprovided. This is a critical part of their story and my story, but it does not address the nature of distribution in localized systems, and fails to consider that locally targeted goods might also be redistributive. Education spending, for example, is often a geographically targeted public good that is left out of social spending calculations, but may in fact be highly redistributive. For instance, Huber and Stephens (2012) attribute recent reductions in inequality in Latin America to education spending, not increased social spending. Rural electrification, a geographically targeted good, is another example of a potentially redistributive spending category that would not be captured by social spending within the national budget. Social spending may be strongly correlated with fiscal redistribution, but may also be a particularly Western European mode of redistribution, reflecting a certain level of development and political history.

Focus on individuals and social groups, and on social spending, has also structured the empirics of the study of the political economy of inequality. Despite common rejection of the representative structure of the RMR model, most scholars nonetheless use measures of inequality that are based on it. When employing a nationally aggregated measure of inequality, including most popularly the Gini coefficient, but also including income ratios and similar calculations, all assume that politics can be approximated as purely national in scope or that voting districts are perfect replicas of the nation. Neither assumption is true in any nation, and in many nations these assumptions obscure critical information about income patterns and voting preferences that are highly relevant to national politics (Beramendi et al. 2015a).

This work is intended to address some of these gaps in the literature on the politics of inequality and to bridge research that I believe is related but which remains largely disconnected from efforts to explain redistribution. An important literature recognizes the importance of interregional differences in wealth on government spending and policymaking at the national level (Alesina and Spolaore 2005; Beramendi 2007, 2012; Bolton and Roland 1997). The predominant research on inequality, for its part, shows that interpersonal inequality fuels distributive conflict and influences fiscal decisions of nations. I link these works to literature on public goods, given preference heterogeneity (Besley and Coate 2003; Cox and McCubbins 2001; Shugart 1999; Volden 2005), and electoral incentives (Carey and Shugart 1995).

Overview of the Argument: Inequality, Institutions and Fiscal Redistribution

Certain political institutions appear to limit the scope of redistribution to reduce income inequality. Specifically, those institutions that constrain the national majority from changing policy at the national level may stand in the way of substantial fiscal redistribution. Figure 1.1 is a plot of the relationship between constitutional constraints on majority power and fiscal redistribution in 2010. Constitutional constraints are measured with an additive index of institutions thought to limit the expression of a single national majority (including federalism, presidentialism, plurality electoral districts, independent judiciaries, and referendum processes) taken from Huber et al. (1993) and expanded by Schmidt (1996). Figure 1.1 shows a clear negative relationship between fiscal

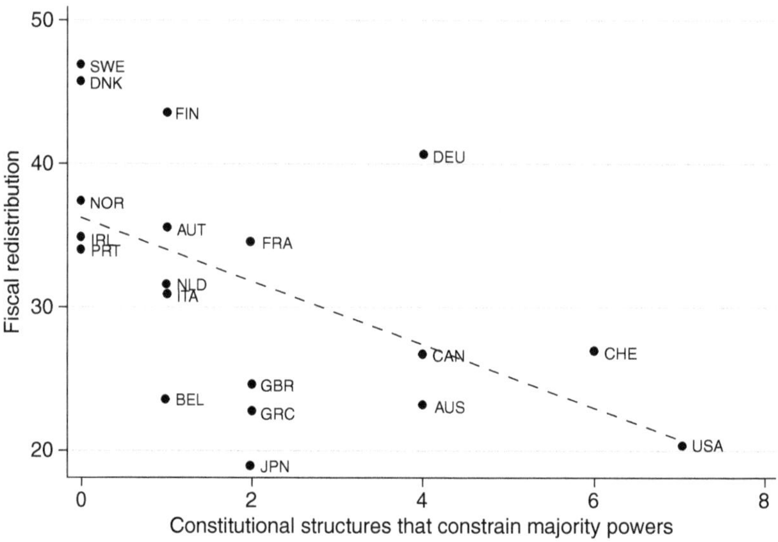

Figure 1.1 Redistribution and Constitutional Structures (sources: fiscal redistribution (Solt 2014); constitutional structures (Huber et al. 1993; Schmidt 1996)).

Note
Fiscal redistribution is measured by the percentage difference in the national Gini coefficient between inequality before and after government taxes and transfers. Constitutional structures that constrain majority power are measured as an additive index of federalism, parliamentary/presidential government, proportional representation/single member districts, bicameralism, and referendum.

redistribution and these constitutional features. As the majority is more constrained from enacting policy, governments are less engaged in equalizing income in these societies.

A bounty of research also addresses the relationship between income inequality and political outcomes, especially fiscal redistribution. As I have explained, these works almost always conceptualize and measure inequality at the individual level, aggregated to one national indicator. I focus additionally on the relationship between interregional inequality and fiscal redistribution. I define fiscal redistribution as the efforts made by the government through taxes and spending to equalize income. In Figure 1.2, I show a snapshot of the relationship between interregional inequality and fiscal redistribution in 2010. Fiscal redistribution is measured by the percentage reduction in the national Gini coefficient of individual income inequality that results from government policies (Solt 2014). The relationship is quite clearly negative; that is, countries with higher interregional inequality also tend to have lower fiscal redistribution. This statistical relationship is very strong, as I will discuss in detail in the next chapter. This book is an effort to link the empirical observations in Figures 1.1 and 1.2 to a theory of political representation.

Political institutions are central to debates on government responses to inequality (Pierson 1995). Certain governmental structures appear particularly conducive to advancing egalitarian policies, while others create roadblocks to redistribution. This book focuses on three institutions consistently associated

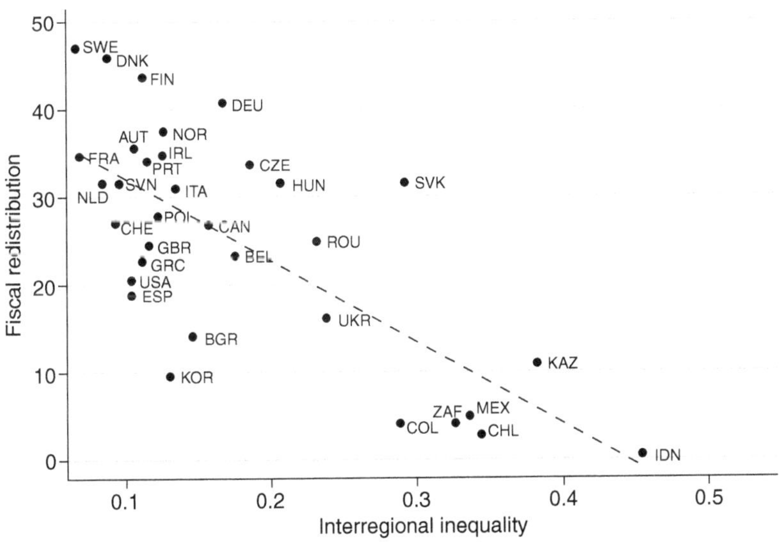

Figure 1.2 Redistribution and Regional Inequality (sources: fiscal redistribution (Solt 2014); interregional inequality (Rogers and Lee 2015)).

Note
Fiscal redistribution is measured by the percentage difference in the national Gini coefficient between inequality before and after government taxes and transfers. Interregional inequality is measured with the adjusted gini coefficient of regional GDP per capita.

with higher inequality and limited redistribution—federalism, majoritarian elections, and presidentialism—and why they contribute to these outcomes. In particular, I argue that each of these institutions reinforces representation of geographic regions by incentivizing politicians to deliver spatially targeted goods to constituents (the "pork" mechanism), by decentralizing and thus fragmenting coalitions in favor of redistribution (the legislative and electoral cohesion mechanism), and by providing blocking power to regions (the veto mechanism).

These institutions not only take focus away from interpersonal distribution, which weakens the power of low-income groups to coalesce in favor of egalitarian reforms, but they also raise the relevance of distribution between regions of low and high income and with different economic profiles. Accordingly, political systems that provide a voice for regions (or fail to dampen that voice) increase distributive concerns but may also erect structural barriers to national coordination for reform.

At the foundation, I argue that national policymaking is a bargaining process between politicians that represent different constituents. Political institutions determine who those constituents are, both in terms of how many there are and where they live. Geography structures electoral districts in nearly all polities, creating the basis for jurisdiction-based representation. Thus representation in all but a few nations is territorialized, but nations vary dramatically in the extent to which politics is oriented toward geographic districts or toward a national scope, and this difference is based on whether other political institutions reinforce or dilute the territorial cleavage. The three mechanisms that I argue reinforce this cleavage through electoral systems and constitutional structures are described below.

The "Pork" Mechanism

Reelection-seeking politicians try to please constituents to win votes (Mayhew 1974). Constituents may be targeted in three broad and overlapping ways—through programmatic policy, pork, and clientelism (Kitschelt 2000). Politicians only deliver these goods to a subset of the population, i.e., their likely or possible voters (Persson and Tabellini 1999). Their subset of voters and how they target them will depend on the nature of the electoral district, ideological positions, and socio-demographic characteristics.

When politicians represent territorial districts, politicians and their constituents tend to favor territorial allocation of government distribution (Milesi-Ferretti et al. 2002; Rehfeld 2005). While national public goods are important to locally elected politicians as well, their efforts may be more ascribed to their party and their districts' rewards are shared. On the other hand, local public goods, or pork, are directly attributable to the efforts of regional politicians and thus valuable for credit claiming (Grimmer 2013). In some political systems, this may take the form of direct transfers from national to local coffers. Accordingly, locally targeted goods are expected to be overprovided in territorial electoral systems and goods allocated to alternative constituencies (including the national constituency) underprovided (Levitt and Snyder 1997). Because budgets are finite, allocating additional resources to pork implies allocating fewer resources to budget categories thought to be redistributive, especially national social spending on health, welfare, and labor market protections.

If territorial politics encourages pork, it is important to establish which types of political institution reinforce the geographic design of electoral constituencies. Electoral rules and ballot structures that allow independence for politicians to represent local (rather than or in addition to national) preferences reinforce territorial cleavages. Specifically, single-member districts and open access to ballots encourage the "personal vote" which often includes a strong element of local representation (Cain et al. 1987). Federalism incentivizes sub-national resource delivery through its associated decentralizing effects on the party system and through regional representation in territorial upper chambers. Parliamentarism strongly dilutes territorial representation because it incentivizes coherent and disciplined national parties. For strong national parties, delivery of broad national goods is more efficient than pork (Cox 1987). Presidentialism does not have the same effect on party discipline, thus failing to dilute regional cleavages equivalently. Where the presidential race is territorialized, such as in the USA, the Electoral College encourages the delivery of pork to swing districts (Kriner and Reeves 2014; Strömberg 2008).

The Veto Mechanism

Political institutions also vary considerably in how many actors they bring to the bargaining table. The more actors involved in the decision and able to block its passage, the more likely the status quo policy will remain (Tsebelis 2002). When the status quo is low redistribution, political institutions with many "veto players" will be less likely to adopt egalitarian reforms. Increased veto points typically increases the heterogeneity of interests within the decision-makers, thus reducing the range of policies that they prefer to the status quo (Tsebelis and Chang 2004).

Related to this, political institutions vary substantially in the extent to which they privilege majorities or protect minority rights (Lijphart 2012; Powell and Vanberg 2000). Minority rights are protected primarily through deliberative mechanisms that give small groups the right to shape, delay, or veto policy change. If the majority of voters are relatively poor, and the minority is rich, institutions that empower minorities provide opportunities for the rich to block redistributive reforms. According to this logic, separation of powers institutions such as federalism and presidentialism should be less redistributive. This idea has considerable empirical support (Persson and Tabellini 1999; Rogers and Lee 2015).

Importantly, political institutions endow regions and social constituencies with distinct powers to affect policy. In many nations, regions are a structuring feature of the constitutionally established systems of representation and administration. Beyond their role as electoral districts, regions also hold special status and powers in many constitutions, including veto powers and protected representation. Social constituencies are not typically protected groups in national constitutions. Rather, social groups' influence comes from their numbers and their role in shaping the nature of contestation in the party system. Their power to enact policy change is heavily dependent on majority status. Regions, conversely, are particularly endowed with blocking powers useful for protecting the status quo (Stepan 2004). Higher interregional inequality incentivizes rich regions to use their constitutional blocking powers to limit redistributive spending (Rogers and Lee 2015).

The Cohesion Mechanism

Some political institutions create barriers to the formation and legislative success of a majority coalition in favor of economic redistribution (Pierson 1995; Steinmo and Watts 1995). They do this by fragmenting parties that represent that majority coalition, both organizationally and ideologically. Federalism and territorial electoral districts provide clear examples. Under both institutions, redistributive coalitions must repeat their campaigns across multiple jurisdictions with different socioeconomic profiles, thus complicating their organizational efforts. With territorial units relevant and with resources targeted geographically, the aggregation of individuals within districts or regions might create very different preference profiles than those of the aggregation of all individuals at the national level. For instance, the poor in a rich region might prefer decentralized welfare over national welfare policy because it could be more generous (Beramendi 2012). Pursuit of the presidential office motivates organizational cooperation and the formation of national parties, but stops short of requiring ideological conformity (Cox 1997; Crisp et al. 2013). Parliamentary systems, on the other hand, encourage organizational and ideological cohesion favorable to unifying a redistributive majority coalition (Becher 2012).

The Book's Contributions

The primary contribution of this work is in its extended treatment of the relevance of territorial representation to the politics of inequality. Previous research relating political geography to redistribution has almost exclusively focused on the "cohesion mechanism" of political institutions. I expand the theoretical linkages of territorial politics to also include the role of targeted local public goods and the veto power of regions. By discussing regions in the context of redistribution, I broaden the discussion of government allocation by including both interregional transfers and pork in order to gain a more complete redistributive picture of nations

My focus on the effect of interregional inequality on redistribution is also relatively new to the literature. I show how institutions might affect outcomes, conditional on the nature of inequality and the currency of bargaining for reelection-oriented politicians. I also add to the small existing literature on interregional inequality in politics a much larger dataset with which to explore the topic.

Beramendi's (2012) seminal book is very much related to this effort. This book extends and adds to that work in several ways. First, I spend more time on the specific institutions that affect the balance of national (i.e., social) or territorial interests and representation in a nation. Beramendi addresses each institution of focus here but particularly emphasizes federalism and whether the party system exacerbates territorial interests or integrates regional politicians into nationally oriented parties. Second, I flesh out in greater detail the theoretical reasons why each institution incentivizes national versus local political concerns. Beramendi also focuses heavily on alternative mechanisms besides income inequality (i.e., labor mobility and regional risk profiles) that drive preferences over fiscal systems. Moreover, his dependent variable is fiscal structures, rather than redistribution.[4] While I build on his research, my frame of analysis is more focused on territorial political institutions and redistribution, and I make use of a larger sample of nations.

Case Selection

In the next chapter, I showcase descriptive statistics and diagrams of interregional inequality, interpersonal inequality, and redistribution for a global sample of nations. These data include observations from 50 nations in an unbalanced panel of the period 1980–2012 in order to give a broad perspective of trends in these variables and whether they appear to have links to the type of political institution.

In related research, I demonstrate the empirical strength of my theoretical arguments (Lee and Rogers 2015; Rogers and Lee 2015). There I show that federalism, localizing electoral rules, and presidentialism are associated with lower government spending, and more spending targeted toward local public goods, and not with those areas of government spending we view as traditionally redistributive. In this book, I expand upon these arguments and provide context using case description of three democracies: the USA, Germany, and Argentina.

The choice of these three federations to illustrate my arguments is motivated by several factors. First, these nations vary considerably in their levels of inequality, both interpersonal and interregional. The USA has notoriously high interpersonal inequality, with Gini coefficients closer to Latin American levels than to those of other wealthy nations. However, the USA has relatively low regional inequality. Even the poorest US state maintains income levels comparable to the richest. Germany has low interpersonal inequality due to considerable government efforts at redistribution. However, because West Germany reunited with considerably poorer and less developed East Germany in 1990, it has elevated levels of interregional inequality for an OECD nation. Argentina has high inequality in both regards. Like the other nations in Latin America, Argentina has Gini coefficients at the upper end of the global scale. Moreover, Argentina's regions are notably divergent. The affluent capital and resource rich regions show income levels far beyond those of most interior regions. These three cases can thus illustrate variation in levels of inequality, types of inequality, and, as we shall see, redistribution.

Related to this, regional inequalities and economic geography resonate strongly in all three nations. The USA has distinct regional economies, in agriculture, manufacturing, finance and trade, as well as agglomerations of specialized industries. Due to many factors—including tax competition, high quality transportation, and dispersed economic endowments—many regions of the country are prosperous and can effectively attract business and labor alike. Germany's economic geography is more polarized than that of the USA but it is certainly more widely distributed than highly concentrated Argentina. Germany's manufacturing regions are largely separated from its agricultural and finance regions. The relative productivity of Germany's regions has varied considerably over time. The addition of the East has brought issues of regional disparity to the forefront of German politics. In Argentina, economic productivity of all kinds—agriculture, manufacturing, finance, and trade—are concentrated in a very limited number of provinces in the Pampas region, and specifically within the capital region and province of Buenos Aires. These two provinces together contribute nearly 70 percent of national GDP. Regional inequality is a major structuring principle of Argentine politics, with both rich and poor regions arguing that they are harmed by existing fiscal and representative structures.

The political institutions of the USA, Germany, and Argentina also vary considerably, yet still share enough in common to serve as comparable cases. All three nations are federal—they hold elections and dole out considerable expenditure at the sub-national level, and have regional representation in a territorial upper chamber. These three federalisms function very differently, however. Germany's "cooperative" federalism is nationalized and integrated by strong parties and a top-down policymaking structure (Lehmbruch 1976). The USA, on the other hand, is considered a competitive federal system, marked by much greater decentralization of policymaking and administration across its states. The interests and rights of states are a perennial issue in US politics. Argentina cannot be characterized as either a cooperative or competitive federation. It is heavily decentralized in expenditure but very centralized in revenue collection. Its fiscal structures incentivize opportunistic behavior on the part of provincial governors (Rodden and Wibbels 2002). Its party system integrates regional actors, but maintains sharp intraparty cleavages based on regional interests (Gibson 1996). Argentina also provides an example of a developing federation to contrast with the experience of the relatively affluent US and German cases.

These three cases show extreme variation in their electoral rules as well. The USA is the pro-typical single-member district system, which strongly highlights local interests. Argentina has closed-list PR, which encourages disciplined parties, yet its ballot access and ways of drawing district lines nonetheless press provincial interests to the fore. Germany stands in between these cases, with a mixed member system. In Germany's lower house, one portion of representatives is chosen by closed-list PR, and the other by single-member districts. This mixture therefore combines the nationalizing incentives of PR with the local focus of single member districts (SMD). Given this substantial variation, political parties in these three democracies function very differently and represent distinct constellations of interests.

These three nations also diverge in their executive structures. Of course, the USA and Argentina are both presidential systems. However, these two presidencies are endowed with very different powers, and this has important implications for the possibility of major policy reform. The US presidency is comparatively weak in its formal policymaking powers, while the Argentine president is relatively strong (Shugart and Carey 1992). In both cases, however, the power of the president strongly depends on the partisan composition of the legislature. Germany contrasts with both of these cases as a parliamentary system, characterized by strong party discipline and executive dominance.

Regarding their levels of redistribution, these three cases represent high, medium, and low levels of the global scale. Figure 1.3 shows the differences across these three cases with regard to their redistribution over time. Germany is among the most redistributive nations in the world. Despite a level of market inequality similar to that of the USA, the government's efforts to redistribute income make net inequality much lower in the German case. Germany's high levels of redistribution make it a counter-example against those who claim that federalism is inimical to redistribution. The USA, conversely, redistributes at low levels for its level of development. Still, Argentina redistributes at considerably lower levels than the "laggard" USA. Even for its level of income, Argentina's does little to equilibrate wealth. Figure 1.3 also indicates that redistribution tends to be very stable over time, suggesting stable features of nations, such as political institutions, may help explain cross-national differences.

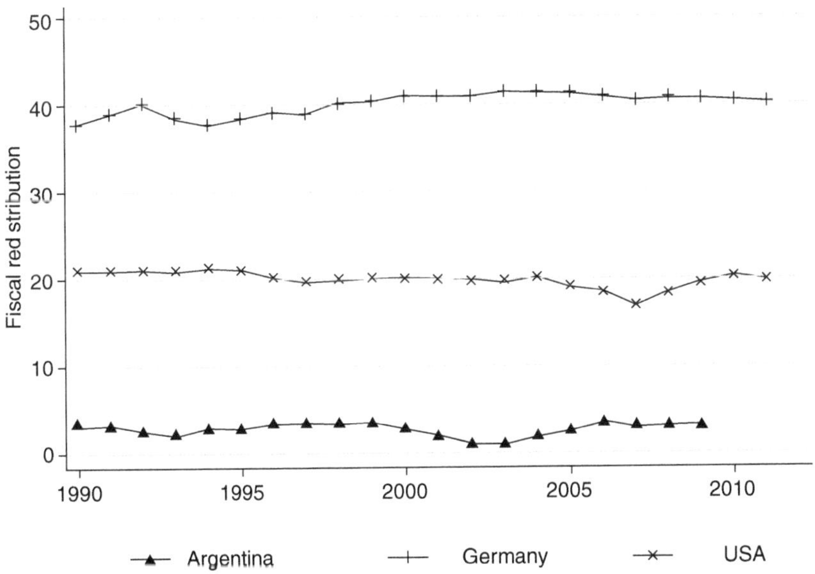

Figure 1.3 Fiscal Redistribution in Argentina, Germany, United States.

Note

Fiscal redistribution is measured by the percentage difference in the national Gini coefficient between inequality before and after government taxes and transfers.

Challenges

The scope of this book is ambitious. However, I cannot do justice to several important matters of clear relevance to the topic. Where possible in the chapters that follow I address concerns outlined below but cannot provide anywhere close to a satisfying theoretical or empirical account.

Endogenous Institutions

Political institutions reflect existing patterns of inequality in their design. That is, political institutions are at least partly endogenous to the level and nature of inequality at the time of their founding (Engerman and Sokoloff 1997; Boix 1999). At the same time, institutions have independent effects on inequality because distributive scenarios shift over time or because institutions were endogenous to power dynamics other than inequality.

Federalism provides a clear example of this concern. The design of fiscal federalism reflects the bargaining process of rich and poor regions with distinct preferences (Bolton and Roland 1997). For example, Spain's decentralization and the constitution of the European Union reflect these tensions (Beramendi 2012). If federalism is designed in reaction to interregional inequality, it is difficult to place causal weight on the political institutions themselves.

At the same time, inequality is much more fluid than political institutions and interregional inequality is not equivalent to interpersonal inequality. Interregional and interpersonal income, while slow moving, do shift over time. Sudden economic shifts in interregional equality are possible with, for example, the discovery of natural resources in a poor region. German reunification provides a clear example of a dramatic increase in interregional inequality with remarkable continuity of existing (Western) political structures. Political institutions, on the other hand, do not often change. Despite dramatic economic changes in the USA, its electoral rules and the design of its presidential system have changed very little. Founders are uncertain about future income distributions and about the effects of institutions, moreover, and cannot design institutions to perfectly represent distributive concerns. With each chapter dedicated to a particular institution, I will therefore address the plausibility of its endogeneity to interpersonal and interregional inequality.

How to Redistribute?

Considerable debate surrounds the best policies to reduce income inequality. Among the many concerns is whether redistribution is most effective through progressive taxation or progressive spending (Kato 2010), whether targeted or universalist programs work best (Korpi and Palme 1998), and whether consumption or investment policies best equilibrate income and opportunity (Beramendi et al. 2015b). Throughout the book, I treat redistribution in extremely broad terms. Many will quibble with this lack of specificity because, among other reasons, the politics in different redistributive policy areas are undoubtedly distinct.

My broad portrayal of redistributive policy is meant to focus the reader on the politics behind the reforms rather than their content. Empirically, I rely on reductions in income inequality that result from government policy (Solt 2014). Theoretically, I consider a policy redistributive when income is transferred from rich to poor through any means. Although this obscures considerable variation in how governments pursue redistribution and why, I believe this simplification is necessary for analytical clarity.

Economic Specificity

Certain economic skills and industries are more mobile and transferrable than others, a concept known as asset specificity. In particular, low-skilled labor has historically moved in response to economic opportunity. The most obvious examples are population transfers from agricultural to manufacturing regions during periods of industrialization. Workers with specific skills, in contrast, tend to be both sectorally and geographically constrained. Despite higher wages, on average, for skilled labor, these workers sometimes demand redistribution as insurance against economic shocks that would leave them particularly vulnerable (Moene and Wallerstein 2001; Varian 1980). Similarly, many industries are geographically specific and they (and their regions) are subject to greater fluctuations in economic outcomes. These industries include, among many others, those that depend on natural resources (e.g., farming, mining, shipping), as well as those that benefit greatly from agglomeration (e.g., high tech industries) (Krugman 1991). Primary products are notoriously subject to global pricing and trends (Blattman et al. 2007). Regions dependent on such industries may seek centralized insurance mechanisms to reduce fluctuations in revenue and population. Even regions with industries that have more inelastic demand and fixed pricing, such as computing and pharmaceuticals, are concerned that overly specialized economies result in unpredictable revenue. Accordingly, economic specificity is a major factor in designs of, in particular, national fiscal structures (Beramendi 2012).

Although economic specificity is clearly important and relevant, it is not a primary empirical variable in this book. Rather, this issue is discussed and analyzed in detail in Beramendi (2012); Beramendi and Wibbels (2010); and Beramendi and Rogers (2015). Economic specificity is of underlying concern throughout the book as a source of economic dynamism in some regions over others, in regional income, and in persistence of regional income over time. It also looms large in the design of political institutions, shaping the representative structures discussed throughout.

Interregional Mobility

Labor mobility is similarly important for political responses to inequality due to risk sharing and concerns for population transfers to more prosperous or generous regions. As discussed above, mobility tends to be higher for the least skilled (and thus lowest paid) workers. With shifts in the economic fates of regions, growing regions can expect a significant influx of individuals at the bottom of the income scale. These individuals may become dependent populations and place stress on the welfare states of the growing regions. Accordingly, it may be in the interest of prosperous regions to transfer income to poorer regions (either through interpersonal or interregional transfers) to avoid an excessive population influx. Similarly, regions with more generous welfare states fear the inflow of a large dependent population that would strain their resources. In short, this suggests reasons why more prosperous regions may seek either more generous centralized redistributive schemes or interregional transfers despite the income transfer implied. Again, despite its relevance, this dynamic will receive less focus than the detailed treatment given in Beramendi (2012). Here, mobility will be more narrowly addressed in the context of whether and how institutions incentivize territorial representation.

Roadmap of the Book

The remaining chapters together serve two main purposes. The first is theoretical, that is, to add geographic concepts and institutional insights into the existing literature on the political effects of inequality. The second is empirical: I present evidence on the extent of interregional inequality and its relationship to redistribution, within a large sample of countries. The book is structured around the institutions of democracy that shape representation on distributive policy. The institution-specific chapters build upon the insights of the theory chapter to add layers of complexity that present a more complete picture of the role of territorial politics on redistribution.

In Chapter 2, I lay out trends in inequality across the world for my sample of developed and developing nations. I define both types of inequality (interpersonal and interregional), describe how they have been measured, and detail empirical concerns with common measures of inequality and redistribution. I include figures and maps illustrating different distributive scenarios that societies face around the globe. Importantly, I describe the extent of regional inequality within nations all over the world, incorporating detailed data on region-level income. This book is the first to systematically present this information with coverage that spans decades for a large number of countries. I also use this chapter to provide an overview of the country case examples that are used throughout the chapters on federalism, electoral rules, and presidentialism. These descriptions provide useful background information on the history, political institutions, and economic geography of Argentina, Germany, and the USA that provides context for the more specific institutional discussion that follows.

Chapter 3 introduces the broad theoretical concerns of the book—that territorial concepts of inequality have not been adequately linked to what we know about the institutional and representative structures of democracies. Specifically, I lay out a framework detailing the necessary conditions for redistribution and relate ways in which territorial constituencies and territorial inequality affect the likelihood for redistribution. I theorize that, at a foundational level, most democratic representation is structured around territorial constituencies that provide incentives for voters and politicians to maximize local public goods.

Constitutional structures—namely federalism versus unitarism, majoritarian versus proportional electoral rules, and presidentialism versus parliamentarism—either reinforce (as with the former institutions) or dilute (as with the latter institutions) the salience of territorial identity and allocative interests in ways that affect redistribution. In particular, federalism, localizing elections, and presidentialism make redistribution less likely because they incentivize the delivery of local public goods, fragment the majority coalition in favor of redistribution, and give votes to powerful minorities, especially regional actors.

Chapter 4 addresses the most obvious institutional structure that highlights regional interests—federalism. Federalism intensifies territorial identities and spatial distributions of income as national politics become a contest between regions to control central resources. The three theoretical mechanisms that link political institutions to lower redistribution are clearly applicable to federalism. First, federalism creates strong incentives for the geographic distribution of goods by national politicians loyal to regional constituencies. This works most clearly through territorial legislative chambers wherein senators seek to maximize resources to their constituency in order to claim credit useful for their political career. Second, the constitutional structures of federalism place multiple veto actors in the way of substantial redistributive policy. Third, federalism empowers rich individuals and regions, which are opposed to redistribution, to limit or block it. Fourth, federalism also clearly fragments the majority coalition that advocates for redistribution by dividing it organizationally, and in terms of its preferences. These dynamics are elucidated by the contrasting federalisms of Argentina, Germany and the USA.

Chapter 5 focuses on territorial constituencies and how they are shaped by electoral rules. Geography structures the constituencies of nearly every representative body in the world. However, nations vary a great deal in whether this latent geographic cleavage is activated. Electoral rules (especially majoritarian and plurality systems) strongly shape the salience of geography by either encouraging local representation, as in SMD systems, or supplanting national party interests as paramount to the interests of politicians in closed-list PR. Territorial constituencies and electoral rules clearly influence the nature of service delivery in democracies, whether to geographic districts or to social constituencies that span districts. Locally oriented electoral rules also fragment the majority coalition for redistribution by making relevant the territorial unit of representation and provoking competition for funding among districts. Like federalism, locally focused electoral rules also challenge the ideological coherence of national political parties that seek to advance redistributive legislation. Argentina (closed-list PR) and the USA (SMD) provide polar examples of constituencies and electoral rules that incentivize national versus local orientation of politicians, respectively. However, Argentina's ballot structure is strongly territorialized, thus making provincial interests relevant in a fragmented but disciplined party system. Germany stands as an intermediate case with its mixed member electoral system intended to activate both national and local representation, based within disciplined and coherent national parties. Interregional inequality shapes the party systems in distinct ways in the three cases.

Chapter 6 addresses the role of executive structure in shaping the balance of territorial and social interests in a political system. Parliamentarism systems should strongly nationalize politics through their incentives for party discipline to both win and hold the government. Pursuit of the presidency also motivates coordination, but non-concurrent elections and fixed terms limit the incentivizes for strong party discipline. Unlike federalism and majoritarian elections, however, it is not altogether clear what role presidents would likely play in the territorial influence on the politics of inequality. On the one hand, presidential systems have additional veto players, making redistributive reforms less likely. On the other hand, presidents may, through formal or partisan powers, be in a unique position to substitute for or unify a fragmented majority coalition in favor of redistribution. In a comparison of health care policy reforms in two different periods of unified leftist government, the USA provides a clear example of how territorial veto gates in a presidential system can block redistribution or moderate it substantially. Argentina provides an example of the president acting as a bridging figure to bring together heterogeneous and territorialized parties. However, the president Carlos Menem in this case bought support from less populated provinces for the purposes of scaling back redistributive policies. Interregional inequality strains the coherence of Argentine parties, and the president used targeted transfers to provinces to overcome governors' resistance to retrenchment. The three mechanisms that link territorial politics to lower redistribution thus also apply to presidential structures.

Chapter 7 concludes with the broad implications of the analysis and extensions of the study. For policy implications, I address the role of institutions in shaping distributive policy outcomes in comparative perspective. With regard to extensions, I focus in particular on the possibility that institutional design is endogenous to the type of inequality that plagues a nation. It is plausible that institutional structures are fundamentally designed, or at least shaped, by the more politically salient form of inequality. Moreover, I suggest possible areas for improvement regarding institutional analysis, the measurement of inequality, and the conceptualization of inequality in the analysis of policy.

Notes

1 For a detailed discussion of interpersonal measures, see De Maio (2007).
2 Or regional constituencies more broadly. This discussion does not depend on the median voter being decisive.
3 These categories normally include: disability benefits, survivors pensions, health benefits, family services and family income support, housing assistance, unemployment benefits, and job market assistance.
4 Of course, fiscal structures affect redistribution.

References

Acemoglu, Daron, and James A. Robinson. *Economic Origins of Dictatorship and Democracy*. Cambridge University Press, Cambridge, 2006.

Alesina, Alberto, and Edward L. Glaeser. *Fighting Poverty in the US and Europe: A World of Difference*. Oxford University Press, 2004.

Alesina, Alberto, and Enrico Spolaore. *The Size of Nations*. MIT Press, 2005.

Ansell, Ben, and David Samuels. "Inequality and Democratization: A Contractarian Approach." *Comparative Political Studies* 45, no. 12 (2010): 1543–74.

Aysan, Ahmet Faruk. *Inequality, Institutions and Redistribution*. Ph.D. Economics, University of Maryland College Park (2005).

Bartels, Larry M. "Economic Inequality and Political Representation." in, *The Unsustainable American State*, edited by L. Jacobs and D. King. Oxford University Press, (2009a): 167–96.

Bartels, Larry M. *Unequal Democracy: The Political Economy of the New Gilded Age*. Princeton University Press, 2009b.

Becher, Michael. "Presidentialism, Parliamentarism, and Redistribution." Paper presented at the General Conference of the European Political Science Association, Berlin, Germany, 2012.

Benabou, Roland. "Unequal Societies: Income Distribution and the Social Contract." *American Economic Review* 90, no. 1 (2000): 96–129.

Beramendi, Pablo. "Inequality and the Territorial Fragmentation of Solidarity." *International Organization* 61, no. 4 (2007): 783.

Beramendi, Pablo. *The Political Geography of Inequality: Regions and Redistribution*. Cambridge University Press, 2012.

Beramendi, Pablo, and Melissa Rogers. *Geography, Capacity, and Inequality*. Duke University and Claremont Graduate University, 2015.

Beramendi, Pablo, and Erik Wibbels. "Foundational Bargains: Distributive Conflicts and Representation in Federations." Paper presented at the Meeting American Political Science Association, Washington, 2010.

Beramendi, Pablo, Melissa Rogers and Alberto Diaz-Cayeros. 2015a. *Barriers to the Left Turn: Distributive Tensions in Latin American Federations*. Manuscript: Duke University, Claremont Graduate University, Stanford University.

Beramendi, Pablo, Silja Häusermann, Herbert Kitschelt, Hanspeter Kriesi, "The Politics of Advanced Capitalism: An Introduction" in *The Politics of Advanced Capitalism*, Cambridge University Press, New York, 2015b.

Besley, Timothy, and Stephen Coate. "Centralized Versus Decentralized Provision of Local Public Goods: A Political Economy Approach." *Journal of Public Economics* 87, no. 12 (2003): 2611–37.

Blattman, Christopher, Jason Hwang, and Jeffrey G Williamson. "Winners and Losers in the Commodity Lottery: The Impact of Terms of Trade Growth and Volatility in the Periphery 1870–1939." *Journal of Development Economics* 82, no. 1 (2007): 156–79.

Bobbio, Norberto. *Left and Right: The Significance of a Political Distinction*. University of Chicago Press, 1996.

Boix, Carles. "Setting the Rules of the Game: The Choice of Electoral Systems in Advanced Democracies." *American Political Science Review* 93, no. 3 (1999): 609–24.

Boix, Carles. *Democracy and Redistribution*. Cambridge University Press, 2003.

Boix, Carles. "Origins and Persistence of Economic Inequality." *Annual Review of Political Science* 13 (2010): 489–516.

Bolton, Patrick, and Gerard Roland. "The Breakup of Nations: A Political Economy Analysis." *The Quarterly Journal of Economics* 112, no. 4 (1997): 1057–90.

Bradley, David, Evelyne Huber, Stephanie Moller, Francois Nielsen, and John D. Stephens. "Distribution and Redistribution in Postindustrial Democracies." *World Politics* 55, no. 2 (2003): 193–228.

Bueno de Mesquita, Bruce, and Randolph M Alastair Smith. "The Logic of Political Survival." MIT Press, Cambridge, 2003.

Cain, Bruce E., John A. Ferejohn, and Morris P. Fiorina. *The Personal Vote: Constituency Service and Electoral Independence*. Harvard University Press (1987).

Carey, John M., and Matthew Soberg Shugart. "Incentives to Cultivate a Personal Vote: A Rank Ordering of Electoral Formulas." *Electoral Studies* 14, no. 4 (1995): 417–39.

Cox, Gary W. *Making Votes Count: Strategic Coordination in the World's Electoral Systems*. Vol. 7: Cambridge University Press, 1997.

Cox, Gary, and Mathew McCubbins. "The Institutional Determinants of Economic Policy Outcomes." In *Presidents, Parliaments, and Policy*, edited by Stefan Haggard and Mathew McCubbins. Cambridge University Press, New York, 2001.

Crisp, Brian, Santiago Olivella, and Joshua Potter. "Party-System Nationalization and the Scope of Public Policy: the Importance of Cross-District Constituency Similarity." *Comparative Political Studies* 46, no. 4 (2013): 431–56.

Cusack, Thomas R., Torben Iversen, and David Soskice. "Economic Interests and the Origins of Electoral Systems." *American Political Science Review* 101, no. 3 (2007): 373.

De Maio, Fernando G. "Income Inequality Measures." *Journal of Epidemiology and Community Health* 61, no. 10 (2007): 849–52.

Dion, Michelle L., and Vicki Birchfield. "Economic Development, Income Inequality, and Preferences for Redistribution." *International Studies Quarterly* 54, no. 2 (2010): 315–34.

Engerman, Stanley L., and Kenneth L. Sokoloff. "Factor Endowments, Institutions, and Differential Paths of Growth among New World Economies." in *How Latin America Fell Behind*, edited by Stephen Haber. Stanford University Press (1997): 260–304.

Gerring, John, Strom C. Thacker, and Carola Moreno. "Centripetal Democratic Governance: A Theory and Global Inquiry." *American Political Science Review* 99, no. 4 (2005): 567–81.

Gibson, Edward L. *Class and Conservative Parties: Argentina in Comparative Perspective*. Johns Hopkins University Press, Baltimore MD, 1996.

Grimmer, Justin. "Appropriators Not Position Takers: The Distorting Effects of Electoral Incentives on Congressional Representation." *American Journal of Political Science* 57, no. 3 (2013): 624–42.

Hacker, Jacob S., and Paul Pierson. "Winner-Take-All Politics: Public Policy, Political Organization, and the Precipitous Rise of Top Incomes in the United States." *Politics and Society* 38, no. 2 (2010): 152–204.

Haggard, Stephan M., Robert Kaufman, and James D. Long. "Inequality and Preferences for Redistribution in the Developing World." *Comparative Political Studies* 48, no. 2 (2013).

Huber, Evelyne, and John D. Stephens. *Democracy and the Left: Social Policy and Inequality in Latin America*. University of Chicago Press, 2012.

Huber, Evelyne, Charles Ragin, and John D. Stephens. "Social Democracy, Christian Democracy, Constitutional Structure, and the Welfare State." *American Journal of Sociology* 99, no. 3 (1993): 711–49.

Iversen, Torben, and David Soskice. "Electoral Institutions and the Politics of Coalitions: Why Some Democracies Redistribute More Than Others." *American Political Science Review* 100, no. 2 (2006): 165–81.

Kang, Shin-Goo, and G. Bingham Powell Jr. "Representation and Policy Responsiveness: The Median Voter, Election Rules and Redistributive Welfare Spending." *Journal of Politics* 72, no. 4 (2010).

Kato, Junko. *Regressive Taxation and the Welfare State: Path Dependence and Policy Diffusion*. Cambridge University Press, 2010.

Kitschelt, Herbert. "Linkages between Citizens and Politicians in Democratic Polities." *Comparative Political Studies* 33, no. 6–7 (2000): 845–79.

Korpi, Walter, and Joakim Palme. "The Paradox of Redistribution and Strategies of Equality: Welfare State Institutions, Inequality, and Poverty in the Western Countries." *American Sociological Review* 63 (1998): 661–87.

Kriner, Douglas, and Andrew Reeves. "The Electoral College and Presidential Particularism." *Boston University Law Review.* 94 (2014): 741.

Krugman, Paul R. *Geography and Trade*. MIT press, 1991.

Lasswell, Harold Dwight. *Politics: Who Gets What, When, How*. P. Smith, New York, 1950.

Lee, Dong-wook, and Melissa Rogers. *Comparing Inequalities: Regional and Interpersonal Income Disparity, Institutions, and Government Spending.* Manuscript, Claremont Graduate University, CA 2015.

Lehmbruch, Gerhard. *Parteienwettbewerb Im Bundesstaat*. Kohlhammer, Stuttgart, 1976.

Levitt, Steven D., and James M. Snyder Jr. "Political Parties and the Distribution of Federal Outlays." *American Journal of Political Science* 39 no. 4 (1995): 958–80.

Lijphart, Arend. *Patterns of Democracy: Government Forms and Performance in Thirty Six Countries*. Yale University Press, 2012.

Lindblom, Charles Edward. "The Market as Prison." *The Journal of Politics* 44, no. 2 (1982): 323–36.

Lindert, Peter H. *Growing Public: Volume 1, the Story: Social Spending and Economic Growth since the Eighteenth Century*. Cambridge University Press, 2004.

Lipset, Seymour M., and Stein Rokkan. *Cleavage Structures, Party Systems, and Voter Alignments: An Introduction*. Free Press, New York, 1967.

Lupu, Noam, and Jonas Pontusson. "The Structure of Inequality and the Politics of Redistribution." *American Political Science Review* 105, no. 2 (2011): 316–36.

Mayhew, David R. *Congress: The Electoral Connection*. Vol. 26: Yale University Press, 1974.

Meltzer, Allan H., and Scott F. Richard. "A Rational Theory of the Size of Government." *The Journal of Political Economy* 89, no. 5 (1981): 914–27.

Milanovic, Branko. "The Median-Voter Hypothesis, Income Inequality, and Income Redistribution: An Empirical Test with the Required Data." *European Journal of Political Economy* 16, no. 3. (2000).

Milesi-Ferretti, Gian Maria, Roberto Perotti, and Massimo Rostagno. "Electoral Systems and Public Spending." *The Quarterly Journal of Economics* 117, no. 2 (2002): 609–57.

Moene, Karle Ove, and Michael Wallerstein. "Inequality, Social Insurance, and Redistribution." *American Political Science Review* 95, no. 4 (2001): 859–74.

Persson, Torsten, and Guido Tabellini. "The Size and Scope of Government: Comparative Politics with Rational Politicians." *European Economic Review* 43, no. 4 (1999): 699–735.

Pierson, Paul. "Fragmented Welfare States: Federal Institutions and the Development of Social Policy." *Governance* 8, no. 4 (1995): 449–78.

Piketty, Thomas, and Emmanuel Saez. "The Evolution of Top Incomes: A Historical and International Perspective." *The American Economic Review* 96, no. 2 (2006): 200–5.

Powell, Bingham Jr., G., and Georg S. Vanberg. "Election Laws, Disproportionality and Median Correspondence: Implications for Two Visions of Democracy." *British Journal of Political Science* 30, no. 3 (2000): 383–411.

Rehfeld, Andrew. *The Concept of Constituency: Political Representation, Democratic Legitimacy, and Institutional Design*. Cambridge University Press, 2005.

Rodden, Jonathan. "Federalism and Inter-Regional Redistribution." *Documents de treball IEB*, no. 3 (2009): 1.

Rodden, Jonathan, and Erik Wibbels. "Beyond the Fiction of Federalism." *World Politics* 54, no. 4 (2002): 494–531.

Roemer, John E. "Why the Poor Do Not Expropriate the Rich: An Old Argument in New Garb." *Journal of Public Economics* 70, no. 3 (1998): 399–424.

Rogers, Melissa, and Dong-wook Lee. *Comparing Inequalities*. Presented at MPSA (Midwest Political Science Association) 2015.

Romer, Thomas. "Individual Welfare, Majority Voting, and the Properties of a Linear Income Tax." *Journal of Public Economics* 4, no. 2 (1975): 163–85.

Rosenstone, Steven J., and John Mark Hansen. *Mobilization, Participation, and Democracy in America (Longman Classics Edition)*. Longman Publishing Group, 2002.

Schmidt, Manfred G. "When Parties Matter: A Review of the Possibilities and Limits of Partisan Influence on Public Policy." *European Journal of Political Research* 30, no. 2 (1996): 155–83.

Shugart, Matthew Soberg. "Presidentialism, Parliamentarism, and the Provision of Collective Goods in Less-Developed Countries." *Constitutional Political Economy* 10, no. 1 (1999): 53–88.

Shugart, Matthew Soberg, and John M. Carey. *Presidents and Assemblies: Constitutional Design and Electoral Dynamics*. Cambridge University Press, 1992.

Solt, Frederick. *The Standardized World Income Inequality Database*. Working paper. SWIID Version 5.0, October 2014.

Steinmo, Sven, and Jon Watts. "It's the Institutions, Stupid! Why Comprehensive National Health Insurance Always Fails in America." *Journal of Health Politics, Policy and Law* 20, no. 2 (1995): 329–72.

Stepan, Alfred. "Toward a New Comparative Politics of Federalism, Multinationalism, and Democracy: Beyond Rikerian Federalism." in *Federalism and Democracy in Latin America*, edited by Edward L. Gibson. Johns Hopkins University Press, Baltimore MD, (2004).

Stiglitz, Joseph. *The Price of Inequality*. Penguin, London, 2012.

Strömberg, David. "How the Electoral College Influences Campaigns and Policy: The Probability of Being Florida." *The American Economic Review* 98, no. 3 (2008): 769–807.

Tsebelis, George. "Veto Players and Institutional Analysis." *Governance* 13, no. 4 (2002): 441–74.

Tsebelis, George, and Eric C. C. Chang. "Veto Players and the Structure of Budgets in Advanced Industrialized Countries." *European Journal of Political Research* 43, no. 3 (2004): 449–76.

Tuschhoff, Christian. "The Compounding Effect: The Impact of Federalism on the Concept of Representation." *West European Politics* 22, no. 2 (1999): 16–33.

Varian, Hal R. "Redistributive Taxation as Social Insurance." *Journal of Public Economics* 14, no. 1 (1980): 49–68.

Volden, Craig. "Intergovernmental Political Competition in American Federalism." *American Journal of Political Science* 49, no. 2 (2005): 327–42.

Weingast, Barry R., Kenneth A. Shepsle, and Christopher Johnsen. "The Political Economy of Benefits and Costs: A Neoclassical Approach to Distributive Politics." *The Journal of Political Economy* 89, no. 4 (1981): 642–64.

2 Interregional and Interpersonal Inequality Around the World

Introduction

The overarching theoretical argument of this book is that territorial delineation of elections, and whether that it is reinforced or diluted by political institutions, influences government responses to inequality. Importantly, inequality matters in every nation, but certain political institutions highlight territorial representation and geographic distribution of government resources that may stand in the way of redistribution. This argument suggests that one should examine territorial spreads of income, and geographic political allocation, for their effect on policymaking.

This chapter serves three purposes. First, I provide a broad overview of the extent of interregional and interpersonal inequality in the world. In descriptive figures and maps, I show levels of regional disparity in a large, diverse sample of nations. These data on regional disparity are new to the research on the political economy of inequality. Second, I demonstrate empirical evidence for one of my central claims—that territorial political institutions encourage prioritization of targeted geographic spending over social spending. Third, I provide an overview of my case countries, Argentina, Germany, and the USA, to give background information useful for subsequent chapters focused on particular institutions.

Inequality in the World

Are interregional and interpersonal inequality observationally equivalent? One can imagine two extreme scenarios. In the first, the level and spread of income in each region is equivalent to the national level. The districts serve as smaller replicas of nation. In the second, all of the poor people live in one region and all of the rich people live in a different region. In both scenarios, the national level of interpersonal inequality is the same. However, the political relevance of regions should be dramatically different. In the first, cross-regional coordination to attain redistributive goals would be optimal. In the second, the political activation of interpersonal inequality should take a regional tone. In order to evaluate which scenario more closely approximates the actual distribution of income across nations, I present data on interregional and interpersonal inequality around the world.

To begin, Figure 2.1 shows the extent of interregional (measured as the Gini coefficient of regional GDP per capita) and interpersonal inequality (measured as the Gini coefficient of household income per capita) in a global sample in 2000. The year 2000 is used to maximize observations in the developing nations. Countries vary widely on both dimensions and the distinct types of inequality appear more serious in certain countries and regions than in others. For example, the Organization of Economic Cooperation and Development (OECD) countries are generally low on both dimensions and Latin American countries high on both. However, interregional inequality, not interpersonal inequality, is stark in many of the featured Eastern European and Asian countries.

The overall correlation between these inequality variables is notable in the global sample, between 0.38 and 0.55 depending on the indicator. Within income groups such as the OECD, however, interregional and interpersonal measures are not statistically related (a pairwise correlation of 0.03). It is not surprising that many countries affected by one type of inequality also show high levels of the other because the measures can capture similar phenomena. For example, if rich individuals were clustered in one region and poor individuals in another, both interregional and interpersonal inequality would be high. This characterizes Peru, for example, where 64 percent of the observed inequality can be explained by geographic location (Faquet and Shami 2008). Within the OECD sample, conversely, interpersonal and interregional income spreads are not equivalent. Figure 2.2 shows these income distributions in the OECD countries alone to

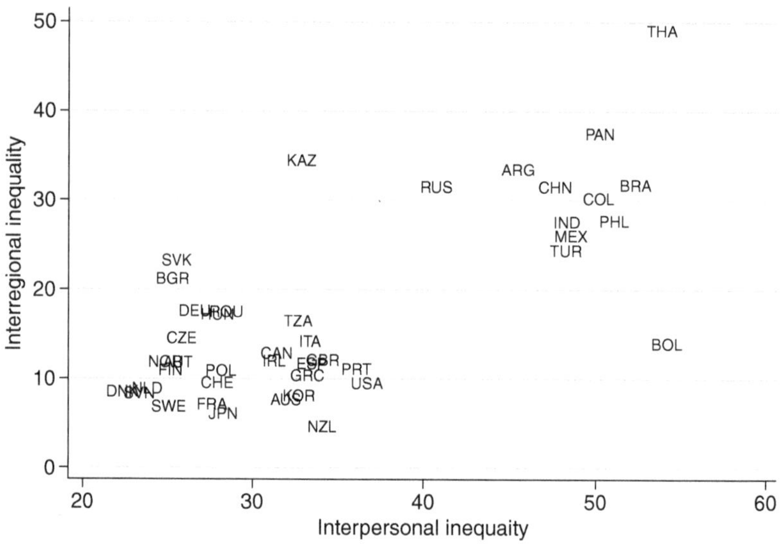

Figure 2.1 Interpersonal and Interregional Inequality, 2000 (sources: Interpersonal inequality, "gini market" (Solt 2014); interregional inequality (Rogers and Lee 2015)).

Notes
Interpersonal inequality is the national Gini coefficient before government taxes and transfers. Interregional inequality is the adjusted Gini coefficient of regional GDP per capita.

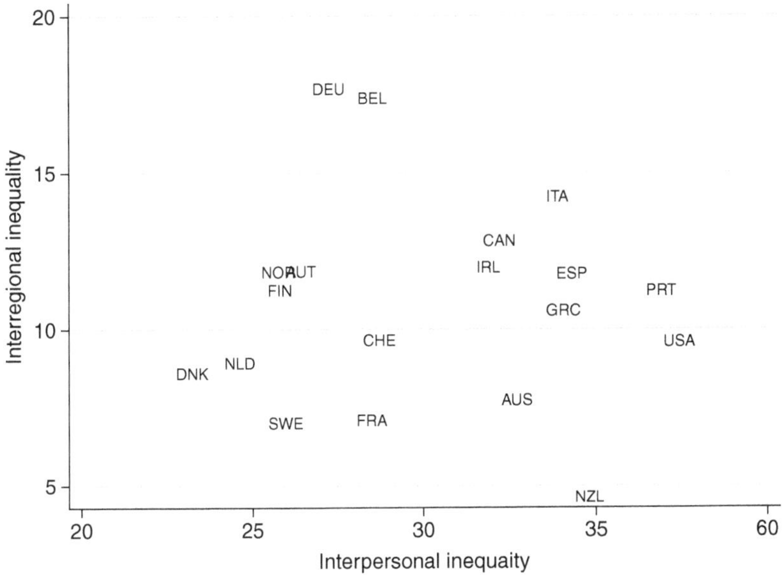

Figure 2.2 Interpersonal and Interregional Inequality in OECD Countries, 2000 (sources: Interpersonal inequality, "gini market" (Solt 2014); interregional inequality (Rogers and Lee 2015)).

Notes
Interpersonal inequality is the national Gini coefficient before government taxes and transfers. Interregional inequality is the adjusted Gini coefficient of regional GDP per capita.

highlight differences in the high income countries that are obscured in the global sample. Certain nations with relatively high regional inequality in GDP per capita, such as Germany and Belgium, have low interpersonal inequality due to substantial government redistribution.[1] Other nations, such as the USA, have high interpersonal inequality but low interregional inequality. The weak association between these inequality indicators suggests that countries often deviate in their patterns of inequality—these indicators represent distinct distributional conflicts within a nation. The theoretical framework in the next chapter explores why we might expect differences in political responses to interregional versus interpersonal inequality.

A scatter plot provides a useful overview of inequality in the world but a map can more clearly illuminate differences across regions of the world. Figure 2.3 is a map of the mean values of interregional inequality for all countries with available data. Because this data includes mean values for the sample, and not values specific to any particular year, the sample is larger and includes several African and South Asian nations not shown in the data above. Figure 2.4 shows a map of global interpersonal inequality measures, using the mean values in the sample. Both maps are color-coded to reflect levels of inequality to highlight regional differences.

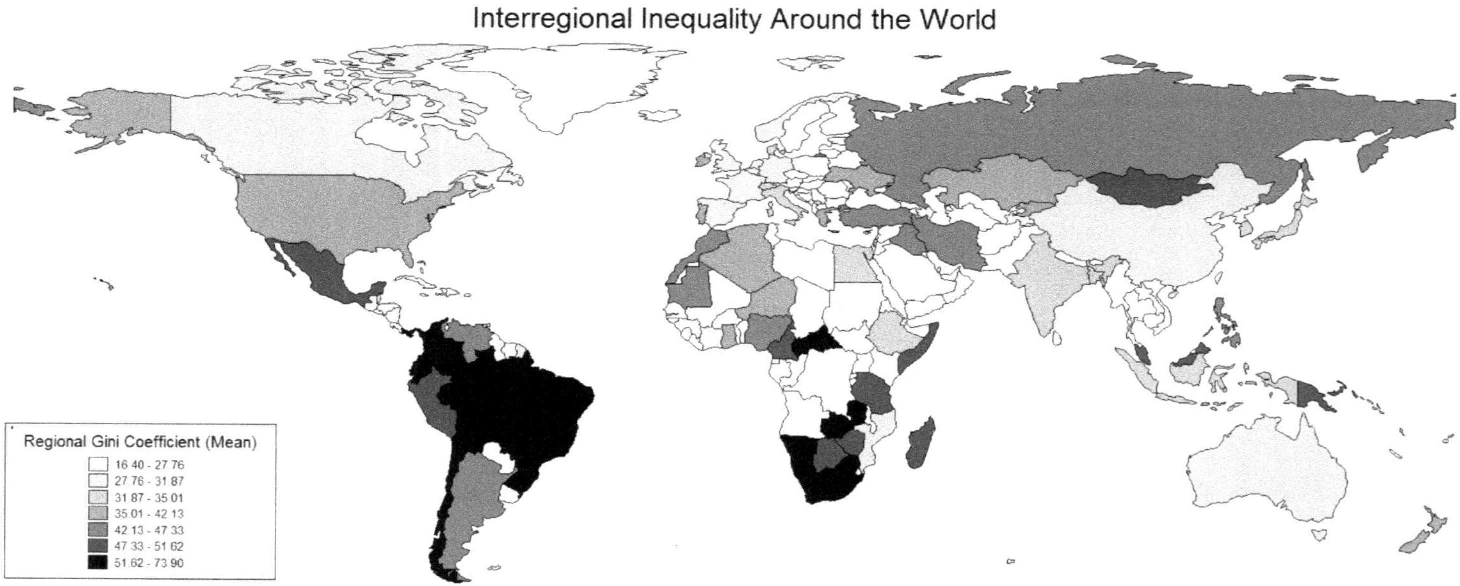

Figure 2.3 Interpersonal and Interregional Inequality, 2000 (source: Rogers and Lee (2015)).

Notes
Interregional inequality in measured with the Gini Coefficient of regional GDP per capita at the mean value for that nation. Some nations have over 40 years of observations, others have only one observation.

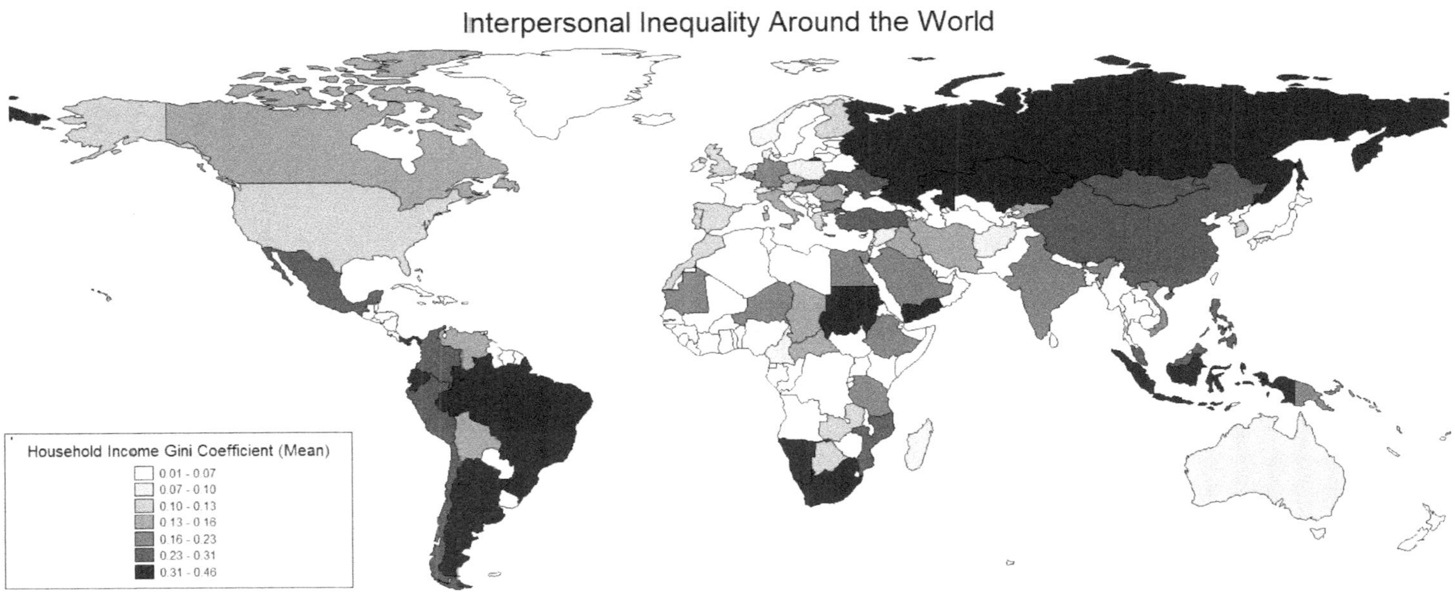

Figure 2.4 Global Map of Interpersonal Inequality (source: Solt (2014)).

Note
Interpersonal inequality is measured with the Gini Coefficient of Household Income per capita measured at the mean value for that nation. Some nations have over 40 years of observations and other have very few.

OECD Nations

The advanced industrial democracies of the OECD show, on the whole, low levels of interregional and interpersonal inequality. The variation within the OECD reveals interesting differences among these wealthy nations. Perhaps not surprisingly, highly redistributive Scandinavian nations are low on both types of inequality. The federal nations show marked variation among themselves. Despite clear regional conflict based at least in part on differences in regional income, Spain has low to moderate levels of interregional inequality within the already low OECD group. The USA and Canada have low interregional inequality while at the same time they are above the mean in interpersonal inequality. Belgium and Germany are just the opposite—they exhibit high interregional and low interpersonal inequality.

Latin America

Latin America is characterized by both high interregional and high interpersonal inequality. Accordingly, as a global region, it stands in contrast to the OECD nations, and forms a group of comparable cases. In a global large N sample, the variance among the Latin American cases is obscured. For example, Venezuela has relatively low regional inequality but high interpersonal inequality. Argentina has relatively high interregional inequality and relatively low interpersonal inequality for Latin America (but still very high in comparative perspective). Interestingly, Venezuela and Argentina have distinct fiscal structures that highlight sub-national preferences (Argentina) or subsume them to national concerns (Venezuela). Likewise, Bolivia and Ecuador have widely different levels of regional inequality and this allows for a viable comparison of countries that have similar levels of development and, currently, similar ideological orientations.

From the theoretical perspective of this book, Latin America is interesting because its nations are presidential but have wide variance in their electoral and constitutional arrangements. Most Latin American nations have PR systems that dilute, to varying extents, the territorial character of representation. However, multipartism combined with presidentialism may encourage policy gridlock, which could hinder the efforts of a majority coalition interested in redistribution (Mainwaring 1993). Argentina provides an example of these dynamics in the case studies.

Asia

Asian countries are broadly characterized by relatively high interregional inequality and relatively low interpersonal inequality. The two largest countries in that zone, India and China, exemplify this distributive tension, which would not be well captured by the Gini coefficient. As India and China's economies expand at high rates, regional disputes may be the most contentious. Evidence of regional tension is already clear in China, and India has highly decentralized political institutions that structure representation around geography (Chhibber and Kollman 1997). Additionally, Thailand's interregional inequality stands out as the worst in the world.

Africa

As a region, Africa is dramatically varied on both interregional and interpersonal inequality. In part, this may suggest that Africa's great diversity limits the validity of continent-wide comparison. Take three examples: Sudan prior to partition (high interregional, low interpersonal), South Africa (high interregional, high interpersonal), Namibia or Zimbabwe (extremely high interpersonal, low interregional inequality). The dynamics in Africa do not appear to be regionally characterized but instead driven by level of development and the influence of natural resources, in addition to domestic factors that have shaped the structure of political institutions. Unfortunately the coverage of regional GDP per capita data is quite limited for Africa.

Measuring Inequality

Social science research commonly employs data on income inequality. These data are almost always nationally aggregated measures of the distribution of interpersonal income. Although many different calculations of inequality are used across the fields, the most common is indisputably the Gini coefficient of household income. In this section, I discuss the possible alternative measures of interpersonal, and especially interregional, inequality, and the theoretical as well as empirical differences between them. At this moment, interregional measures of inequality are nearly absent in political science research.

Measuring Interpersonal Inequality

Interpersonal inequality is typically measured at the individual or household level, and captures differences in the distribution of individuals across income brackets (often quintiles). These data are taken from national income surveys that may not be strictly comparable in their calculations. The Luxembourg Income Study (LIS) standardizes the results of these income studies into broadly comparable income data for the countries that make their data available. Other scholars, such as Deininger and Squire (1996) and Solt (2009) have expanded upon the LIS data to include more developing nations. The data for these non-LIS countries are considered of poorer quality, however.

The way to calculate the spread of interpersonal income is dictated by the scholar's theory. For example, Piketty and Saez (2006a) measure inequality as the percentage of income held by the top 1 percent of income earners in a nation. They present a theoretical argument about the concentration of income at the very top of the distribution. Other scholars are more concerned about how income differs between the top earners and the bottom, between the middle and the bottom, or the top and the middle. Such values can be captured in ratios of the income held by these groups. As stated, the most commonly used measure is the Gini coefficient, which measures the inequality among incomes in a frequency distribution. A Gini of zero represents perfect equality, with all individuals having the same income. A value of one represents perfect inequality: all income is held by one individual. In practice, Gini coefficients tend to range between 0.2 (Slovenia is currently the lowest at 0.24) and 0.7 (South Africa, the highest, is estimated to be close to 0.7).

In addition to the choices scholars make about how to measure distributions, they must also evaluate the theoretical importance of different types of incomes and aggregation. For example, scholars may be concerned with income spreads before taxes and government transfers (market inequality) or after taxes or transfers (net inequality). The measure of redistribution that I employ throughout this book is the percentage difference between these two values. For those interested in the role of government in reducing inequality, both measures are relevant; for those concerned with the effect of inequality on other outcomes, such as health, net inequality is more likely relevant.

Income can also be measured at the individual or household level. Piketty and Saez (2006a), for example, use individual tax returns to measure inequality, thus capturing individual income. Most other studies use household income as the appropriate unit because it better captures the material conditions of most individuals and shows a more even distribution. For instance, children and stay-at-home mothers earn no income, but they have access to resources within the shared household setting. Hence, standardized household income per capita is the standard in most social science studies. Similarly, most studies exclude pensioners or include them in a separate category of income. Retired individuals earn no income and thus countries with aged populations (such as most OECD nations) would appear more unequal than they truly are by the inclusion of the elderly in their sample. This problem is reduced when a full account of income (from government or private pensions) is available and can be incorporated into the data.

Scholars must also consider whether the most important aspect of inequality is in income or wealth. Income refers to the sum of all the wages, salaries, profits, interests payments, rents, and other forms of earnings received on a yearly basis (Case and Fair 2007). Wealth includes the sum of accumulated income and assets minus liabilities. The difference between income and wealth could be important in, for example, the intergenerational transfer of inequality (both wealth and debt transmitted to future generations). Income measures are much more widely available and thus are employed most commonly. Both income and wealth measures, however, are widely thought to be truncated because the most affluent individuals avoid participation in government surveys.

In addition to standard income inequality measures, levels of poverty can capture important differences in the material condition of citizens. The distinction can be conveyed by a simple explanation. Imagine a wealthy nation in which income inequality is high because the very top of the income distribution is extremely wealthy while the poorest population still maintains a high standard of living. This nation may have the same Gini coefficient as a desperately poor nation in which the richest individuals live comfortably but the poorest are destitute. Measures of poverty would pick up the difference between these two nations.

Measuring Interregional Inequality

The concept of interregional inequality captures variation in levels of income and development across regions within a nation, and how nations vary in their spread of regional income. To take a commonly understood example, most people can recognize the differences in income in rich New York versus relatively poor Mississippi. Similarly, Mexico City (the nation's capital district) far outpaces the income of its rural south, including Oaxaca. These measures capture the difference between New York and Mississippi, and Mexico City and Oaxaca, and whether the disparity between the US states is more or less than the disparity between the Mexican states. In all measures, the difference is greater in Mexico than the USA.

The interregional inequality measures I use throughout this book relate regional GDP per capita, the country's average GDP per capita, and the number of regions in that country (Kessler and Lessmann 2010; Lessmann 2011). The regions I employ as sub-national territorial units are equivalent to the state, province, department, or NUTS (Nomenclature of Territorial Units for Statistics) Level 2, in the case of OECD nations.[2]

Throughout the empirical research in this book, I use the Gini coefficient of regional GDP per capita. From research on political geography and regional convergence, I adopt three formulae most commonly used for calculating interregional inequality: the region-adjusted Gini coefficient (*ADGINI*), the coefficient of variation (*COV*), and the population-weighted coefficient of variance (*COVW*). The formulae are listed below, with y representing regional GDP per capita, n the number of regional units, and p the population. All three measures are usable in cross-national analysis and highlight three distinct inequality concepts (relative deprivation, dispersion, and populated-weighted dispersion) (Lessmann 2009; Portnov and Felsensten 2005). This allows for the "intra-country" variance information to be translated into the numerically continuous index of "inter-country" variance. In the case of the region-adjusted Gini coefficient, the value of zero denotes that a country is evenly developed across its regions; the value of one represents extreme inequality. The indicators do not change depending on the number of regions involved, are not sensitive to shifts in average GDP level, and satisfy the Pigou–Dalton principle.[3]

1 *ADGINI—Measure of Deprivation*

$$\frac{2\sum_{i=1}^{n} iy_i}{n\sum_{i=1}^{n} y_i} - \frac{n}{n-1}$$

2 *COV—Measure of Dispersion*

$$\frac{1}{y}\left[1/n\sum_{i=1}^{n}(\bar{y}-y_{\text{i}})^2\right]^{1/2}$$

3 *COVW*—Population-Weighted Measure of Dispersion

$$\frac{1}{y}\left[1/n\sum_{i=1}^{n}p_i(\bar{y}-y_i)^2\right]^{1/2}$$

These three regional disparity measures represent different notions of inequality. *COV* and *COVW* are measures of dispersion and *ADGINI* is a measure of deprivation. Dispersion and deprivation are two ways to conceptualize spatial differences in wealth (see Protnov and Felsensten 2005). The dispersion measure *COV* only captures the distribution of income across districts. *COVW* factors in population weights of the regions to the overall distribution measure. The *ADGINI* is the Gini coefficient of regional income. Compared to COV and COVW it retains more meaningful information about the extent of relative deprivation. In *ADGINI*, additional weight is given to regional incomes as they veer farther away from the mean of the regional income distribution. This calculation makes the *ADGINI* measure more sensitive to changes in the upper or lower tail of this distribution. I use the ADGINI throughout the book for easy comparison with the interpersonal Gini coefficient. None of the empirics shown are affected by the choice of interregional inequality indicator.

The regional population, GDP, and GDP per capita data I employ come from Cambridge Econometrics, EUROSTAT, the OECD, the Economic Commission of Latin American Countries, and national accounts. Using GDP per capita rather than income to capture regional inequality has several advantages, both theoretical and empirical. Theoretically, regional GDP is an important concept for politicians trying to improve the conditions in their particular region. GDP captures economic productivity and changes in economic tides, which should reflect opportunities for its citizens and their relative standard of living. Thus regional GDP per capita is not merely a proxy for income but an important indicator of the regional endowments and likely distributive conflict. Empirically, using regional GDP data allows for a much larger global dataset than does income data, and including more countries and more time coverage allows for better econometric estimation. Moreover, region-level GDP per capita and regional household income per capita are very highly correlated (see discussion and data availability in Lee and Rogers 2015).

Of course, GDP per capita is not a direct measure of citizens' income. Interregional inequality is also captured with actual income levels as collected in national income surveys. Where possible, I also present these data. For these measures, I employ household income data measured per adult equivalent.[4] For the cases of Germany and the USA, I include data from the LIS. Argentina does not participate in the LIS so I use data from their national income survey, the Encuesta Permanente de Hogares (EPH). The EPH only surveys metropolitan areas, including at least one city in each province. These data can thus only capture the urban sectors of Argentina. Because these data have not been standardized by the LIS, they should not be considered directly equivalent to the US or German data. However, they should be internally valid, meaning the data for Buenos Aires and Tierra del Fuego, for example, are directly comparable.

Sources of Interpersonal Inequality

In this book, because I look at political dynamics related to income inequality, I do not address the sources of income inequality directly. Of course, governments have strong effects on the level of inequality through income redistribution. By examining redistribution, I am in part looking at the sources of inequality.

Inequality also emerges from many economic, social, and demographic factors that I briefly mention here but leave to the bountiful research on the topic to treat more satisfactorily. Differences in income result from different endowments of goods (physical, human, and social capital), luck, and effort among a population. Government policies have strong effects on investments in these different forms of capital and whether individuals have equal opportunity to attain them (Beramendi et al. 2015).

Research on interpersonal inequality has been growing recently because of the well-documented rise in inequality since the early 1970s in wealthy nations. This research looks at the causes of this surge, and the variation in government responses. Certain global trends, such as increased trade, technological advancement and deindustrialization, and free movement of capital and people, have led to increased market inequality in wealthy nations. However, only some countries have increased net inequality because the government has not compensated those who have struggled under these structural economic changes (Brune and Garrett 2005).

Developing nations have mixed trends in interpersonal inequality in recent years, likely related to their varied levels of development (Kuznets 1955). Latin American nations' inequality has been falling since the early 2000s from their peak in the 1990s (Lustig et al. 2013). Broad economic and social trends, such as urbanization and industrialization, appear to be contributing to rising inequality in China and India. Much of the rest of the world shows no clear pattern (Milanovic 2010).

Sources of Interregional Inequality

Interregional inequality emerges from a combination of economic geography and political processes. Regions have different endowments, much of which comes from nature, such as land and location that attract industry, investment, and human capital. In particular, access to markets has made coastal cities prosperous and arable land has proved a boon to agricultural commodity producers. Natural resources such as oil or minerals are another clear example. Other regions are prosperous through the specific efforts of governments to attract investment and capital, whether through the development of human capital (Seoul is a popular examples of this) or friendly business environments (e.g., tax havens or low tax states). Natural features are nonetheless the strongest predictors of economic output, even in service economies decoupled from most land-specific factors (Gallup et al. 1999).

In many nations, economic productivity is geographically concentrated in a small number of regions. Endowments tend not to be spread evenly across space, and economies of scale and production encourage agglomeration (Baldwin and

Krugman 2004). Thus, most nations have a degree of regional inequality that emerges from natural endowments that can be somewhat offset by government policies to disperse productivity across regions.

Governments have means to affect the distribution of income and productivity across regions. The dispersion of income can be straightforwardly achieved with income subsidies to poor regions, either directly to individuals, or as intergovernmental transfers to regions. To spread productivity, in contrast, national or regional governments must make specific efforts to attract business to places that lack natural or existing human or capital endowments. This is most achievable in industries dependent primarily on human capital. For example, US federal government investment in the military industry in Phoenix dramatically increased the size of the population and economy there. Brazil's national government hoped to even out the regional dominance of São Paolo by placing the capital Brasilia (and its workers and economic activity) in the Amazon. South Korea and Japan's national governments took the approach of investing in the education and skills of their populations to attract business in the absence of natural endowments suitable for primary production.

Just as it is not straightforward that interpersonal inequality leads to individual income redistribution, it is not clear that interregional inequality leads to regional redistribution. Governments are not machines that seek to equilibrate income, but rather political entities composed of agents with diverse interests. In particular, citizens and politicians from rich regions want to keep their wealth and status. Accordingly, regional transfers and national investment in particular regions are contentious political issues because they imply regional redistribution. Moreover, political institutions may be structured to reinforce existing economic disparities, whether interpersonal (Sokoloff and Engerman 2000) or interregional (Beramendi 2012; Beramendi and Wibbels 2010).

Measuring Fiscal Redistribution

Redistribution to Individuals

Governments primarily address inequality through their revenue and expenditure functions. In particular, redistributive policies tax resources from one group (typically the rich) and spend relatively more on a different group (usually the comparatively poor). Nations vary in how they (re)distribute. Some opt for progressive policies through the taxation function and others more through spending on the less well off (Kato 2010; Beramendi and Rueda 2007). Some redistribute through direct income transfers, and others (especially social democratic governments) invest in public goods (such as public education and health) intended to enable individuals to improve their economic condition. If the poor get more out of government than they put into it, which is always difficult to measure, then that system of government may be said to be progressive. Precisely how progressive (regressive) that system is depends on the degree to which the rich subsidize (or benefit from) government services in that nation. This topic is the subject of a very large literature in the social sciences. For a summary, see Lambert (2001).

Redistribution through Interregional Transfers

A logical concern with my discussion of redistribution is that it is too narrow. Governments redistribute through policies targeted to individuals but also through intergovernmental transfers to regions. Centralization of policymaking is not necessary for egalitarian policies if politicians can agree to equilibrate resources across regions and each region can decide how best to spend its money. This option is part of the menu of redistributive options that I consider, and explore in depth in the case examples.

Where regional transfers fit into the redistributive matrix is subject to several important considerations. First, are interregional transfers progressive, meaning they redistribute income from rich to poor regions? A concern with decentralization of policy is that decentralization of resources will mean that rich regions have a large pot to use and the poor regions a small pot. Inequality in regional resources can make for a very different level and quality of government provision across territories in the same nation (Prud'homme 1995). In a progressive regional transfer system, rich regions give to poor regions so that all regions have the same sized pot of money. I find reason for skepticism that regional transfers of this type are always progressive, as is discussed in the Argentine case. Transfers in Argentina go disproportionately to less populated (but not necessarily poor) regions that are overrepresented in the malapportioned legislature (Gervasoni 2010). The German example shows that transfers can be redistributive—we see a progressive formula in intergovernmental provisions that complements the strong centralized social welfare system. The USA stands as an intermediate case with effects from malapportionment and population-based formulae that do not necessarily send resources to the most needy areas (Lee 1998).

Second, how will interregional transfers be used? If we see regional transfers as a mechanism to reduce income inequality, we need to ask if transfers are used in this manner. Redistributing income, construed broadly, could mean improving the material condition of citizens or improving the economic foundations of the regions to provide opportunities for citizens to earn more income. In the former, we would expect intergovernmental transfers to fund social spending such as healthcare, unemployment insurance, or job training. US states, for example, receive money from the federal government to fund the low-income healthcare subsidy Medicaid. In the latter, transfers could be used to spur local economic growth. An example of this could be transfers used for infrastructure investments that improve transportation. Of course these two categories are not mutually exclusive—Medicaid subsidies could help some local business environments. In either of those cases, however, transfers may reduce inequality in the long run. In contrast, transfers may be allocated as rents to local elites or used for clientelistic purposes to gather votes for national parties from local constituencies. This possibility is addressed in the case of Argentina's federal system.

Interregional transfers are a subset of geographically targeted spending from the central government (Milligan and Smart 2005).[5] An alternative that I highlight throughout this book is the provision of local public goods within national budgets. National governments that allocate pork are also transferring to regions, but with a specific earmark (meaning regional politicians cannot decide how to spend the money) and distributive characteristic. All of these options fit within a menu of redistributive options available to nations. Territorialized systems simply take somewhat greater advantage of the interregional transfers and pork options than do centralized systems.

Social Allocation and Local Public Goods

A central mechanism linking certain institutions to redistribution is the fact that territorial constituencies encourage politicians to target political allocation to geographic zones. Political institutions either reinforce or dilute the territorial cleavage, moving nations in the direction of more geographically oriented spending or more national social spending. This seems theoretically plausible, but it is empirically observable?

Lee and Rogers (2015) address this question directly by examining the effects of different types of inequality (interpersonal and interregional) and different political institutions on government spending. They first examine the effects on the level of government spending, which is presumed to be broadly redistributive in a progressive tax system, and then look at government policy priorities—the distribution among the spending categories in a nation. These policy priorities capture the trade-offs in government spending between local public good and social spending, and show which nations are dedicating resources to which type of spending.

Lee and Rogers find that interpersonal and interregional inequality predict overall spending, but in different directions. As interregional inequality grows, government spending decreases significantly. This result is very consistent and robust to multiple empirical specifications, changes in the measurement of inequality and the control variables, and an instrumental variables approach. Consistent with RMR, as interpersonal inequality grows, government spending also tends to grow. This result, however, is more tenuous. The significance fluctuates with the specification of the model and changes in control variables. This mixed result is consistent with the idea that the effects of interpersonal inequality strongly depend on institutional conditions that affect the salience of national social class interests and the power of the majority coalition of the poor. Importantly, the three institutions in focus in this analysis—federalism, territorial elections, and presidentialism—are strongly and significantly associated with lower government spending. This is supporting evidence that these institutions do appear to hinder efforts at redistributively oriented groups from achieving their desired policy goals.

Government policy priorities capture how they allocate their resources (Jacoby and Schneider 2009). The governments of the USA and Germany, for example, spend similar amounts relative to GDP.[6] However, the USA allocates a much higher percentage of that money to national defense, whereas Germany spends a much higher percentage on social welfare. Thus differences in level of spending can obscure differences in the allocation of spending that are very important to the question of redistribution.

In Lee and Rogers (2015), they calculate central government policy priorities for OECD nations from 1990 to 2010. Policy priorities reflect relative allocation to spending categories and not total allocation. These scores use Jacoby and Schneider's (2009) unfolding method to show the spatial relationship between different spending categories. This method shows which types of spending tend to occur together. For example, the countries that allocate a large amount to social spending also tend to allocate a large amount to health spending. On the other side, those countries that tend to spend more on national defense also allocate more to domestic security and public order. Jacoby and Schneider argued that spending categories spatially cluster in this way, and that these clusters reflect differences in the ways that governments target their citizens—i.e., whether through particularistic spending to individuals or public goods to localities.[7] Importantly, this measure incorporates all categories of spending, and not just social spending as a percentage of GDP, to evaluate how a country's distributive system operates.

In Figures 2.5 and 2.6, I show the results from Lee and Rogers' analysis of policy priorities in OECD nations. Figure 2.5 shows how spending categories

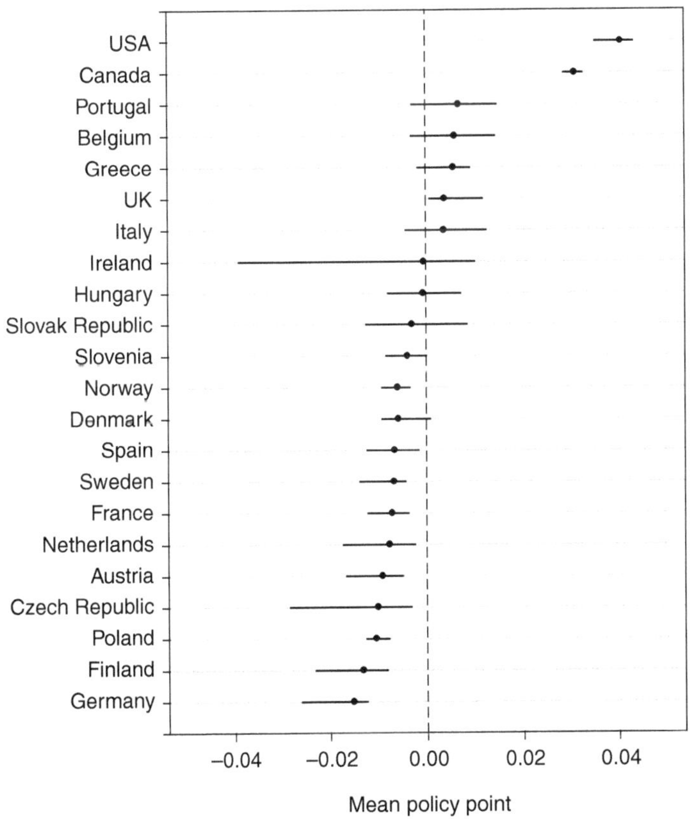

Figure 2.5 Policy Point Locations, OECD 1990–2010.

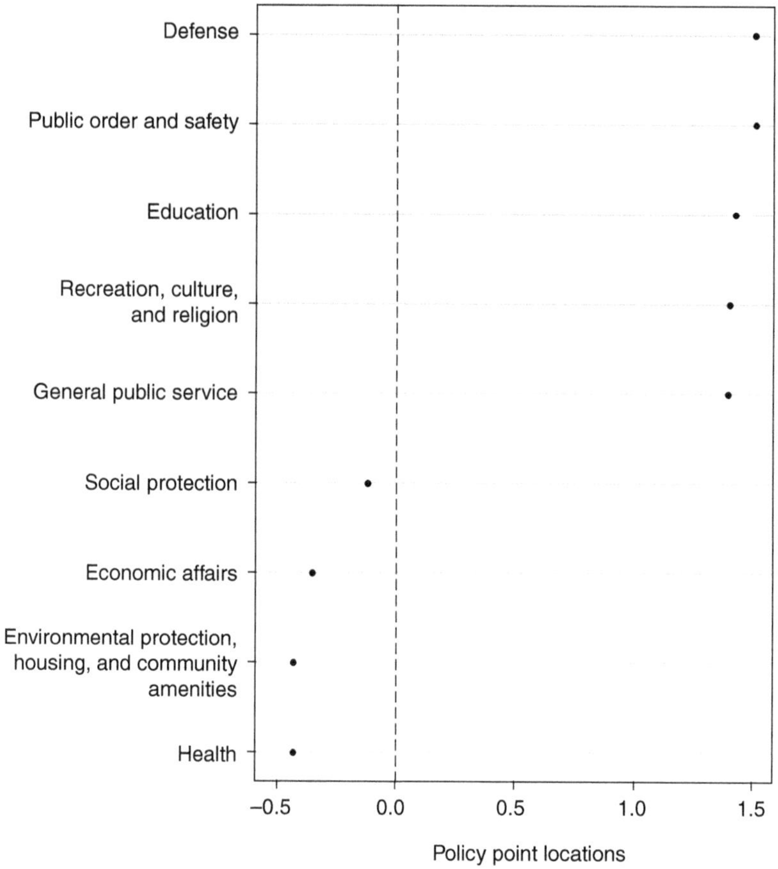

Figure 2.6 Policy Priorities, Country Mean 1990–2010.

cluster in this sample of nations. On the left side of the figure, one sees spending that tends to be targeted to social groups (especially the less well off), including social protection, health, housing and community amenities.[8] On the right side are national defense, public order and safety (domestic), general public services (which includes transfers from the central to sub-national governments), and education. The policy point location in Figure 2.5 shows a clear trade-off between spending on social welfare and spending on local public goods. It also shows that nations seem to cluster their spending on one of these two broad allocative methods.

In Figure 2.6, we see where the OECD countries fall on this policy priority matrix. Countries on the left side of the table take a negative value and spend more on the categories shown in the left of Figure 2.5 (health, social protection, economic services, environmental protection and community amenities). Countries on the right side of Figure 2.6 take a positive value, and spend more on the categories shown in the right of Figure 2.5 (national defense, domestic public order and safety, general government services, and education).[9]

The country positions in Figure 2.6 capture differences in spending allocation among OECD nations often noted by scholars of comparative politics i.e., the differences in the spending patterns in traditionally liberal countries and that found in more social democratic countries. These differences are captured in the polarization of spending categories. For example, highly egalitarian countries (e.g., Germany, Denmark, Norway, and Sweden) cluster together as spending more on social categories. On the other side, the countries that we expect to spend quite differently, including on categories thought to enhance capitalist markets (especially order and infrastructure), do so predictably (e.g., the USA, Canada, and Ireland).

If my theoretical framework is accurate, we should see predicable effects of political institutions and inequality on these spending allocations. The political institutions that I classify as reinforcing territorial cleavages should be associated with greater spending on locally targeted public goods. Their alternatives should dilute the territorial cleavage and reduce incentives for local targeting. Accordingly, these institutions should be associated with more spending that can be targeted to particular social groups (class, age, race, language, ethnicity, etc.). In Table 2.1 below, I show the abbreviated results of the detailed regression analysis in Lee and Rogers (2015). These results give strong support for the relationship between territorial institutions and territorial spending.

The models in Table 2.1 show the relationship between government policy priorities and the three political institutions in focus in this book. The dependent variable is the mean policy point location of the OECD countries in the sample. Consistent with the values on the x-axis of Figure 2.5, a negative score means that a country spends more on social categories, and a positive score indicates that more is spent on local public goods. Thus the positive and significant value for federalism suggests that federal nations spend more on local public goods and less on social spending than do unitary systems. The negative and significant values for parliamentarism mean that those systems allocate more to social spending than do presidential systems. The positive and significant value for plurality electoral systems suggests these rules are associated with higher spending on local public goods and intergovernmental transfers.

The results in Table 2.1 support the first mechanism that links political institutions to inequality—i.e., politicians' incentives to deliver either territorialized goods or broad social goods to constituents. Localizing electoral rules, here measured as plurality rules, are significantly related to more spending on geographically targetable goods. Likewise, federalism and presidentialism are also associated with significantly more spending on the categories that are more easily targeted to localities. These results also point to an important trade-off that is influenced by political institutions—systems that are spending more on local goods spend less (in relative terms) on social spending. Incentives to target localities under localizing political institutions therefore suggest one underexplored reason why certain systems redistribute less income.

In addition to political institutions, the effects of interpersonal and interregional inequality on government spending also reveal results that are interesting for this study. As inequality grows, what is the effect on spending? For both

Table 2.1 Institutional Predictors of Government Policy Priorities

	Base	*Base*	*Full*	*Robust*
	[1]	*[2]*	*[3]*	*[4]*
Inequality Types				
Gini (Regional GDP per capita)	–0.055***		–0.054***	–0.055***
	(0.005)		(0.007)	(0.008)
Gini (Household Income)		–0.014**	–0.013*	–0.021***
		(0.006)	(0.007)	(0.003)
Political Institutitons				
Parliamentary System	–0.661***	–0.609***	–0.662***	–0.661***
	(0.058)	(0.101)	(0.060)	(0.051)
Plurality Electoral Rule	0.385***	0.357***	0.359***	
	(0.077)	(0.098)	(0.087)	
Average District Magnitude				–0.003***
				(0.001)
Federal Government	0.150***	0.120*	0.125**	
	(0.054)	(0.071)	(0.062)	
Territorial Bicameralism				0.028
				(0.021)
Controls				
Population (Logged)	–0.061	–0.154**	–0.041	0.133***
	(0.049)	(0.072)	(0.058)	(0.019)
Trade (% of GDP)	0.004***	–0.000	0.004***	0.003***
	(0.001)	(0.001)	(0.001)	(0.001)
Real GDP (Output)	–0.024*	–0.003	–0.027	–0.054***
	(0.014)	(0.018)	(0.017)	(0.013)
% Population >65	–0.051***	–0.009	–0.049***	–0.093***
	(0.008)	(0.017)	(0.013)	(0.013)
Lagged Dependent Variable	0.902***	0.893***	0.903***	0.911***
	(0.014)	(0.017)	(0.018)	(0.015)
Constant	2.050***	1.316**	2.600***	4.184***
	(0.190)	(0.657)	(0.273)	(0.322)
Number of Observations	47	47	47	47
Countries	19	19	19	19
χ^2	100,465	6,011	261,276	188,636

Source: Lee and Rogers (2015).

Notes

Two-tailed test signficant at $***p<0.01$, $**p<0.05$, $*p<0.1$. All independent variables are calculated as 5 year average values. All models are Feasible Generalized Least Squares regressions, corrected for heteroskedastic and first-order panel-specific error structures.

types, greater inequality is associated with significantly higher spending on social goods. The reason this would be the case for interpersonal inequality is straightforward—as inequality grows, the poor demand more redistributive spending. The policy priority measure suggests that rising interpersonal inequality is linked to relatively more spending on social goods, but this does not necessarily mean that these governments spend more overall or that they provide higher levels of social goods.

The effect of interregional inequality is more interesting. Why would greater divides between regions lead to more social spending? Lee and Rogers argue this is reflective of a distributive conflict between rich and poor regions on the one hand and equal and unequal regions on the other. Redistributive local public goods spending would mean that rich areas are subsidizing targeted spending to poor areas; this necessarily involves an income transfer across regional borders. Redistributive social spending, conversely, would mean that the poor citizen would be getting more resources, regardless of their region. Rich regions therefore have an incentive to push for greater social spending under these circumstances because they can benefit from subsidies to their own poor population. Local public goods, on the other hand, are by definition excludable based on location. Since rich regions also tend to be urban and unequal, this provides incentives for them to support social spending in their own interests. Recall, furthermore, that increased regional inequality leads to lower spending and lower tax capacity (Beramendi and Rogers 2015). This finding reveals a shift in emphasis, not an increased commitment to social spending, as interregional differences in income grow.

However, it also points to a problem of bargaining in territorialized political institutions. I argue throughout that localizing political institutions incentivize targeted spending to regions. Localized spending is valuable to politicians and to constituents, and works as a bargaining chip in forming national coalitions for policy reform (Diaz-Cayeros 2006). However, as interregional inequality grows, localized spending is increasingly redistributive from rich to poor regions. This may be a source of contention in localized political systems—as interregional inequality grows, rich regions are paying more to bargain for national policies. Under these institutional circumstances, growth in regional disparities may result in more policy gridlock. This dynamic appeared after German reunification as the territorial Bundesrat increased its use of veto and delaying powers on budget matters (Gunlicks 2002).

Overview of the Cases

In this section, I provide a broad overview of the three case examples used in the chapters focused on individual institutions. This overview is intended to provide background on the political systems and the extent and nature of interregional and interpersonal inequality within these nations.

United States of America

The USA features a diverse economic geography with varied economic productivity spread throughout the nation. The USA has regional variation in service sector industries, natural resources, transportation, and other features. Despite these differences, income is spread relatively evenly in the USA, in comparative perspective. Figure 2.7 below shows median household income levels by state in 2013 with data from LIS.[10] The richest state, Massachusetts, had an average household income (before taxes and transfers) of $60,968, and the poorest state,

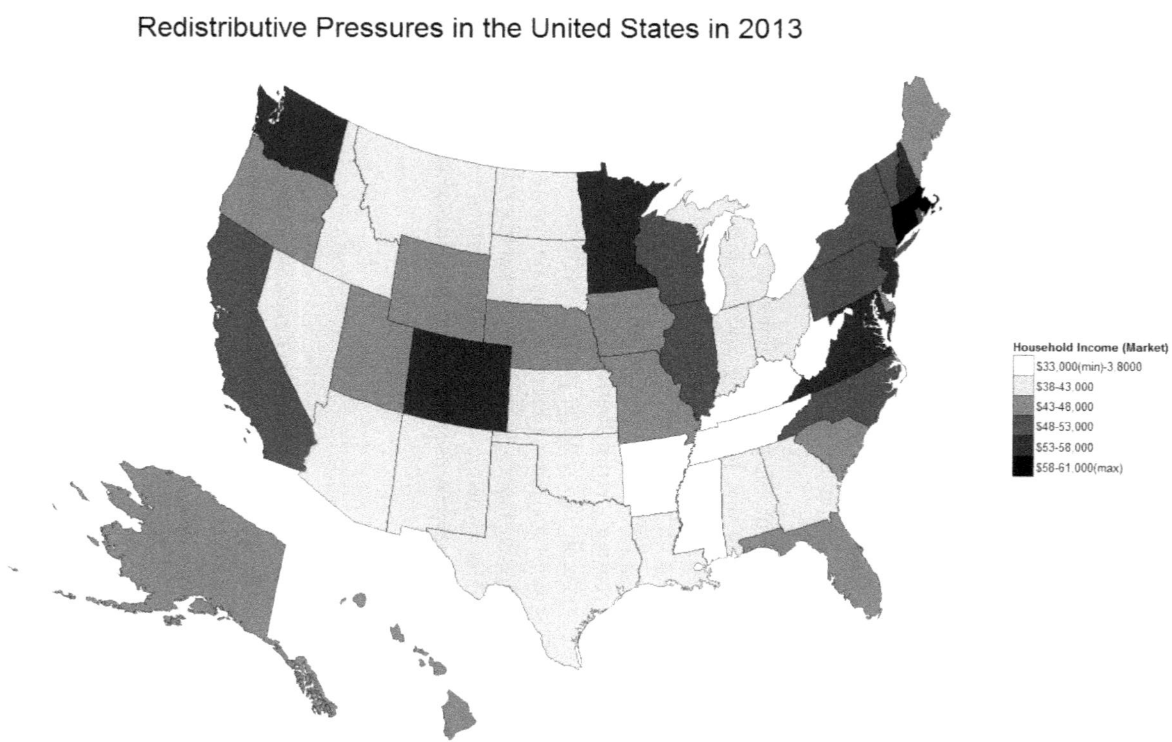

Figure 2.7 Map of Median Household Income, by US State (source: Luxembourg Income Study).

Note
Values represent household income per capita (market value) in current US dollars.

Arkansas, had an average household income of $33,663 in that year. While on a percentage basis this makes the income in Massachusetts seem much higher than in Arkansas, these differences are dwarfed by the disparities in other nations. Moreover, these income calculations do not factor in the cost of living, which is certainly lower in Arkansas than Massachusetts.

Redistribution in the United States

Redistributive spending and tax policies in the USA are subject to the nominal, contentious process in the separation of powers system. Unlike in Germany, spending and tax policies are strongly decentralized, limiting the tools of a motivated national government to enact transformational reform.

On the spending side, US redistributive spending is a "marble cake" of heterogeneous federal, state, and local policies. Program management is highly fragmented and citizens in similar circumstances in different states face very different levels and quality of services. With the exception of old age pensions (Social Security), most redistributive programs are state-run, means-tested and focused on the poorest members of society. Significant changes in spending programs at the national level are rare, given the contentious politics of redistribution, and the difficult policy process of passing both legislative houses and a president under frequent conditions of divided government. Programs, moreover, atrophy due to failure to adjust them to changing economic conditions, which has a similar effect as legislated retrenchment (Hacker and Pierson 2010). Changes to state programs must pass similar institutional separation of powers systems in the states. Many states also have long-standing conservative legislative majorities that oppose redistribution.

Most redistributive spending is funded through progressive income taxes at the national and state levels in the USA. Income tax rates in the USA are moderate by international standards but relatively progressive in structure. Certain states do not collect taxes on income, so draw more from sales, property, and other taxes. Unlike most nations, the USA does not collect a national consumption (sales) tax. Most national redistributive programs in Western Europe and Latin America rely heavily on national consumption taxes (Beramendi and Rueda 2007; Ha and Rogers 2015). Changes in tax policy are extremely controversial at the national and state levels. Reforms to national income taxes (both personal and corporate) since the 1980s have generally reduced the progressivity of the tax structure and reduced government revenue (Piketty and Saez 2006b). States face limitations in tax policy due to interstate competition for businesses and residents (Tiebout 1956). These factors constrain policymakers even in states inclined to increase program generosity.

US Institutions

The political institutions of the USA are characterized by separation of powers and territorial constituency structures. The US presidential system features a powerful legislative branch and a largely reactive president with limited policy tools. Presidents and legislatures, even those composed of a majority of the President's party, often clash, with resulting policy gridlock. Presidents have a legislative veto and informal agenda-setting powers through cooperation with their co-partisans in the legislature. Presidents have often been first-movers in major redistributive policy reform, such as Social Security (F. Roosevelt), income subsidies (L. Johnson), and health care (L. Johnson and Obama). The US presidential contest is strongly territorial because of the Electoral College, which compiles votes by state into (in nearly all states) a winner-take-all allocation of seats. This institution incentivizes presidential candidates to spend time in and distribute resources to "swing" states (Kriner and Reeves 2014).

Electoral rules for the US Congress are also strongly territorial. In the upper house, the Senate, the constituency is the state. In the lower house, the House of Representatives, the first order constituency is the state, which is subsequently subdivided into electoral districts of roughly equivalent population size. In both bodies, members have incentives to target territorial goods to their districts (Cain et al. 1987). SMD rules in both houses encourage local bipartism, and the contest for the presidency encourages national bipartism (Cox 1997). Given the substantial differences in regional ideology and diversity in regional economic structures, the two national parties feature substantial internal heterogeneity of policy preferences. This heterogeneity and regional orientation is thought to undermine efforts of national coalitions interested in income redistribution.

US federalism is the institution most frequently cited as a barrier to a comprehensive welfare system (Pierson 1995; Skocpol and Amenta 1986). Within this structure, states retain many strong policy-making powers. This includes jurisdiction over lucrative taxes, most notably on income and consumption.[11] Both of these taxes are usually reserved exclusively for national governments and both affect the progressivity of the tax structure. Spending is also considerably decentralized in the USA, including on areas central to the welfare state, such as healthcare and low-income subsidies. States with weak economies or ideological opposition to redistribution have tools to limit its generosity within their borders. Federalism also scuttles the organizational coherence of redistributive coalitions in the USA because their efforts must be duplicated across states, and because multiple veto actors can block or delay the passage of preferred policies. Moreover, given the territorial structure of representation and service delivery, the wealth of states and internal distributions of income may divide redistributive coalitions across diverse states.

Regional preferences and economic differences clearly played a role in the design of US political institutions (Beramendi and Wibbels 2010). The constituency structure and co-equal powers of the House of Representatives and the Senate, for example, represent a bargain between small and large states that bolster the voting power of the small states. The federal structure placing strong powers in the hands of states also reflects the diverse economic geography and asset specificity of the states (Beramendi 2012).

Germany

As seen in Figure 2.4 above, Germany's Länder (states) vary considerably in economic productivity (regional GDP per capita). Figure 2.8, however shows a more compact income distribution. These relatively uniform household income results (even on market income) reveal the effects of considerable redistribution across regions and individuals in Germany. While the income standards are high in the highly productive regions of the south, including Bavaria and Hesse, the household income differences across the west and east are relatively muted. Remarkably, certain Western Länder (e.g., Saarland) show similar income levels to the poorest Eastern Länder (e.g., Thuringia).

Reunification marked a dramatic change in Germany's economic geography. Each of the East German Länder that joined the Federal Republic of Germany in 1990 was poorer than the poorest West German Länder. Redistributive efforts by the national government have equilibrated income somewhat, as can be seen in the partial convergence of Eastern Länder with poorer Länder in the West in Figure 2.8. Importantly, the change in interregional inequality associated with reunification has heightened territorial identities and territorial political conflict

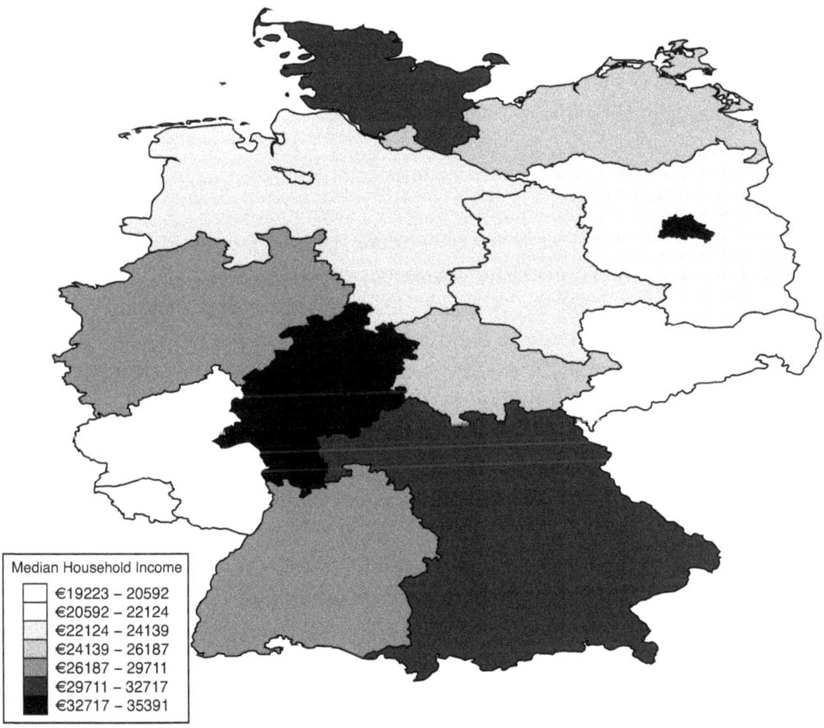

Figure 2.8 Map of Median Household Income, by German Länder (source: Luxembourg Income Study).

Note
Values represent household income per capita (market value) in current Euros.

(Jeffrey 1999). As a result, redistribution in Germany, whether through transfers to the Länder governments or through centralized social welfare, involves a substantial income transfer from rich to poor regions. Both interregional and interpersonal inequality thus stand as important political issues in Germany, and the government does much to address both.

The design of German institutions has changed frequently with political upheaval in the nineteenth and twentieth centuries. The current German federal system was shaped in the period after World War II in consultation with Allied forces. That war had the effect of reducing regional inequalities because it destroyed productive cities (Berlin, Bremen, etc.) Germany's Länder after the war until the late 1970s and 1980s were broadly homogenous in productivity, and distributive tensions among them limited (Jeffrey 1999). Accordingly, the agreed upon institutions reflected concerns that were shared across regions with social protection and efficient national risk pooling (Manow 2005).

The nature and level of interpersonal and interregional inequality in Germany changed significantly in 1989 with reunification. This exacerbated a growing regional inequality that had become apparent in the 1980s and led to increasing tension within the territorial Bundesrat. Prior to reunification, the tension was between increasingly affluent regions in the southwest of Germany and declining industrial regions in the northwest. After reunification, the even greater West–East divide added to these distributive conflicts and contributed to the expanded role of the Bundesrat (Gunlicks 2002).

Redistribution in Germany

Germany has one of the most generous welfare states in the world. Germany was the historical first mover in the development of welfare benefits through Bismark's reforms of the 1870s. Bismark designed the social insurance system along occupational lines. Despite the tremendous flux in institutions in the early twentieth century, Germany's welfare system is very similar in structure to its original design. However, unlike in Bismark's system, revenue is pooled between occupational classes (white and blue collar) to reduce disparities in system generosity. At the same time, because contributions are the primary source of funding, German social spending is not highly progressive but is primarily a system of social insurance (Manow 2005).

The financing of Germany's social spending sets it apart from other generous systems in Europe. Funding is established through employer and employee contributions to a specialized fund. This fund is somewhat separate from other categories of national spending; it is not funded through general taxation and it does not require legislative action to respond to changes in economic conditions because it has automatic adjustments. This "para-state" fiscal arrangement allows the welfare state to avoid the contentious politics of taxing and spending, especially in the Bundesrat. Manow (2005) argues that this fiscal arrangement clouds political responsibility, allowing politicians to claim credit for its generosity or to criticize its profligacy, without incurring the costs of legislating for it.

This has lead to a common pool problem that arguably results in overspending on the welfare state in Germany.

German Institutions

Germany's institutions are highly nationalized despite their federal and territorial design. Germany's federation assigns policymaking authority to the central level, and policy implementation and administration to the Länder. The central government distributes large intergovernmental transfers to administer policies within the Länder. These transfers are considerably progressive—they are more generous to the poor regions than to the rich ones. Länder legislatures are elected by their populations to form a Länder government. The cabinet members of the Länder government serve as representatives to the Bundesrat.

The Bundesrat is the most obvious manifestation of territorial representation in national politics. This upper house holds an absolute veto over any policy considered to affect the administration or fiscal policies of the Länder governments. Originally this was thought to constitute about 10 percent of legislation but that interpretation has increased to around 55 percent of legislation (Manow 2005). Because Länder share responsibility for the collection of every major tax in Germany, the Bundesrat is a very significant veto player in revenue policy (Gunlicks 2002). They also hold a suspensive veto over policies considered unrelated to Land policy. However, these tools are not applicable to the largely autonomous para-state financing of the welfare state.

Germany's electoral rules in the lower house, the Bundestag, are defined by territory and administered according to two electoral designs—SMD and closed-list PR. In the SMDs, the territorial design has two levels. First, like the US House, the country is divided into its Länder, and then districts of roughly equal population are carved out within each Land. The PR competition designates Länder as electoral districts, and determines the district magnitude according to regional population. The PR system encourages multipartism, with typically three to five significant parties. In both methods of designing constituencies, territory is an organizing principle, but the localizing effect is considerably stronger in the SMDs. The mixed member design was intended to provide the best of both worlds by incentivizing both nationally oriented policies and responsiveness to local constituencies in the national legislature (Shugart and Wattenberg 2001).

The parliamentary structure in Germany is dominated by the chancellor (prime minister) and cabinet, both of which are supported by coalitions of disciplined, ideologically cohesive parties. Parties work to bridge differences between their regional representatives in the Bundesrat and the more nationally oriented Bundestag. The executive–legislature fusion and cohesive parties in the German case show a strong contrast to the presidential systems with decentralized, heterogeneous parties in the US case and the disciplined but fragmented parties in the Argentine case.

Argentina

Argentina has very high regional disparity and interpersonal inequality in comparative perspective. Figure 2.9 demonstrates how income is spread across Argentina's provinces. The darker shades denote wealthier provinces and the lighter shades denote poorer provinces. The map clearly shows pockets of relative wealth and pockets of relative poverty within the nation. Specifically, the capital city of Buenos Aires and the Patagonian provinces of the south (Santa Cruz and Tierra del Fuego) have considerably higher median incomes ($42,000–$60,000 Argentine Pesos per year) than the provinces of the north, such as Formosa, Chaco, Santiago del Estero and Corrientes ($18,720–$20,400) per year. These income differences are indicative of very different levels of economic development within the same nation. Unlike in Germany, however, the Argentine governments do little to equilibrate regional economic productivity or interpersonal income.[12]

Argentina's populace, like that in Germany and the USA, includes a large contingent that supports government redistribution. Like the other nations of Latin America, Argentina has very high levels of income inequality and a large population below the poverty line. The labor movement in Argentina has historically been among the most powerful seen outside of Western Europe. The country experienced notable anarchist and syndicalist unrest during the 1920s. In the past and the current period, strikes and protests by unions have been common. With an educated, activist population and a large latent demand for redistributive policies, Argentina seems on the face of it a likely case for substantial welfare reform.

Redistribution in Argentina

A motivated national majority in Argentina faces structural barriers to significant redistribution on the tax and spending side. Argentina underperforms in tax collection overall and in particular on income taxes (Bergman 2003). The country relies heavily on relatively inefficient consumption taxes—both on trade and VAT—collected at the national level. Argentina's tax sharing structure, moreover, has the national government collecting most revenue (income, consumption, trade) and the provinces spending most of it. This creates, as in Germany, an obfuscation of fiscal responsibility that results in under collection at the national level and overspending at the provincial level (Rodden and Wibbels 2002).

Redistributive spending is fragmented and privatized in Argentina as in the USA. Health care, for example, is largely a private good, with approximately 78 percent of spending occurring through private provision or contributory social insurance, and the provinces filling in the gaps (Cavagnero et al. 2006). A web of union-based systems (Obras Sociales) organized by occupation provides health insurance for some formal sector employees. A high percentage of the population (around 38 percent) lacks health insurance (ibid.) Pensions and social insurance are similarly decentralized and limited in their scope.

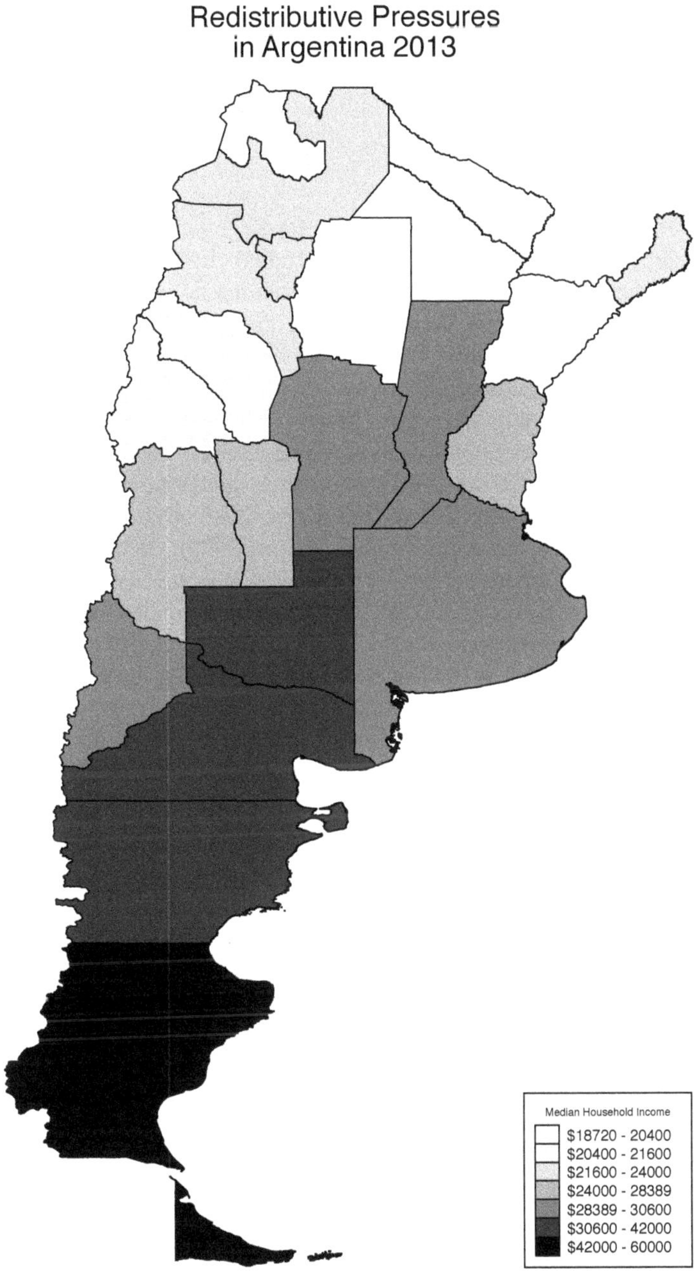

Figure 2.9 Map of Median Household Income, by Argentine Province (source: Encuesto Permanente de Hogares).

Note
Values represent household income per capita (market value) in current Argentine Pesos.

The pensions system in particular has struggled with deficits due in part to contributors underreporting income or simple evasion. The responsibility for provision of welfare programs has fluctuated over time between central and provincial administrations, with change in the 1990s shifting most of the responsibilities to the provinces (Lloyd-Sherlock 2005).

Argentine Institutions

Throughout Argentina's history, the central political conflict has been regional (Rock 1987; Gibson 1996). Politicians from the capital city and its surrounding province have fought to centralize control away from interior provinces and the remaining provinces have sought autonomy from the powerful Porteños. This regional dispute between the capital city and the surrounding provinces on one side, and the interior, peripheral provinces on the other, extends to the academic debate on Argentina's institutions as well. Most of the literature sides with the capital, depicting the interior provinces as leeching (Sawers 1996; Tommasi et al. 2001), profligate (Jones et al. 2000), sometimes authoritarian (Gervasoni 2010; Gibson 2005), clientelist (Gibson and Calvo 2000; Calvo and Murillo 2004; Stokes 2005) and economically stunted (Sawers 1998). Others emphasize the role of the most developed provinces in stifling development in the interior provinces by creating resource dependence and thrusting unfunded mandates on ill-prepared provincial governments (Eaton 2001; Bonvecchi and Lodola 2011). Still others explain both sides as evidence of a bargain among the provinces to build national coalitions (Diaz-Cayeros 2006; Gibson 1996).

The debate on the Argentine case is similarly divided on the strength of federalism and the role of the party system within it (Benton 2009; Diaz-Cayeros 2006). Most scholars agree that the provinces have wide powers to spend and make policy within their territories (Remmer and Wibbels 2000; Bonvecchi and Lodola 2011). At the same time, the central government retains powers of intervention into provincial affairs and collects much of the tax revenue in Argentina (Diaz-Cayeros 2006). Nobody questions that regional transfers sit at the heart of bargaining in national politics (Rogers 2014).

Argentina's presidential system reserves strong legislative powers for the president, including decree authority, bill introduction, and the line-item veto. At times, these tools allow the president to reform policy without majority support in the legislature. However, presidents always require support from provincial governors, and governors' agents in the legislature, for major reform efforts (Levitsky 2003). Support from governors is frequently secured with targeted transfers to regions (Bambaci et al. 2002). Like the USA, Argentina had a very territorialized presidential contest with an electoral college, yet this institution was replaced in 1994 with a popular contest. Argentina thus serves as an interesting case for whether the presidency works as a "bridging" institution that nationalizes and coheres fragmented interests, or whether it works to reinforce existing regional cleavages.

Argentina illustrates the difficult balance that must be struck by political parties organizing for national policy in a nation characterized by diversity in level of development, and in political and economic structures. Argentina's parties are strongly federal—provincial party leaders control nominations to the national legislature and have a strong pull in selecting presidential candidates (Jones 1997; Jones et al. 2000). Nonetheless, the national parties are highly disciplined in the legislature (Molinelli 1991; Mustapic 2000). Legislative seats are decided according to closed-list PR, which incentivizes strong loyalty among members to party leaders. Paradoxically, Argentina's parties appear to be both fragmented and united and regional differences appear to fall away in national policymaking yet remain strong in party formation. Certainly, regional divides have been critical in the formation and strength of Argentina's parties (Gibson 1996). Malapportionment of the legislature, which bolsters considerably the representation of the less populated provinces, also shapes the coalition behavior of parties (Eaton 2001; Gibson and Calvo 2000.) The overrepresented provinces in Argentina are in the interior of the country. Importantly, as can be seen in Figure 2.9, these interior provinces with a strong voice in the legislature differ greatly in their average income level and likely preferences for redistribution.

Conclusion

This chapter provides the empirical backbone of the theoretical and substantive chapters that follow. The first section of this chapter documented the extent of interregional and interpersonal inequality for a large sample of nations across the world. These two measures of inequality were shown to capture different phenomena and to vary widely across and within global regions. Also within that section were brief overviews of how inequality is measured, as well as broad theories of how inequality comes about.

In the second section, I addressed the empirical support for the claim that underlies an important theoretical mechanism in the book—that territorial politics incentivize politicians to deliver more targeted local public goods and to engage in less social spending. This analysis featured a variable that is new to the literature on comparative politics—namely, government policy priorities—adopted from my previous research. The three institutions of focus in Chapters 4–6 (federalism, localizing electoral rules, presidentialism) were shown here to be strongly associated with greater provision of geographically oriented spending relative to social spending in this regression analysis.

The third section provided an overview of interregional inequality and the political institutions of the USA, Germany, and Argentina. The economic geography of these three nations varies considerably, with important implications for interregional inequality and political representation. Their institutional settings vary considerably but also overlap in ways that allow for meaningful comparison. The USA and Argentina have similar presidential and federal designs, but Argentina shares more in common with Germany in its proportional electoral rules. Each has unique history that has shaped its particular responses to income inequality.

Notes

1 These two country examples also show the important difference in regional GDP per capita and regional household income. These nations have big spreads in productivity, but thanks to redistributive social spending, have low variation in standards of living.
2 I attempt to capture electorally relevant territories in my income measures but cannot match every voting district with existing data. The level I use is typically the unit of representation for territorial upper houses, the district level for geographically oriented lower houses, and the administrative locus for fiscal and other policy decentralization.
3 Any income transfers from the richer to the poorer regions reduce inequality (Pigou 1912).
4 I use the "square root scale" in which household income is divided by the square root of household size. This recognizes diminishing costs per added member of a household. For example, the scale implies that a household of four has needs twice as large as a single-person household.
5 In the central budget categories discussed in the empirical section below, interregional transfers make up the majority of the "General Public Service" category for most countries. Not surprisingly, high spending in this budget category occurs frequently in the nations that also spend a lot on local public goods categories.
6 On average, Germany tends to spend more than the USA relative to GDP.
7 For a full description of the policy priority methodology and theoretical foundations, see Jacoby and Schneider (2001, 2009) and Lee and Rogers (2015).
8 The OECD cases show that "economic affairs" spending is high in countries with high social spending. This trend has been noted in OECD literature (OECD Government at a Glance 2011). This category includes state-run banks and other industries, more commonly high in nations with large public sectors.
9 National defense is typically considered a national public good, not a local public good. However, the nature of military spending tends to be highly geographic because it is targeted to particular districts that house military bases and support facilities.
10 In the previous charts, I used regional level GDP per capita to represent income because of much wider coverage available for GDP. State GDP per capita and income are highly correlated. There is also good reason to believe that both income level and state GDP are very important motivators of preferences for national government outcomes.
11 The US national government also taxes income.
12 They do, of course, redistribute in the form of interregional transfers. These do not serve to equlibrate regional income, however (Delgado and Russo 2000).

References

Baldwin, Richard E., and Paul Krugman. "Agglomeration, Integration and Tax Harmonisation." *European Economic Review* 48, no. 1 (2004): 1–23.

Bambaci, Juliana, Tamara Saront, and Mariano Tommasi. "The Political Economy of Economic Reforms in Argentina." *The Journal of Policy Reform* 5, no. 2 (2002): 75–88.

Benton, Allyson L. "What Makes Strong Federalism Seem Weak? Fiscal Resources and Presidential–Provincial Relations in Argentina." *Publius: The Journal of Federalism* 39, no. 4 (2009): 651–76.

Beramendi, Pablo. *The Political Geography of Inequality: Regions and Redistribution.* Cambridge University Press, 2012.

Beramendi, Pablo, and Melissa Rogers. *Geography, Capacity, and Inequality*. Duke University and Claremont Graduate University, 2015.

Beramendi, Pablo, and David Rueda. "Social Democracy Constrained: Indirect Taxation in Industrialized Democracies." *British Journal of Political Science* 37, no. 4 (2007): 619–41.

Beramendi, Pablo, and Erik Wibbels. "Foundational Bargains: Distributive Conflicts and Representation in Federations." Paper presented at the Meeting of the American Political Science Association, Washington, 2010.

Beramendi, Pablo, Silja Häusermann, Herbert Kitschelt, and Hanspeter Kriesi, "The Politics of Advanced Capitalism: An Introduction" in *The Politics of Advanced Capitalism*, Cambridge University Press, New York, 2015.

Bergman, Marcelo S. "Tax Reforms and Tax Compliance: The Divergent Paths of Chile and Argentina." *Journal of Latin American Studies* 35, no. 3 (2003): 593–624.

Bonvecchi, Alejandro, and Germán Lodola. "The Dual Logic of Intergovernmental Transfers: Presidents, Governors, and the Politics of Coalition-Building in Argentina." *Publius: The Journal of Federalism* 41, no. 2 (2011): 179–206.

Brune, Nancy, and Geoffrey Garrett. "The Globalization Rorschach Test: International Economic Integration, Inequality, and the Role of Government." *Annual Review of Political Science* 8 (2005): 399–423.

Cain, Bruce E., John A. Ferejohn, and Morris P. Fiorina. *The Personal Vote: Constituency Service and Electoral Independence*. Harvard University Press, Cambridge MA, 1987.

Calvo, Ernesto, and Maria Victoria Murillo. "Who Delivers? Partisan Clients in the Argentine Electoral Market." *American Journal of Political Science* 48, no. 4 (2004): 742–57.

Case, Karl E., and Ray C. Fair. *Principles of Microeconomics*. Pearson Education, Harlow UK, 2007.

Cavagnero, Eleonora, Guy Carrin, Ke Xu, and Ana Mylena Aguilar-Rivera. "Health Financing in Argentina: An Empirical Study of Health Care Expenditure and Utilization." *Innovations in Health Financing: Working Paper Series*, no. 8 (2006).

Chhibber, Pradeep, and Ken Kollman. *The Formation of National Party Systems: Federalism and Party Competition in Canada, Great Britain, India, and the United States*. Princeton University Press, Princeton NJ, 2004.

Cox, Gary W. *Making Votes Count: Strategic Coordination in the World's Electoral Systems*. Vol. 7: Cambridge University Press, 1997.

Deininger, Klaus, and Lyn Squire. "A New Data Set Measuring Income Inequality." *The World Bank Economic Review* 10, no. 3 (1996): 565–91.

Delgado, Felisa Ceña, and José Luis Russo. "Evolución De La Convergencia Y Disparidades Provinciales En Argentina." *Revista de Estudios Regionales*, no. 57 (2000): 151–75.

Diaz-Cayeros, Alberto. *Federalism, Fiscal Authority, and Centralization in Latin America*. Cambridge University Press, 2006.

Eaton, Kent. "Decentralisation, Democratisation and Liberalisation: The History of Revenue Sharing in Argentina, 1934–1999." *Journal of Latin American Studies* 33, no. 1 (2001): 1–28.

Faguet, Jean-Paul, and Mahvish Shami. *Fiscal Policy and Spatial Inequality in Latin America and Beyond*. World Bank, Washington DC, 2008.

Gallup, John Luke, Jeffrey D. Sachs, and Andrew D. Mellinger. "Geography and Economic Development." *International Regional Science Review* 22, no. 2 (1999): 179–232.

Gervasoni, Carlos. "A Rentier Theory of Subnational Regimes." *World Politics* 62, no. 2 (2010): 302–40.

Gibson, Edward L. *Class and Conservative Parties: Argentina in Comparative Perspective*. Johns Hopkins University Press, Baltimore MD, 1996.

Gibson, Edward L. "Boundary Control." *World Politics* 58, no. 1 (2005): 101–32.

Gibson, Edward L., and Ernesto Calvo. "Federalism and Low-Maintenance Constituencies: Territorial Dimensions of Economic Reform in Argentina." *Studies in Comparative International Development* 35, no. 3 (2000): 32–55.

Gunlicks, Arthur B. "The Impact of Unification on German Federalism." *German Politics* 11, no. 3 (2002): 131–52.

Ha, Eunyoung, and Melissa Rogers. *Shifting the Burden in Global Markets: Partisan Effects on Tax Revenue in Less Developed Countries*. Claremont Graduate University, California, 2015.

Hacker, Jacob S., and Paul Pierson. "Winner-Take-All Politics: Public Policy, Political Organization, and the Precipitous Rise of Top Incomes in the United States." *Politics and Society* 38, no. 2 (2010): 152–204.

Jacoby, William G., and Saundra K. Schneider. "Variability in State Policy Priorities: An Empirical Analysis." *Journal of Politics* 63, no. 2 (2001): 544–68.

Jacoby, William G., and Saundra K. Schneider. "A New Measure of Policy Spending Priorities in the American States." *Political Analysis* 17, no. 1 (2009): 1–24.

Jeffery, Charlie. "Party Politics and Territorial Representation in the Federal Republic of Germany." *West European Politics* 22, no. 2 (1999): 130–66.

Jones, Mark P. "Evaluating Argentina's Presidential Democracy: 1983–1995." *Presidentialism and Democracy in Latin America*, edited by Scott Mainwaring and Matthew Soberg Shugart, Cambridge University Press, (1997): 259–99.

Jones, Mark P. "Explaining the High Level of Party Discipline in the Argentine Congress." in *Legislative Politics in Latin America*, edited by Scott Morgenstern and Benito Nacif. Cambridge University Press, New York, (2002): 147–84.

Jones, Mark P., Pablo Sanguinetti, and Mariano Tommasi. "Politics, Institutions, and Fiscal Performance in a Federal System: An Analysis of the Argentine Provinces." *Journal of Development Economics* 61, no. 2 (2000): 305–33.

Kato, Junko. *Regressive Taxation and the Welfare State: Path Dependence and Policy Diffusion*. Cambridge University Press, 2010.

Kessler, Anke, and Christian Lessmann. "Interregional Redistribution and Regional Disparities: How Equalization Does (Not) Work." Discussion paper for Centre for Economic Policy Research, vol. 8133 (2010).

Kriner, Douglas, and Andrew Reeves. "The Electoral College and Presidential Particularism." *Boston University Law Review* 94 (2014): 741.

Kuznets, Simon. "Economic Growth and Income Inequality." *The American Economic Review* 45 (1955): 1–28.

Lambert, Peter. *The Distribution and Redistribution of Income*. Manchester University Press, 2001.

Lee, Frances E. "Representation and Public Policy: The Consequences of Senate Apportionment for the Geographic Distribution of Federal Funds." *The Journal of Politics* 60, no. 1 (1998): 34–62.

Lee, Dong-wook, and Melissa Rogers. *Comparing Inequalities: Regional and Interpersonal Income Disparity, Institutions, and Government Spending*. Manuscript, Claremont Graduate University CA, 2014.

Lessmann, Christian. "Fiscal Decentralization and Regional Disparity: Evidence from Cross-Section and Panel Data." *Available at SSRN 936874* (2009).

Lessmann, Christian. "Regional Inequality and Decentralization: An Empirical Analysis." CESifo working paper: Public Finance, 2011.

Levitsky, Steven. "From Labor Politics to Machine Politics: The Transformation of Party-Union Linkages in Argentine Peronism, 1983–1999." *Latin American Research Review* 38, no. 3. 2003

Lloyd-Sherlock, Peter. "Health Sector Reform in Argentina: A Cautionary Tale." *Social Science and Medicine* 60, no. 8 (2005): 1893–903.

Lustig, Nora, Luis F. Lopez-Calva, and Eduardo Ortiz-Juarez. "Declining Inequality in Latin America in the 2000s: The Cases of Argentina, Brazil, and Mexico." *World Development* 44 (2013): 129–41.

Mainwaring, Scott. "Presidentialism, Multipartism, and Democracy: the Difficult Combination." *Comparative Political Studies* 26, no. 2 (1993): 198–228.

Manow, Philip. "Germany: Cooperative Federalism and the Overgrazing of the Fiscal Commons." In *Federalism and the Welfare State*, edited by Herbert Obinger, Stephan Leibfried, and Frances G. Castles. Cambridge University Press, New York, (2005): 222–62.

Milanovic, Branko. *The Haves and the Have-Nots: A Brief and Idiosyncratic History of Global Inequality*. Basic books, New York, 2010.

Milligan, Kevin, and Michael Smart. "Regional Grants as Pork Barrel Politics." CESifo Working Paper Series No. 1453. Available at SSRN: http://ssrn.com/abstract=710903 (2005).

Molinelli, N. Guillermo. *Presidentes Y Congresos En Argentina: Mitos Y Realidades*. Grupo Editor Latinoamericano, 1991.

Mustapic, Ana María. " 'Oficialistas Y Diputados': Las Relaciones Ejecutivo-Legislativo En La Argentina." *Desarrollo Económico* (2000): 571–95.

Pierson, Paul. "Fragmented Welfare States: Federal Institutions and the Development of Social Policy." *Governance* 8, no. 4 (1995): 449–78.

Pigou, Arthur Cecil. *Wealth and Welfare*. Macmillan and co., London, 1912.

Piketty, Thomas, and Emmanuel Saez. "The Evolution of Top Incomes: A Historical and International Perspective." *The American Economic Review* 96, no. 2 (2006a): 200–5.

Piketty, Thomas, and Emmanuel Saez. "How Progressive Is the US Federal Tax System? A Historical and International Perspective." National Bureau of Economic Research, Cambridge MA, 2006b.

Portnov, Boris A., and Daniel Felsenstein. "Measures of Regional Inequality for Small Countries." In *Regional Disparities in Small Countries*, edited by Daniel Felsenstein and Boris A. Portnov. Springer, New York (2005): 47–62.

Prud'Homme, Remy. "The Dangers of Decentralization." *The World Bank Research Observer* 10, no. 2 (1995): 201–20.

Remmer, Karen L., and Erik Wibbels. "The Subnational Politics of Economic Adjustment: Provincial Politics and Fiscal Performance in Argentina." *Comparative Political Studies* 33, no. 4 (2000): 419–51.

Rock, David. *Argentina, 1516–1987*. University of California Press, 1987.

Rodden, Jonathan, and Erik Wibbels. "Beyond the Fiction of Federalism." *World Politics* 54, no. 4 (2002): 494–531.

Rogers, Melissa Ziegler. "Taxing with Dictators and Democrats: Regime Effects, Transfers and Revenue in Argentina's Provinces." *Journal of Politics in Latin America* 6, no. 1 (2014).

Rogers, Melissa, and Dong-wook Lee. *Electoral Geography, Inequality, and Representation*. Manuscript, Claremont Graduate University CA, 2015.

Sawers, Larry. *The Other Argentina: The Interior and National Development*. Westview Press, Boulder CO, 1996.

Shugart, Matthew, and Martin P. Wattenberg. *Mixed-Member Electoral Systems: The Best of Both Worlds?* Oxford University Press, 2001.

Skocpol, Theda, and Edwin Amenta. "States and Social Policies." *Annual Review of Sociology* 12 (1986): 131–57.

Sokoloff, Kenneth L., and Stanley L. Engerman. "History Lessons: Institutions, Factors Endowments, and Paths of Development in the New World." *The Journal of Economic Perspectives* 14, no. 3 (2000): 217–32.

Solt, Frederick. *The Standardized World Income Inequality Database*. Working paper. SWIID Version 5.0, October 2014.

Stokes, Susan C. "Perverse Accountability: A Formal Model of Machine Politics with Evidence from Argentina." *American Political Science Review* 99, no. 3 (2005): 315–25.

Tiebout, Charles M. "A Pure Theory of Local Expenditures." *The Journal of Political Economy* 64, no. 5 (1956): 416–24.

Tommasi, Mariano, Sebastian Saiegh, Pablo Sanguinetti, Ernesto Stein, and Mauricio Cárdenas. "Fiscal Federalism in Argentina: Policies, Politics, and Institutional Reform [with Comments]." *Economia* 1, no. 2 (2001): 157–211.

3 Theoretical Foundations

Territorial Political Incentives and the Limits to Redistribution

Organization is not always necessary to obstruct; it is essential, however, for the promotion of a sustained program in behalf of the have nots.

(Key 1949, p. 305)

Certain political institutions, notably federalism, localizing electoral rules, and presidentialism, appear to work against citizens' efforts to increase redistribution and use the tools of government to reduce inequality. Among the variety of reasons this may be the case is that each of these institutions reinforces territorial interests in political representation, to the detriment of national class-based coalitions. In this chapter, I focus on the theoretical reasons why territorial politics helps to explain differences across institutions in their effect on redistribution.

To introduce the theoretical construct, I begin with a thought experiment: under what conditions are democratic governments likely to introduce redistributive reform? While this is the motivating question for most research on social welfare, no literature of which I am aware details the conditions necessary for significant changes in a nation's distributive system. Two major insights come out of this discussion. First, after examining the many pieces required for redistributive reform in institutionalized democracies, it is not surprising that most countries redistribute very little. Redistribution is far from automatic, as simplified modeling may suggest, but rather an arduous political process with many possible roadblocks. Second, political institutions highlight many different possible cleavage structures, most notably territorial, that complicate the pursuit of redistribution by a majority coalition of low-income voters.

After laying out these conditions, I link them to the three mechanisms I argue push political institutions away from national class cleavages and social policy distribution, and toward territorial identities and targeted local goods. I divide my discussion into sections based on each of the three mechanisms: pork, party cohesion, and veto powers. The logic of these mechanisms is linked to the institutional characteristics of federalism, localizing elections, and presidentialism that reinforce the relevance of geography in politics. To show contrast, I also discuss their alternatives: parliamentarism, proportional representation, and unitary government. These dilute territorial claims by encouraging voters and strategic politicians to organize around other principles, most notably social class.

The Analytical Framework: Elements and Premises

I start with an inductive exercise: under what conditions will democratic governments respond to income inequality with redistributive policy? The answer to this question may seem obvious—democracy implies responsiveness to the needs and wants of the majority of citizens, rendering redistribution essentially automatic as inequality grows (Romer 1975, Meltzer and Richard 1981). However, a very large literature in the social sciences shows that redistribution is not a certain output of democratic representation. Rather, inequality may heighten political conflict and lead those who stand to lose from redistribution to vigorously protect the status quo in democracies (Aysan 2005). High inequality may lead elites to block democratization in the first place (Acemoglu and Robinson 2006) or to limit state capacity to reduce the ability of the state to redistribute once democracy is in place (Soifer 2013).

A look around the world suggests that achieving high levels of income redistribution, even in societies that can plausibly afford it and with politically empowered citizens, is unusual. Extensive fiscal redistribution is uncommon and primarily European. How can we explain why a set of policies that should ostensibly be so popular in nearly every nation remains so rarely put into place?

Existing literature on redistribution has offered many necessary conditions for redistributive policy. The following list provides as close to a full account as I can piece together from the literature.

1 Interpersonal inequality is a salient policy issue to politicians and citizens.
2 A programmatic party or coalition of programmatic parties desires redistributive policy change.
3 The redistributively oriented programmatic party or coalition gains office and has sufficient authority to press controversial legislation over objections.
4 Constitutional rules favor centralized policymaking.
5 There is societal motivation to press for redistribution and there are resources available to those who favor redistribution to incentivize politician behavior.
6 There are legal protections of property rights.
7 There is sufficient tax capacity to fund expensive redistributive policy.

I have certainly missed some important points and glossed over many complex and nuanced issues. The point of the exercise is to highlight the opportunities for institutions, in addition to socio-demographic and economic pressures, to play a role in the pursuit of redistributive reform in a nation. These elements are not meant to be understood as mutually exclusive, since each is informed by overlapping political institutions and societal inputs. I briefly discuss each element in turn and then relate these conditions to the three mechanisms that link institutions to redistribution. The central theme that I highlight in this section is that redistribution is more likely where political institutions encourage the nationalization of party and issue competition, and constituents' interests.

Interpersonal Inequality is Salient

In most research on the topic, inequality is assumed to be a highly salient (indeed, the most salient) concern in political systems. Politics, under this simplification, is a distributive game with all actors focused on securing their share of resources. Political institutions act as a barrier or lubricant to advancing these goals. Even where cleavages other than that between rich and poor predominate, such as those based on ethnic, religious, or other identities, disparities in income often overlay those conflicts.

Concerns with economic inequality are certainly fundamental to the politics in any nation, but the form this debate takes and whether it results in a focus on interpersonal redistribution varies considerably. For instance, in the USA, recent scholarship has argued that voters either do not prioritize economic redistribution in their policy preferences or they underestimate its extent and importance (Campbell 2010). Rather, in that nation, politics is framed around a narrative of economic growth, with redistributive elements (such as higher taxes or spending) seen as inimical to that ultimate goal (Hacker and Pierson 2010). The barriers to inequality's policy salience may thus be behavioral—voters may see growth as more important than redistribution, voters may not evaluate redistribution in straightforwardly self-interested terms (Ansell and Samuels 2010; Dion and Birchfield 2010), or voters may not be informed about the extent of income inequality (Campbell 2010). Alternatively, parties may not provide voters with the policy options to reduce inequality that they seek (Miller and Scofield 2008; Roemer 1998).

Low redistribution in developing countries with severe inequalities is also explained by deficiencies in parties. In many developing nations, voters may prefer redistribution but are not provided with programmatic parties that prioritize such transformations.[1] Low-income voters that may benefit from systemic redistribution may also be swayed by clientelist distribution over broad reforms. Inequality under this portrayal of politics in less-developed nations is salient and relevant, because politicians exploit this issue to win votes from low-income constituents, while substantive redistribution remains limited (Levitsky and Roberts 2013). This view of parties in less-developed countries is increasingly being questioned, however, with literature citing those nations' structural, institutional, and economic barriers to reform in addition to failings of the left (Soifer 2013; Ha and Rogers 2015).

The ways in which political institutions structure the balance of national (class) politics versus territorial politics stand to play a very important role in the salience of inequality and redistribution in national politics. While distributive concerns may indeed be important in every nation, territorial politics may interfere with the policy priority to reduce interpersonal inequality or its collective support. Redistribution among individuals may be secondary, according to voters but especially politicians, to distribution among regions and within regions. If elections are territorial and electoral rules incentivize locally targeted goods, we should see an undersupply of broad redistributive social reforms (Milesi-Feretti et al. 1999). Even if national income inequality is salient, it competes with these other distributive concerns for attention in political allocation. If the "solutions" to interpersonal, interregional, and intraregional inequality are equivalent, then a broad coalition representing interests of interpersonal and geographic income distributions should be expected. If, however, these solutions differ and thus compete for resources, territorial politics can be an institutional barrier to redistribution.

A Programmatic (Leftist) Party (Coalition) Desires Redistributive Policy Change

For the pro-redistributive coalition to achieve its policy goals, it needs to organize into cohesive programmatic political parties that advocate and legislate for policies to reduce inequality. This necessary condition implies at least two sub-conditions. First, leftist parties need to be cohesive enough to form a majority block that passes redistributive policy. Second, parties need to be programmatic—i.e., oriented toward substantive policy change rather than clientelism or distribution according to private concerns (Kitschelt 2000).[2] Importantly, a programmatic party is defined by consistency in its ideological orientation toward national policies affecting (national) groups. Kitschelt (2000) defines programmatic parties as pursuing "policy programs that distribute benefits and costs to *all* citizens, regardless of whether they voted for the government of the day or not" (Kitschelt 2000, p. 845 emphasis added). Parties oriented toward purposeful distribution to a specific district or region would not typically be considered as ideologically coherent.[3]

Not only is a programmatic party necessary, it must be oriented toward redistribution. Typically redistribution is advanced by parties with leftist or center-left ideologies (Huber and Stephens 2001).[4] The Conservative party in Britain is programmatic and nationalized and, when in power, has extensive authority to change the status quo. We have no expectations that they would want to substantially redistribute income, however. To capture a majority often requires joining with outside parties or other groups not so committed to pro-poor reform, and this may compromise the left's redistributive goals (Przeworski 1985).

Because change from the status quo distributive system requires (at least) majority support, often across multiple institutions, leftist parties must also be cohesive in order to advance reform. Cohesion requires coordination of votes and policy proposals. Political institutions certainly affect party discipline and cohesion (Strøm 1990). Fragmentation of the left is thought to come from natural heterogeneity of interests, activated by power-separating institutions, within the low-income coalition. Importantly, regional interests are an important source of this heterogeneity. Advocates of redistribution from different parts of a nation may have very different views of its desirable scope and nature.

To explain whether nations have cohesive and programmatic leftist parties oriented toward redistribution, we must therefore look to the nature of political institutions, to social and territorial heterogeneity, and to their interactions. In particular, significant literature has shown that closed-list PR, and parliamentary and unitary institutions promote programmatic parties that mute intra-party heterogeneity (Bowler et al. 1999; Iversen and Soskice 2006). Not often in focus in this literature, however, is that each of these institutions mutes heterogeneity arising from territorial interests.

The Redistributively-Oriented Party Gains Sufficient Power to Change Policy

Given the two previous conditions—that national income inequality is salient and that a cohesive, programmatic leftist party advocates redistribution—the likelihood of policy change depends on whether this leftist party is able to gain enough votes and seats to change policy. These seats may need to constitute a majority or supermajority, and may need to span several institutions, such as bicameral chambers, legislatures and presidents, sub-national legislatures and governors, or judiciary branches. The ability of even the most cohesive majorities to change the status quo varies considerably depending on institutions that separate power within a nation.

Constitutional Rules Favor Centralized Policymaking

Policy change is broader and more comprehensive where it is implemented at the central government level. Conversely, policy enacted under multi-level governance is characterized by gaps in generosity and by inconsistencies in implementation and scope that are caused by different preferences and veto points (Obinger et al. 2006). Accordingly, most scholars argue that significant redistribution is much more likely where constitutional rules favor centralized policymaking and where redistributive programs are largely the national government's domain (Pierson 1995; Skocpol and Amenta 1986).

Centralized policymaking can occur through several mechanisms relevant to this study—namely, unitary government, unicameralism, parliamentarism, and closed-list PR. Centralized policymaking feeds into and is made possible by several of the other conditions for redistribution described above, especially programmatic, cohesive parties and leftist parties with enough votes to pass their distributive agenda. Empirically, unitary government, PR, and parliamentarism are linked to higher taxation and more government spending (Cameron 1978; Persson and Tabellini 1999; Milesi-Ferretti et al. 1999).

Centralized policymaking greases the wheels for redistributive reform because it implies that fewer actors are required to agree to or veto a policy. Adding a veto player either has no effect on the status quo or makes it more likely to remain in place (Tsebelis 2011). Presidentialism and federalism, in particular, are considered veto-heavy institutions that allow minority opinions to block reforms desired by the majority. However, presidentialism may be an important institution for encouraging policy change where party systems are fragmented (Shugart 1999). Federalism may also allow for pockets of innovation and limited reform that would not be possible in a centralized setting (Finegold 2006).

Societal Motivation and Resources Available to Incentivize Political Change

Theories of representative democracy argue that politicians legislate policy change to reflect societal interests.[5] For each policy passed, a significant constituency has demanded this policy change and demonstrated its support, through votes or money or both, to elected officials. Accordingly, for redistributive reform to emerge from a crowded policy agenda, there must be significant societal motivation to address inequality.

The (strong) demand for redistribution is often taken as given based on income distribution and preferences assumed to emerge from individuals' positions within those distributions. Neither preferences for redistribution nor the priority that voters place on its reform can be taken for granted, however. The poor vote less often, reducing demand for redistribution (Rosenstone and Hansen 2002; Benabou 2000). Ansell and Samuels (2010) and Dion and Birchfield (2010) find that assumed preferences of the poor and rich for redistribution were not entirely borne out in survey research. In the USA, there is some evidence that people either do not think that redistribution is an appropriate role of government or that government should not compensate those that are poor because of incentive effects (Campbell 2010). For voters to have preferences on redistributive policy, moreover, policy needs to be transparent enough for its distributive effects to be recognized and voters need to understand the extent of inequality (Bartels 2005; Norton and Ariely 2011).

The latent assumption of a strong demand for redistribution also comes from a belief that rising inequality makes redistribution more salient and voters more motivated to push for reform (Romer 1975; Meltzer and Richard 1981; Brady 2004). However, research suggests that inequality may drive down political engagement, discussion, and voter turnout rather than encouraging them (Solt 2008). Recent scholarship also questions the foundations of the distributive coalition. Milanovic (2000) finds that the median voter does not usually benefit from redistribution. Lupu and Pontusson (2011) argue that middle class voters are swing voters and not obviously part of the redistributive coalition. Accordingly, inequality that grows between the top and the middle of the income distribution should drive more redistribution as the middle class sides with the poor in favor of redistribution. Inequality that pulls the middle and top away from the poor, however, should not result in significant reform because these two social actors will team up against the poor. Thus changes in inequality may influence the strength and composition of the distributive coalition, and do so in ways that interact with existing political institutions.

Technological advances may also influence the translation of societal demand for reform into policy change. With certain innovations, such as those in social media, societal demand for reform can be more cheaply, directly, and quickly expressed to elected officials. Other media technologies such as television, however, have made elections more expensive and have made parties increasingly detached from grass-roots bases (Dalton and Wattenberg 2000). Accordingly, money has become more important to winning elections. Systematic evidence from the USA shows that campaign resources increasingly come from the rich and not from social organizations like unions (Bonica 2013; Hacker and Pierson 2010). If the poor vote less often, if election funding comes from the wealthy, and if the masses (with little money to influence politics) are swayed by arguments framing politics against redistributive issues, politicians will not be eager to press for redistributive reform.

Legal Protections of Assets

Contributions such as those of Acemoglu and Robinson (2006) and Boix (2003) argue that the adoption and design of political institutions are contingent on levels of inequality. In particular, affluent citizens are concerned about democratic voting because of majority preferences for redistribution. For the rich incumbents to be willing to accept democratic institutions (if they indeed accept them) they must have some way to retain most of their assets or have the option to exit. Under this logic, those nations with mobile assets may be more likely to introduce reforms that could result in significant redistribution because the rich can move their wealth abroad. Conversely, those nations whose most important assets are fixed in space, such as land, will have a difficult transition to democracy and will likely adopt political institutions that severely limit the possibility for redistributive reform (Boix 2003; Sokoloff and Engerman 2000).

While very important, most scholarship on redistribution is contemporary and thus largely leaves the role of state intervention aside because the universe of cases (OECD) has already achieved democracy and all have strong property rights regimes. However, this issue is not irrelevant even in the OECD cases because of the important role of taxation in redistribution. Burdensome taxation is pertinent in all nations, and concerns with the nationalization or seizure of assets loom large in the minds of asset holders in developing nations particularly.

Sufficient Tax Capacity to Fund Expensive Redistributive Policy

Most research on redistributive policy examines Western European nations that have high tax capacity—i.e., the ability to collect high levels of revenue relative to GDP and to collect from the most difficult types of taxes, especially progressive income taxes (Lieberman 2002; Rogers and Weller 2013). Though not often recognized, high tax capacity is a precondition for expensive redistributive spending. Importantly, high tax capacity and substantial redistributive spending likely come from similar political processes whereby relatively affluent citizens surrender resources in a quasi-voluntary manner (Levi 1989). This link between input (taxes) and output (spending) may seem so obvious that it is often assumed in literature on inequality and redistribution. However, elites may purposefully under-invest in tax capacity in order to limit redistribution (Soifer 2013) or the same conditions that lead to low economic development may also limit tax capacity (Beramendi and Rogers 2015).

Interregional economic profiles and inequality are fundamental concerns for tax policy. The major national taxes—those on trade, consumption, and income—fall disproportionately on particular areas of a nation. Trade taxes place a greater burden on the exporting and (typically affluent) coastal zones. Consumption taxes are collected primarily from (affluent but unequal) urban areas. Income taxes come largely from the most economically advanced areas of the country, including industrial and service sector zones, and less from agricultural areas. Adoption of income taxes in particular may reflect desires by landed interests to impose the tax burden on capitalists (Mares and Queralt 2013; Baack and Ray 1985). Reduction in trade taxation consistent with globalizing reforms benefits exporting regions, but the consumption and income taxes used to replace it also fall on those same exporting regions (Ha and Rogers 2015). In short, the taxation needed to fund redistributive policy falls disproportionately on particular regions that are also often the wealthiest, and thus have an important regional and interpersonal dynamic. Affluent regions and individuals therefore have incentives to avoid developing tax capacity if they expect the burden to fall heavily on themselves (Beramendi and Rogers 2015). As interregional inequality grows and as the most affluent regions become wealthier still, their incentives to fund redistributive national governments diminish further.

Mechanisms: Territorial Politics and Institutional Effects

In the discussion above, I provided a synthesis of the conditions that make redistributive reform more likely in a nation. An important theme of many of these conditions is the nationalization of political institutions and constituents' interests. In this section, I address the theoretical reasons why territorializing political institutions make redistributive reform less likely. An important contribution from this discussion is that the territorial nature of political institutions is directly important to redistribution, not simply because these same institutions tend to fragment power. Separation of powers is critical, but the effects on constituency interests and politicians' incentives inherent in the spatial divide of districts provide an important link to distributive outcomes.

In theory, territorialized systems can produce significant redistribution. For example, if all districts have similar economic profiles, it can be efficient to join together in centralized welfare as a form of risk-sharing and to take advantage of economies of scale in these services. Even if economic geography differs, it may make sense to redistribute through central or interregional transfers to poorer regions to reduce population transfers to more productive regions. Decentralization can even result in higher redistribution than that produced by centralized systems. This could be the case if rich regions are highly unequal and would prefer to redistribute, but in such a manner as to not share across regions, or if they are blocked by relatively egalitarian but somewhat poorer regions (Beramendi et al. 2015). Nonetheless, the conditions under which territorialized systems are most likely to redistribute are through nationalized party systems, such as in Germany (Beramendi 2012).

Territorial politics discourage redistribution in three ways discussed in detail in this section. First, territorial electoral constituencies, especially when coupled with decentralizing electoral rules, encourage politicians to deliver local goods that take away resources for national social spending. Second, territorial politics fragment the coalition in favor of redistribution both ideologically and organizationally. Third, territorial institutions provide special tools to regions to block (redistributive) policy. Before examining these mechanisms, I first address the possible concerns that institutions are endogenous to territorial conflict over distributive issues.

Endogeneous Territorial Inequality

In the following discussion of the mechanisms that lead territorial political systems to redistribute less to poor individuals, it is reasonable to ask whether territorial institutional design is itself a response to interpersonal inequality. Riker (1964) and Przeworski (2004), among many others, have expressed reasonable concern that institutions are epiphenomenal. Institutions may not shape actors' behavior, but instead reflect the underlying political dynamics that are the true source of political outcomes. With regard to the study at hand, the political institutions that I argue shape distributive outcomes may in fact be designed to reflect inequality, and also perhaps the distributive outcomes I seek to explain. To avoid circularity, I avoid a causal claim—that institutions drive redistribution—but rather point to which types of distributive concerns (territorial or social class) appear to structure political competition in different types of political systems, and accordingly how we should understand the role inequality plays in these political systems. Inequality of individuals and regions is considered at least somewhat endogenous within this framework, in an effort to better explain what these institutions do and whether institutional designers may or may not have intended this outcome. I assume a combination of endogenous and exogenous roles for inequality within the design of these institutions.

Are interpersonal and interregional inequality motivating factors for institutional adoption or design? Distribution of interpersonal income appears to be a concern regarding the adoption of national democracy in the first place (Boix 2003; Acemoglu and Robinson 2006).[6] However, the structure of inequality does not appear to be a motivation for the adoption of a federal system (Riker 1964). The adoption of presidential versus parliamentary systems also does not seem to be an endogenous response to inequality but tends to reflect colonial legacies or institutional spillover from nearby nations (Shugart and Carey 1992).

The *design* of political institutions, on the other hand, is quite possibly shaped by distributions in income. Contributions by Boix (1999), Cusack et al. (2007), Beramendi and Queralt (2014), and Ahmed (2010), suggest that interpersonal inequality is a relevant factor in the design of electoral *rules*. Under this logic, incumbent leaders choose electoral rules based on their beliefs about the relative balance of power of conservative, liberal, and socialist voters (that represent different income classes) in the political system. In contrast, Rehfeld (2005) argues that territorial designation of national electoral *districts* is a "default" choice motivated in the past by complications of distance but is now devoid of theoretical motivation. Beramendi and Wibbels (2010), for their part, maintain that the distribution of income across and within regions influences the design of the fiscal and representative structures of federalism. In particular, rich regions will look to block transfers to poor regions under these designs, particularly by limiting the fiscal tools of the center.

While endogeneity is a concern for all analyses of the effects of political institutions, there are several reasons to start by taking institutions as at least partially exogenous to explore their role in the politics of inequality. Territorial representation appears to motivate geographically targeted pork irrespective of inequality, for example (Rehfeld 2005). Local goods are the currency of parties in highly territorialized systems, as opposed to social spending in more nationalized systems. This design reflects a particular political logic that can certainly affect redistribution, but is not necessarily informed by politicians concerns about inequality. Before we can ask if systems that favor pork are designed in response to inequality, we first have to look at pork as a substitute for the types of goods thought to directly reduce income inequality. If systems that favor territorial goods are found to underprovide social welfare, this will represent an important theoretical explanation for the differences observed in distributive outcomes.

Second, if we know that territorial politics divides the coalition for redistribution, we need to ask (1) if it is a general condition that any political reform in a fragmented system is less likely, and (2) how the "content" of politics is changed by territorial jurisdictions. In the first case we are looking at political institutions that are veto-heavy and resistant to all policy change. Of course there is good reason to believe that wealthy elites design institutions that strongly favor the hardly redistributive status quo. This mechanism is distinct, however, from one whereby changing constituencies influences what is salient in politics and how voters and politicians think about their preferences. Before we can start to examine whether designers choose institutions to affect distributive outcomes, we need to understand the effects these institutions have on the politics of inequality in the first place.

Delivery of Goods to Constituencies

A significant literature in political science addresses incentives for politicians to deliver either programmatic policies or targeted geographic goods to constituents. This literature is highly relevant to how and whether inequality is addressed by the political system (economic redistribution) but few scholars have considered whether the nature of political distribution (tactical redistribution) is related to the political economy of inequality (Dixit and Londregan 1996). I argue that the pursuit of geographically targeted spending reduces the resources available for programmatic policies, especially national social spending. In line with the conditions that make redistribution more likely, as outlined above, institutions that incentivize local distributions are to some degree incompatible with programmatic redistributive parties.

National policy emerges from bargains across and within constituencies to advance shared interests. Constituencies affect the nature of these bargains. As Rehfeld (2005) puts it, policy outcomes differ based on "what kinds of logs are being rolled," and whether bargains are based on targeted benefits to localities, to economic classes, to occupational groups, to racial or ethnic groups, etc. (p. 10). For Rehfeld, log-rolling based on territorial constituencies should result in greater emphasis on geographic distributions of national resources to the detriment of allocations based on other principles, including national class differences.

Research on institutions and their localizing incentives offers important insights about the nature of service delivery and what we should expect from politicians under different institutional structures. Electoral rules designed around geographic districts, especially majoritarian ones, incentivize local orientation and thus prompt distribution to districts over distribution to national groups (Weingast et al. 1981). Mechanically, geographic orientation makes politicians care about what their particular district needs and gets, because voters can most clearly evaluate politicians for reelection on the basis of local goods (Milesi-Feretti et al. 2002; Grimmer 2013). Under these circumstances, parties allow for considerable heterogeneity to win votes across a diverse constituent base in a national party. In certain institution environments, targeted geographic spending ("pork" or regional transfers) is more efficient for gathering votes than broad social policy (Huber and Ting 2013; Cain et al. 1987; Cox and McCubbins 2001). The geographic orientation of political representation thus affects the "currency" of political compromise. Geographically oriented institutions that encourage these outcomes most clearly include federalism and territorial electoral districts especially with single members.[7]

Conversely, representative institutions that encourage a national policy orientation incentivize politicians to rationally pursue the interests of national groups represented by their political party (Austen-Smith and Banks 1988). The most obvious national groups represented within parties are social constituencies, such as groups formed on the basis of economic class, but they could also be other national groups, including quite narrow ones. Strongly nationalizing institutions, such as high district-magnitude PR, unitarism, and parliamentarism, encourage unified coalitions of voters and politicians that are focused on national social interests. The most efficient way to target national groups is to provide goods that span a large segment of individuals rather than by targeting particular geographic territories. Redistributive social welfare policies most often fall into these categories of goods.

A country's place on a continuum between representation of local versus national interests is affected by many different institutions within the nation, and also by the geographic spread of social groups (Rickard 2012) and the (de)centralization of government resources (Chhibber and Kollman 2004). The defining institutional features include electoral rules (Milesi-Ferretti et al. 2002; Persson et al. 1998), constitutional structure (Cox 1997; Persson and Tabellini 2004), political decentralization (Bakke and Wibbels 2006; Beramendi 2007), veto authority (Cox and McCubbins 2001), and the interaction of all of these rules (Beramendi 2012). These broadly recognized attributes of political institutions have been shown to be important to many government outcomes, including redistributive government spending, but have not been linked to economic inequality (with the exception of the studies on political decentralization).[8]

Policy targeted to local constituencies can include several different categories of goods. The most widely acknowledged is constituency service, in which politicians provide direct benefits to individuals within their district. The most common examples are intervening on behalf of constituents in federal bureaucracies (social security administration, veterans' administration, etc.) and providing selective goods such as nominations to a national military academy (Fenno 1978; Cain et al. 1987). Targeted expenditures on public goods, such as highways, hospitals, or schools, are also local goods. In addition, politicians can also target tax breaks or beneficial regulation to their districts. Most commonly, these benefits are aimed at a particular industry that spans districts but, given concentration of certain industries in certain districts, this legislation entails concentrated benefits and diffuse costs (Rickard 2012).

Regional budget transfers, I argue, have similar properties to national pork in their role in political bargaining and in substitution for national social spending (Milligan and Smart 2005). Regional transfers are money directly transmitted from the national government to local authorities to fund their programs.[9] National governments have some degree of discretion over how these resources are distributed across regions. Typically regions also have some discretion in how they are spent. In federal nations in particular, transfers can be distributed strategically to build political coalitions at the national level (Diaz-Cayeros 2006). These allocations constitute a large percentage of many national budgets and are discussed at length in the institution-specific chapters.

If we accept that certain political institutions incentivize targeted geographic spending and that this takes away resources that could be spent on social welfare, we must examine the relationship between pork (or transfers) and redistribution. Local public goods and regional transfers fund many budget categories with potentially redistributive effects. For example, primary public education spending is a locally targeted good in most countries, and it is strongly redistributive (Lloyd-Sherlock 2009). Transportation infrastructure enables commerce that creates employment that should lower income disparities. Local hospitals funded by national resources, for example veterans' hospitals, improve access to care for income-strapped populations. Similarly, funds for low-income housing reduce inequality by boosting the spending power of the poor. Subsidies for rural electrification improve the standard of living and economic prospects for otherwise impoverished regions. Regional transfers pay for nearly the full range of spending categories, including social spending. It is not obvious, therefore, that heavy spending on local public goods or transfers to sub-national governments are inimical to egalitarian outcomes.

On the other hand, pork and transfers may limit redistribution because centralized social spending is more effective in reducing inequality, and because much of the locally targeted pork and regional transfers is not progressive in intent or result. Economists studying the most effective policies to reduce income inequality have consistently shown that targeted benefits to individuals (especially income subsidies, unemployment insurance, and healthcare subsidies) reduce inequality more effectively than spending in other categories (Levy and Schady 2013) and that the central government is in the best position to do it (Brown and Oates 1987; Korpi and Palme 1998). All spending may be somewhat progressive, but social spending appears to have the most direct effect on inequality and poverty (Kenworthy and Pontusson 2005). Regional transfer programs, on the other hand, vary considerably in their progressivity (Beramendi et al. 2015). Even if pork is broadly consumed within the locality, moreover, its effects on income inequality are generally expected to be indirect, muted, and long term.

The three institutions of focus in this book have different theoretical relationships to pork. The link for electoral institutions was made above—territorial constituencies affect which "logs are rolled" and electoral rules influence whether parties are able to dilute the geographic cleavage. Electoral rules that let voters select individuals, especially in one district such as SMDs, make targeted local public goods particularly useful to politicians. Without control of ballot access, parties have weaker tools to centralize parties' ideological platforms and to efficiently reward members using broad social goods. Electoral rules that give these tools to parties enable the centralization of platforms and politicians' careers. In these circumstances, rewarding members is most easily done with national policies that benefit their constituents across all regions.

Federalism similarly encourages territorialization of interests and service delivery in several possible ways. The first is territorial bicameralism with strong upper chambers that only exist in federal systems. Not all federal systems have territorial chambers and some that do are weak, such as Canada's Senate. With strong territorial bicameralism, senators have a clear mandate to bring resources back to their regional constituency. A second mechanism works through "compounded representation" whereby constituents in multi-tiered systems evaluate their interests at the national level in territorial terms (Tuschhoff 1999). Thus, their political identity takes on a territorial component that politicians wish to satisfy. Importantly, in federal systems, electoral districts are nearly always organized at the regional level, and so electoral rules and federalism correlate on this dimension.[10]

Presidentialism matters for the distribution of territorial goods for at least two reasons. The first is not so much what presidentialism does, but what it does not do, in comparison with parliamentary systems. Because parliamentary systems require strong party discipline based on a unified national platform to maintain government, they discourage party heterogeneity of any kind, including that based on regional interests. Moreover, members are not empowered to press regional interests in strongly disciplined systems. Conversely, because the executive does not depend on the confidence of the legislature, presidential systems have lower incentives for discipline. Accordingly, presidential systems do not encourage parties to tamp down regional (or any other) heterogeneity within their ranks (Mainwaring and Shugart 1997). Second, presidentialism, as a national SMD, encourages targeted distributions to voters whose support is necessary to cross the 50 percent threshold. This may take the form of geographically targeted distributions where elections are organized territorially. This will most obviously be the case where elections for the president are restricted, such as in the U.S. Electoral College (Kriner and Reeves 2014). Presidents may also target resources to particular districts to help the electoral chances of co-partisans, or to compensate those who supported their legislative agenda (Kriner and Reeves 2015).

In sum, territorial constituencies incentivize (or in the case of presidentialism fail to override) geographic allocation of spending. The national pie, therefore, goes more toward pork or regional transfers than welfare spending. If legislative agendas and economic resources are limited, territorial concerns should "crowd out" redistributive claims by social constituencies.

Providing Blocking Powers to Minorities

Political institutions are important to redistributive outcomes because they structure the rules to achieving policy change. In addition to establishing constituencies, institutions also create voting rules by which national policy is decided. In simple terms, institutions determine whether policy is made by majoritarian or consensus principles (Lijphart 2012; Powell and Vanberg 2000). Majority-enhancing institutions concentrate power in the hands of the majority, leaving little policy role for minorities. Consensus institutions, on the other hand, limit the tools of the majority by giving minorities access to the bargaining table or tools to shape or override majority-led policy initiatives. In this section, I argue that the consensus political institutions linked to federalism and presidentialism provide regional actors with distinct policy tools to affect distribution, and that regional actors might be particularly opposed to centralized redistribution.

Lijphart describes majoritarian institutions as centralizing power and consensus institutions as dividing power. Examples of majoritarian institutions include parliamentarism, SMD, and unitarism, among others. Consensus institutions divide power, thus requiring more voices to be heard in the policy process; these include presidentialism, federalism, bicameralism and PR. In theory, the consensus–majoritarian divide should be linked to redistribution. Majoritarian institutions should encourage redistribution because they allow the relatively poor to control the government alone (Boix 1999). Institutions that give voice to minorities, on the other hand, may prove a hindrance to redistribution if representatives of the rich use these means to constrain redistributive spending. Empirically, however, the majoritarian–consensus dichotomy does not satisfactorily explain redistribution. PR is linked to lower inequality and higher redistribution and SMD the opposite (Iversen and Soskice 2006; Persson et al. 1998. Federalism is linked to higher inequality and lower redistribution. Parliamentarism is associated with higher redistribution and lower inequality (Kang and Powell 2010).

Separation of powers institutions, which include federalism, bicameralism, and presidentialism, among others, are put in place to limit the central government. Advocates of power-dividing institutions, such as Madison (1787) and Riker (1982) argue they protect individual rights against a powerful central government or a tyranny of the majority. These institutions can also prove a particular hindrance to centralized redistributive reform advanced by a majority of poor individuals.

While the possibility that separation of powers institutions may limit redistributive reform is widely recognized, few acknowledge the particular role of political geography and territorial politics in these dynamics. Regions are a distinct type of veto actor in many democratic systems. In the case of federalism, regions have policy tools codified in constitutions, such as special representation in legislatures, judicial bodies to adjudicate their claims, and policy areas that they exclusively control (Lee and Rogers 2015). Politicians representing regions thus have great power to shape policy outcomes in many nations.

Why should it matter that regions have unique powers in political institutions? If income is unevenly distributed across jurisdictions, representatives of constituencies at different levels of income may have different preferences for government spending and allocation (Bolton and Roland 1997). This conflict should become more heated the greater the spread in income distribution across places or people. As inequality grows, distributive conflict should escalate as the poor demand higher levels of government spending, and the rich, accordingly, look to block it. The rich increasingly have incentives to limit redistributive policies that they increasingly fund. With rising inequality the benefits of cooperation between classes decline for the rich and increase for the poor due to differences in their demand elasticities for government spending (Guiranno 2009). This strengthens the bargaining position of the rich, who will have to be persuaded of the value of government spending in order to change the status quo. Accordingly, inequality will not drive up spending if the rich have the means to block it in a representative system.

Regions have strong tools and, often, strong incentives to block redistribution as inequality grows. Extensive redistribution, as discussed above, most often involves a centralization of authority. This threatens the autonomy of regional politicians, who will only support it if they view the benefits to their region as surpassing their loss in autonomy (Beramendi 2012). From this perspective, regional representatives of rich areas and those who seek to preserve regional authority (even at the cost of beneficial fiscal flows) will block national redistributive efforts. This scenario played out in the USA during the New Deal as certain wealthy states and poor Southern states banded together to successfully block many proposed centralized redistributive policies (Finegold 2006; Beramendi 2012). Thus political and economic geography shape redistribution, and regions hold a unique position in representative structures that allows them to influence the political economy of inequality. The following discussion details how federalism, presidentialism, and plurality electoral rules should affect the role of regions and the majority coalition that favors redistribution.

The political economy of inequality helps to explain why the majoritarian–consensus dichotomy does not consistently explain redistributive outcomes. Voting institutions structure the balance of power between the majority (poor individuals) and the minority (rich individuals).[11] Unitary government and parliamentarism appear to empower the majority of poor individuals because they enhance majority power and limits the dissenting role of rich people and regions that prefer autonomy. Plurality elections, on the other hand, may empower majorities within individual districts, but at the national level they promote party heterogeneity and encourage pork. The geographic foundation of plurality elections limits the *national* majoritarian and centralizing influences relevant for redistributive policy reform.

The separation of powers institution that most clearly links regionalism to reduced redistribution is federalism. Federalism matters for national policymaking because it is associated with a range of other political institutions that place regions at the bargaining table in national politics. The most obvious is territorial bicameralism whereby states are the bases for constituencies in the national upper chamber. Senators thus have strong incentives to represent the heterogeneous interests of states and to deliver resources back to them. Some federal systems decide policies through intergovernmental policy agreements between the national executive and regional governors. Canada and Argentina, for example, use this mechanism frequently for important policy areas affecting both levels of government. In this setting the division of powers between government levels is negotiated, as is policy content at both levels. Federal nations also have national courts to adjudicate intergovernmental conflict. In the USA, the Supreme Court has frequently limited the authority of the federal government in the area of redistributive policy (Finegold 2006). In each of these associated institutions, more political actors come to the bargaining table, increasing the number of veto points, and thus make reform more difficult.

Malapportionment in territorial upper chambers (or lower chambers) may also affect redistributive policy change. By definition, malapportionment is deviation away from population-based principles toward territorial ones. For example, the US Senate's apportionment formula is two senators for each state. Given variance in regional populations, malapportionment gives disproportionate weight to the sparsely populated regions over the densely populated ones. If regions are uniform in income level and distribution, malapportionment should not affect distributive outcomes except by region-based representation incentivizing territorial representation above national representation. If, however, overrepresented regions are poorer or richer than average, then redistribution should be more or less likely, respectively, as regions vote for their interests. In many nations, less populated states have particular antipathy toward centralization of authority and centralized redistribution specifically (Samuels and Snyder 2001; Beramendi et al. 2015). With voting power that outpaces their size, less populated states can strongly influence policy outcomes (Ardanaz and Scartascini 2013). Sparsely populated regions also make particularly attractive coalition partners because their votes are relatively cheap to "buy" with strategic distributions (Gibson and Calvo 2000). Accordingly, in malapportioned systems, the distributive preferences of the sparsely populated regions may be further amplified as they are more likely to be in the majority coalition. If they are richer than average or can be bought off by the anti-redistribution coalition with regionally targeted transfers, malapportionment can work against redistribution. Empirically, malapportioned states redistribute less. This dynamic is discussed in the cases of the USA and Argentina in Chapter 4.

Importantly, constitutional and representatives powers are available to regions and, typically, not to other potential constituency groupings, such as economic class or racial, ethnic, or linguistic groups.[12] These powers given to regions are veto points, thus endowing, in particular, minority regions with tools to preserve the status quo or shape policy in their interest. If the minority regions have preferences that are distinct from the majority—say, for example they are richer than most, and more economically dynamic or egalitarian than most—they may use these tools to block national redistribution that does not benefit them (Lee and Rogers 2015).

Presidentialism also increases the number of veto points available to the anti-redistribution coalition. In highly simplified terms, if the rich cannot capture the legislature, they might be able to capture the presidential office, or vice versa, with both institutions having strong powers on budget and other policy outcomes in presidential systems.[13] In parliamentary systems, on the other hand, the executive dominates the policy process. If the majority captures both offices in a presidential system, the additional veto points may not be relevant if their preferences are the same. However, given different territorial constituencies even co-partisan presidential and legislator preferences are expected to diverge (Carey and Shugart 1992). Presidentialism thus infuses a territorial "separation of purpose" into its distinct constituencies that can inject regional politics into its separation of powers.

Interestingly, the president may also be a bridging figure under conditions of societal heterogeneity that could result in greater redistribution (Shugart 1999). As the only politicians with a national constituency in otherwise territorial political systems, the executive has incentives to advance policies in the best interest of the majority of the nation. Taken in the context of societal or regional interests, the president may be most favorable to the interests of the poor majority in favor of redistribution. President Cardoso's efforts to advance redistribution against the strongly territorial Brazilian Senate with an anti-redistributive minority, provides an ultimately unsuccessful example (Stepan 2004). It is not obvious, however, that the president would consider redistribution in the interest of the national majority. Presidents may, for instance, be advocates for robust economic growth or balanced budgets, even when they represent the left (Kiewict and McCubbins 1988). These two policy preferences frequently attributed to presidents could in fact be inimical to expensive redistributive efforts. This balance is considered in more detail in Chapter 6 on executive systems.

Electoral rules may also provide blocking powers to minorities through the creation of constituencies and through fragmentation of the party system. Territorializing electoral constituencies can, intentionally or not, lead to representation of minority groups that happen to be majorities in a particular geographic zone. Most obviously, "majority–minority" congressional districts in the USA boost representation of national minorities (i.e., African Americans) in the national legislatures by increasing their representation within a single district. National minorities may also gain disproportionate representation by virtue of their voluntary spatial spread. Republicans more likely to be opposed to redistribution, for example, may be advantaged by territorial representation because they spread more evenly across suburban and rural districts. Democrats, on the other hand, tend to cluster in cities and thus "waste votes" by dominating elections in urban districts (Rodden 2010; Bishop 2009). This effect will be most obvious in SMDs but could also characterize territorial representation with low district magnitude.

Proportional electoral rules should result in greater voice for national minorities (Lijphart 2012; Rogowski and Kayser 2002). Because groups can be represented with a smaller fraction of the vote, ideologies or preferences of minorities can gain effective representation and, if they join a government coalition, strong control over particular policy areas. In theory, the minority of rich voters could form a coalition with other minority parties to form a ruling coalition that rejects redistribution. For this to result, legislative politics would need to have multidimensional issue space so that some of the majority poor would join (non-majority) parties for reasons other than redistribution (Roemer 1998). This multidimensionality is clearly present in most political systems, and may undermine redistributive outcomes. However, multidimensionality is also present in majoritarian electoral systems, which similarly take policy focus off redistribution within parties toward other policy areas with majority support (Tavits and Potter 2014).

While proportional rules appear in theory to benefit minorities, thus giving the rich opportunities to undermine redistribution, this does not appear to be the dominant effect in reality. Rather, proportional rules seem to better capture the interests of the median voter than do majoritarian rules (Powell and Vanberg 2000). The median voter is likely to be a member of any government coalition that forms from multiple parties. Majoritarian institutions, on the other hand, are subject to greater challenges of electoral coordination that may result in the election of minority or extreme parties and accordingly non-majoritarian policy choices (Cox 1997). In either case, electoral rules can shape the power of minorities (in this discussion, those antagonistic toward redistribution) to block policy aimed at reallocating wealth.

Fragmenting the Redistributive Coalition

Political institutions matter fundamentally for redistribution because they can fragment, either organizationally or ideologically, the majority coalition that would benefit from redistribution (Huber et al. 1993). The majority is thought to be able to advance its (salient) redistributive interests through the formation and electoral success of a programmatic party on the left. Where political institutions make party cohesion difficult or interpersonal inequality less salient, the redistributive aims of leftist parties may be hindered. Territorial constituencies limit party cohesion by weakening the link between voters and national policy concerns and by promoting intraparty preference heterogeneity. Similarly, territorial constituencies pit regions against each other in a competition for regionally targeted national spending. With territorial aggregation of preferences in districted systems, moreover, inequality among regions affects the preferences of constituents in regions of different income level and spread, and highlights interregional and intraregional inequalities. Each of these factors hinders societal support for redistribution and undermines the power of a centralized, programmatic party interested in pursuing reform.

Electoral institutions that territorially segment representation, or that encourage policy heterogeneity within its ranks more generally, undermine the pursuit of redistribution. Electoral rules encourage heterogeneity (and implicitly reduce the salience of interpersonal inequality) through several related mechanisms. First, they can encourage the "personal vote" whereby politicians have incentives to distinguish themselves from co-partisans for electoral gain (Cain et al. 1987; Carey and Shugart 1995). This is most likely in SMD or in territorial bicameralism where politicians' appeals are likely to be more tailored to territorial interests. Because personal appeals require deviations from the party platform in favor of local appeals, the personal vote should reduce party cohesion. Overall, territorial constituencies can create heterogeneity of appeals that detract from a majority coalition pressing for redistribution.

Electoral constituencies can also foster heterogeneity of preferences by segmenting the latent majority coalition that could benefit from redistribution. Regions have different levels of wealth and intraregional distributions of income. These characteristics of regions inform relative preferences for national redistribution that can undermine solidarity of the majority (Beramendi 2007). For example, poor individuals in rich regions would likely prefer a regional approach to redistribution over a national one because it could be more generous on a per capita basis. Poor individuals in poor regions, on the other hand, would strongly prefer a national redistributive scheme that would entail subsidization by the rich regions. Accordingly, the poor in rich and poor regions face a conflict over the optimal solution to redistribution, whether local or national, that is informed by economic geography.

Fragmenting the majority coalition in favor of redistribution may also occur through multipartism. The institutions that encourage this outcome include PR and low party thresholds that enable smaller parties to compete effectively for seats. Fragmentation of parties may hinder the coalition for redistributive reform by "allowing" greater expression of heterogeneous interests through separate parties. In low threshold PR, issue multidimensionality is also more common (Powell 2004). Parties competing on identities other than strictly class, such as ethnic, language, and post-modern concerns (environmentalist, civil liberties) reduce the salience and urgency of redistributive reform (Roemer 1998). Frequently, redistributive parties must join coalitions with parties representing other issue dimensions, such as the Greens or linguistic parties, which lack programmatic ambitions on this issue (Przeworski 1985). Accordingly, separate parties render the discipline of members more difficult and complicate the agenda-setting process, both of which are crucial in passing controversial redistributive reform.

Majoritarian parties are an interesting phenomenon in this sense. With strictly national distributive concerns driving preferences, a two party system should be a boon for the cause of redistribution. Given that low income voters are the majority of any system, limited room for parties means the left will likely coalesce into a single, electorally dominant party (Boix 1999). However, two-party systems are characterized by heterogeneous parties that must compromise to appease their regionally and ideologically varied members (Downs 1952).

Majoritarian parties, empirically speaking, are linked with lower redistribution than are their proportional counterparts (Powell and Vanberg 2000). Majoritarian electoral rules may also encourage middle class voters to join in coalition with the wealthy to limit progressive taxation (Iversen and Soskice 2006).

Even given a strong ideological demand to reduce inequality, certain political institutions are expected to organizationally fragment the coalition for redistribution. Many authors argue that federalism in particular undermines the organizational capacity of welfare advocates, such as unions and coalitions of the poor. Because significant welfare policy occurs at the sub-national level, advocates must continually repeat their efforts and do so in different political and institutional contexts. This creates collective action problems in cross-regional coordination (Pierson 1995; Obinger et al. 2005). Federalism also has strong effects on party systems, typically requiring decentralization of much of the organizational efforts and even policy platforms (Chhibber and Kollman 2004). However, some parties in federal systems are able to centralize their organizations when combined with other institutions that encourage party cohesion and when regional issues are shared (such as when labor mobility is high or when economic shocks affect many regions).

Importantly, localizing institutions should not only undermine organizational capacity but also "permit" heterogeneity of preferences in these coalitions, including ones informed by interpersonal and interregional differences in income levels and distributions. Decentralization of representation changes the nature of the distributive game in ways that can encourage cross-class coalitions for fiscal structures that benefit their regions (Beramendi 2012). In particular, rich and poor alike in affluent regions may be better off providing their own welfare systems rather than funding a central pot that is disproportionately spread to other regions.

Beramendi (2012) argues that a territorially aggregating party system is able to overcome the fragmentation created by power-dividing institutions. In particular, parliamentarism and PR work to offset the territorialization inherent in federal systems. The reason is that national party leaders pay the cost for dilution of their party brand name. If regional party members are poor representatives of the national platform, this hurts the party as a collective. Accordingly, national elites have strong incentives to use both carrots and sticks (e.g., advancing or blocking careers, increasing or withholding regional transfers) to keep local politicians in line. Where party systems are not centralized, national leaders lack these incentives and tools. This helps to explain why certain federal systems, such as Germany with its mixed-member representation and parliamentary government, are highly redistributive while others, such as the USA, with its SMD and presidentialism, have more limited redistribution.

Germany's Bundesrat (the upper house formed by constituencies of the regional Länder) provides an example of both regional veto power, as described above, and how party organizations can overcome territorial interests. The Bundesrat has a vote on all policies that affect Länder governance. This mandate can be broadly or narrowly construed. As regional inequality grew dramatically with the reunification of Germany, the Bundesrat became increasingly active, including most prominently in budget negotiations (Gunlicks 2002). Germany's strongly nationalized party system, on other hand, keeps the Bundesrat from being an immovable obstacle to majority party interests in the popular chamber. To overcome the Bundesrat veto, political parties simultaneously organize votes in the lower house where policy originates and in the upper territorial house that has veto or delay authority. Parties take a regional approach by convincing co-partisans from the Länder delegations to support the legislation (Saalfeld 2002).

Executive selection and survival also has a strong influence on party cohesion, including incentives for left parties to adhere to consistent party platforms and vote in unity. Parliamentarism, because creating and maintaining the governing coalition requires voting unity, inspires strong party discipline and selection of like-minded politicians into the party fold (Strøm 2000). Presidentialism, on the other hand, lacks the unifying threat of the vote of confidence, as executive and legislative parties members are born and die independently. Certainly there are incentives for party cooperation across branches in presidential systems to pass legislative agendas and to manage the interdependence due to electoral coattails, but these mechanisms should be weaker than in parliamentary systems (Samuels 2004). Presidentialism can thus coexist with substantial heterogeneity within parties and fragmentation in the party system because there is no forceful mechanism to eliminate it. In fact, the legislative powers of the president may at times substitute as a mechanism to advance policy despite fragmented coalitions (Shugart 1999).

The reasoning in this section highlights what is often considered about the representative function of political institutions—how they construct majorities—but rarely addressed in research on the politics of inequality. In most of this literature, the majority is assumed to be all of the poor, regardless of district. However, the majority in particular institutions might be better conceptualized as (rich or poor, equal or unequal) districts in addition to an aggregation of individuals. Even if institutions empower the majority, this majority may not be the national coalition of poor individuals as is often assumed.

Summary of Theoretical Expectations

In the sections above, I first put forward the conditions favorable for the adoption of redistributive policy. In contrast to the bare-bones assumptions of the RMR median voter model, these conditions reveal many barriers to redistribution even when the majority of citizens may benefit from it. In doing so, I highlighted both the role of political institutions in shaping those conditions, and how changes in inequality (interpersonal or interregional or both) may inform the likelihood of conditions for redistribution being met.

Second, I laid out the theoretical mechanisms that, I argue, make redistribution less likely under certain institutional conditions. In particular, I suggest that these institutions (federalism, territorialized electoral rules, and presidentialism) reinforce territorial cleavages in national politics. This shift in relevance from purely national to local concerns makes redistribution less likely in three primary ways. First, politicians target localities with local goods because they are not rewarded for broad national policies. Second, territorial politics is associated with institutional vetoes that privilege minorities, including rich individuals and especially the rich regions that pay disproportionately for redistribution. Third, territorial politics fragment the coalition that favors redistribution, both organizationally and ideologically.

Importantly, with territorial politics and a fragmented coalition, the number of relevant "units" of inequality grows. While national levels of inequality are always relevant in national political debates, in territorial systems interregional and intraregional inequality also become focal. If national parties are fighting on behalf of national constituents to maximize their share of the pie, so too are regionally minded politicians looking to shift resources to their region.

In the chapters that follow, I provide greater detail and case examples of how these institutions "activate" different redistributive concerns in national systems. Each institution is given its own chapter, specifying how the causal mechanisms laid out in this chapter apply to each. Country case examples are provided throughout each chapter, with particular attention given to three nations that vary on these institutions, their level of development, and their welfare states: the USA, Germany, and Argentina.

Notes

1 Baker and Greene (2011) and Zechmeister (2006) argue that parties' distributive orientations in developing countries are similar to those seen in industrialized nations.
2 Of course this is an oversimplification. Parties are not exclusively programmatic, clientelistic, or oriented toward private goods but typically are some combination of two or three of these characteristics. Certain policies that may have redistributive elements, such as import substitution industrialization, often occur under policies that are considered "populist" more than programmatic (Kaufman and Stallings 1991). Programmatic neoliberal reform was coupled with clientelistic exchange in Argentina (Levitsky 2003).
3 Certainly every national policy has regional implications. Thus programmatic parties may take positions that help some regions and hurt others. Parties' positions on trade openness provide an example. Openness will help export- oriented regions and hurt those with industries unable to compete in global markets. Such a national position is different than advocating specific allocation to certain regions based on distributive interests, and is not a coherent ideological program.
4 Again this requires a caveat. Conservative parties may set the status quo by advancing their own welfare policies to preempt much more transformative reform by the opposition.
5 Of course, other theorists argue that policymaking reflects rent-seeking (Krueger 1974). For the purposes of this discussion, it does not matter whether politicians support policies to win votes or win votes because they support policies.
6 Haggard and Kaufman (2012) question the link between inequality and regime change on empirical and theoretical grounds.
7 Rehfeld (2005) is very clear that we should not conflate constituencies with voting rules. It is electoral constituencies based on territory, he argues, that incentivize pork delivery, not SMDs, in the US case. If those SMDs were organized based on occupation, for example, the result would be targeted delivery of occupational benefits, not local ones.
8 Related to this discussion, Beramendi (2012) models the interactions of regional and interpersonal inequality with centripetal and centrifugal institutions. Beramendi's

primary focus is on three institutional sources of political decentralization: federalism, territorial upper houses, and the party system.

9 Nations vary in how they manage these transfers (Rodden 2002). Also, different transfers within the same country have different political properties i.e., useful for presidents or useful for governors. See Bonvecchi and Lodola (2011).

10 Rehfeld points out that most representative bodies are built on more than one constituency dimension. For example, the US House of Representatives forms constituencies first at the state level that are subdivided within to match population within geographically contiguous areas. The US Senate, on the other hand, has only one constituency level, the state. Germany's legislature, in contrast, combines territorial SMDs with territorial but much larger proportional districts in their mixed-member system.

11 While we know that rich individuals are the minority in every nation, it is not so clear whether rich or poor regions are the majority in all nations.

12 Of course some other identity groups, such as linguistic, racial or ethnic groups also have constitutionally protected representation. Belgium and Switzerland provide clear examples of this. However, regional representation is much more common.

13 Presidential systems vary in the role played by legislatures and presidents in the budget process (Alesina et al. 1999). The US has a relatively limited role for the president: non-binding agenda setting and "blanket" veto. In Argentina, the president sets the agenda on budgets and has a line item veto. Chile provides an unusual case in which the president sets the budget and the legislature may only revise it downward (Baldez and Carey 1999)

References

Acemoglu, Daron, and James A. Robinson. *Economic Origins of Dictatorship and Democracy*. Cambridge University Press, 2006.

Ahmed, Amel. "Reading History Forward: The Origins of Electoral Systems in European Democracies." *Comparative Political Studies* 43, no. 3 (2010).

Alesina, Alberto, Ricardo Hausmann, Rudolf Hommes, and Ernesto Stein. "Budget Institutions and Fiscal Performance in Latin America." *Journal of Development Economics* 59, no. 2 (1999): 253–73.

Ansell, Ben, and David Samuels. "Inequality and Democratization: A Contractarian Approach." *Comparative Political Studies* 45, no. 12 (2010): 1543–74.

Ardanaz, Martin, and Carlos Scartascini. "Inequality and Personal Income Taxation the Origins and Effects of Legislative Malapportionment." *Comparative Political Studies* 46, no. 12 (2013): 1636–63.

Austen-Smith, David, and Jeffrey Banks. "Elections, Coalitions, and Legislative Outcomes." *The American Political Science Review* 82, no. 2 (1988): 405–22.

Aysan, Ahmet Faruk. "Inequality, Institutions and Redistribution." Ph.D. Economics, University of Maryland College Park (2005).

Baack, Bennett, and Edward John Ray. "Special Interests and the Adoption of the Income Tax in the United States." *The Journal of Economic History* 45, no. 3 (1985): 607–25.

Baker, Andy, and Kenneth Greene. "The Latin American Left's Mandate: Free-Market Policies and Issue Voting in New Democracies." *World Politics* 63, no. 1 (2011): 43–77.

Bakke, Kristin, and Erik Wibbels. "Diversity, Disparity, and Civil Conflict in Federal States." *World Politics* 59, no. 1 (2006): 1–50.

Baldez, Lisa, and John M. Carey. "Presidential Agenda Control and Spending Policy: Lessons from General Pinochet's Constitution." *American Journal of Political Science* 43, no. 1 (1999): 29–55.

Bartels, Larry. "Homer Gets a Tax Cut: Inequality and Public Policy in the American Mind." *Perspectives on Politics* 3, no. 1 (2005): 15–31.

Benabou, Roland. "Unequal Societies: Income Distribution and the Social Contract." *American Economic Review* 90, no. 1 (2000): 96–129.

Beramendi, Pablo. "Inequality and the Territorial Fragmentation of Solidarity." *International Organization* 61, no. 4 (2007): 783.

Beramendi, Pablo. *The Political Geography of Inequality: Regions and Redistribution*. Cambridge University Press, 2012.

Beramendi, Pablo, and Didac Queralt. *The Electoral Origins of the Fiscal State*. (2014). www.didacqueralt.com/bq_electoral_origins_dec14.pdf

Beramendi, Pablo, and Melissa Rogers. "Geography and Capacity." Presented at the workshop on Inequality and Conflict, ETH Zurich, April 16–18 2015.

Beramendi, Pablo, and Erik Wibbels. "Foundational Bargains: Distributive Conflicts and Representation in Federations." Paper presented at the Meeting of the American Political Science Association, Washington, 2010.

Beramendi, Pablo, Melissa Rogers, and Alberto Diaz-Cayeros. *Barriers to the Left Turn: Distributive Tensions in Developing Federations*. Manuscript, Duke University, Claremont Graduate University, and Stanford University, 2015.

Bishop, Bill. *The Big Sort: Why the Clustering of Like-Minded America Is Tearing Us Apart*. Houghton Mifflin Harcourt, New York, 2009.

Boix, Carles. "Setting the Rules of the Game: The Choice of Electoral Systems in Advanced Democracies." *American Political Science Review* 93, no. 3 (1999): 609–24.

Boix, Carles. *Democracy and Redistribution*. Cambridge University Press, 2003.

Bolton, Patrick, and Gerard Roland. "The Breakup of Nations: A Political Economy Analysis." *The Quarterly Journal of Economics* 112, no. 4 (1997): 1057–90.

Bonica, Adam. "Ideology and Interests in the Political Marketplace." *American Journal of Political Science* 57, no. 2 (2013): 294–311.

Bonvecchi, Alejandro, and Germán Lodola. "The Dual Logic of Intergovernmental Transfers: Presidents, Governors, and the Politics of Coalition-Building in Argentina." *Publius: The Journal of Federalism* 41, no. 2 (2011): 179–206.

Bowler, Shaun, David M. Farrell, and Richard S. Katz. *Party Discipline and Parliamentary Government*. The Ohio State University Press, 1999.

Brady, Henry E. "An Analytical Perspective on Participatory Inequality and Income Inequality." in *Social inequality*, edited by Kathryn M. Neckerman. Russell Sage Foundation, New York (2004): 667–702.

Brown, Charles C., and Wallace E. Oates. "Assistance to the Poor in a Federal System." *Journal of Public Economics* 32, no. 3 (1987): 307–30.

Cain, Bruce, John A. Ferejohn, and Morris P. Fiorina. *The Personal Vote: Constituency Service and Electoral Independence*. Harvard University Press, Harvard CT, (1987).

Cameron, David R. "The Expansion of the Public Economy: A Comparative Analysis." *American Political Science Review* 72, no. 4 (1978): 1243–61.

Campbell, Andrea Louise. "The Public's Role in Winner-Take-All Politics." *Politics and Society* 38, no. 2 (2010): 227–32.

Carey, John, and Matthew Soberg Shugart. "Incentives to Cultivate a Personal Vote: A Rank Ordering of Electoral Formulas." *Electoral studies* 14, no. 4 (1995): 417–39.

Chhibber, Pradeep, and Ken Kollman. *The Formation of National Party Systems: Federalism and Party Competition in Canada, Great Britain, India, and the United States*. Princeton University Press, Princeton NJ, 2004.

Cox, Gary. *Making Votes Count: Strategic Coordination in the World's Electoral Systems*. Cambridge University Press, 1997.

Cox, Gary W., and Mathew McCubbins. "The Institutional Determinants of Economic

Policy Outcomes." in *Presidents, Parliaments, and Policy*, edited by Stephan Haggard and Mathew McCubbins. Cambridge University Press (2001): 21–63.

Cusack, Thomas, Torben Iversen, and David Soskice. "Economic Interests and the Origins of Electoral Systems." *American Political Science Review* 101, no. 3 (2007): 373.

Dalton, Russell J., and Martin P. Wattenberg. *Parties without Partisans: Political Change in Advanced Industrial Democracies*. Oxford University Press, 2000.

Diaz-Cayeros, Alberto. *Federalism, Fiscal Authority, and Centralization in Latin America*. Cambridge University Press, 2006.

Dion, Michelle, and Vicki Birchfield. "Economic Development, Income Inequality, and Preferences for Redistribution." *International Studies Quarterly* 54, no. 2 (2010): 315–34.

Dixit, Avinash, and John Londregan. "The Determinants of Success of Special Interests in Redistributive Politics." *Journal of Politics* 58 (1996): 1132–55.

Fenno, Richard F. *Home Style: House Members in Their Districts*. Little Brown, Boston, 1978.

Finegold, Kenneth. "The United States Federalism and Its Counter-Factuals." In *Federalism and the Welfare State. New World and European Experiences. Cambridge*, edited by Herbert Obinger, Stephan Leibfried and Francis G Castles, Cambridge: Cambridge University Press, (2005): 138–79.

Gibson, Edward, and Ernesto Calvo. "Federalism and Low-Maintenance Constituencies: Territorial Dimensions of Economic Reform in Argentina." *Studies in Comparative International Development* 35, no. 3 (2000): 32–55.

Grimmer, Justin. "Appropriators Not Position Takers: The Distorting Effects of Electoral Incentives on Congressional Representation." *American Journal of Political Science* 57, no. 3 (2013): 624–42.

Guiranno, Michele. "Regional Income Disparity and the Size of the Public Sector." *Journal of Public Economic Theory* 32, no. 3 (2009): 321–46.

Gunlicks, Arthur. "The Impact of Unification on German Federalism." *German Politics* 11, no. 3 (2002): 131–52.

Ha, Eunyoung, and Melissa Rogers. *Shifting the Burden in Global Markets: Partisan Effects on Tax Revenue in Less Developed Countries*. Manuscript, Claremont Graduate University, CA, 2015.

Hacker, Jacob, and Paul Pierson. "Winner-Take-All Politics: Public Policy, Political Organization, and the Precipitous Rise of Top Incomes in the United States." *Politics and Society* 38, no. 2 (2010): 152–204.

Haggard, Stephan, and Robert R. Kaufman. "Inequality and Regime Change: Democratic Transitions and the Stability of Democratic Rule." *American Political Science Review* 106, no. 3 (2012): 495–516.

Huber, Evelyne, and John D. Stephens. *Development and Crisis of the Welfare State: Parties and Policies in Global Markets*. University of Chicago Press, 2001.

Huber, Evelyne, Charles Ragin, and John D. Stephens. "Social Democracy, Christian Democracy, Constitutional Structure, and the Welfare State." *American Journal of Sociology* 99, no. 3 (1993): 711–49.

Huber, John D., and Michael M. Ting. "Redistribution, Pork, and Elections." *Journal of the European Economic Association* 11, no. 6 (2013): 1382–403.

Iversen, Torben, and David Soskice. "Electoral Institutions and the Politics of Coalitions: Why Some Democracies Redistribute More Than Others." *American Political Science Review* 100, no. 2 (2006): 165.

Kang, Shin-Goo, and G. Bingham Powell Jr. "Representation and Policy Responsiveness: The Median Voter, Election Rules and Redistributive Welfare Spending." *Journal of Politics* 72, no. 4 (2010): 1014–28.

Kaufman, Robert, and Barbara Stallings. "The Political Economy of Latin American Populism." In *The Macroeconomics of Populism in Latin America,* edited by Rudiger Dornbusch and Sebastian Edwards. University Of Chicago Press (1991): 15–43.

Kenworthy, Lane, and Jonas Pontusson. "Rising Inequality and the Politics of Redistribution in Affluent Countries." *Perspectives on Politics* 3, no. 3 (2005): 449–71.

Key, V. O. "Southern Politics in State and Nation." Alfred A. Knopf, New York, 1949.

Kiewiet, D. Roderick, and Mathew D. McCubbins. "Presidential Influence on Congressional Appropriations Decisions." *American Journal of Political Science* 32, no. 3 (1988): 713–36.

Kitschelt, Herbert. "Linkages between Citizens and Politicians in Democratic Polities." *Comparative Political Studies* 33, no. 6–7 (2000): 845–79.

Korpi, Walter, and Joakim Palme. "The Paradox of Redistribution and Strategies of Equality: Welfare State Institutions, Inequality, and Poverty in the Western Countries." *American Sociological Review* 63 (1998): 661–87.

Kriner, Douglas, and Andrew Reeves. "The Electoral College and Presidential Particularism." *Boston University Law Review.* 94 (2014): 741.

Kriner, Douglas L., and Andrew Reeves. "Presidential Particularism and Divide-the-Dollar Politics." *American Political Science Review* 109, no. 1 (2015): 155–71.

Krueger, Anne O. "The Political Economy of the Rent-Seeking Society." *American Economic Review* 64, no. 3 (1974): 291–303.

Lee, Dong-wook, and Melissa Rogers. Comparing Inequalities: *Regional and Interpersonal Income Disparity, Institutions, and Government Spending.* Manuscript, Claremont Graduate University CA, 2015.

Levi, Margaret. *Of Rule and Revenue*. Vol. 13: University of California Press, 1989.

Levitsky, Steven. "From Labor Politics to Machine Politics: The Transformation of Party-Union Linkages in Argentine Peronism, 1983–1999." *Latin American Research Review* 38, no. 3 (2003): 3–36.

Levitsky, Steven, and Kenneth Roberts. The Resurgence of the Latin American Left. Johns Hopkins University Press, Baltimore MD, 2013.

Levy, Santiago, and Norbert Schady. "Latin America's Social Policy Challenge: Education, Social Insurance, Redistribution." The Journal of Economic Perspectives 27, no. 2 (2013): 193–218.

Lieberman, Evan S. "Taxation Data as Indicators of State-Society Relations: Possibilities and Pitfalls in Cross-National Research." *Studies in Comparative International Development (SCID)* 36, no. 4 (2002): 89–115.

Lijphart, Arend. *Patterns of Democracy: Government Forms and Performance in Thirty-Six Countries.* Yale University Press, New Haven CT, 2012.

Lloyd-Sherlock, Peter. "Social Policy and Inequality in Latin America: A Review of Recent Trends." *Social Policy and Administration* 43, no. 4 (2009): 347–63.

Lupu, Noam, and Jonas Pontusson. "The Structure of Inequality and the Politics of Redistribution." *American Political Science Review* 105, no. 2 (2011): 316–36.

Madison, James. "The Federalist No. 10." *Daily Advertiser*, November 22, 1787.

Mainwaring, Scott, and Matthew Soberg Shugart. *Presidentialism and Democracy in Latin America.* Cambridge University Press, 1997.

Mares, Isabela, and Didac Queralt. "The Origin of the Modern Fiscal State." Paper presented at the CES workshop, Amsterdam, 2013.

Meltzer, Allan, and Scott F. Richard. "A Rational Theory of the Size of Government." *The Journal of Political Economy* 89, no. 5 (1981): 914–27.

Milanovic, Branko. "The Median-Voter Hypothesis, Income Inequality, and Income Redistribution: An Empirical Test with the Required Data." *European Journal of Political Economy* 16, no. 3 (2000): 367–410.

Milesi-Ferretti, Gian Maria, Roberto Perotti, and Massimo Rostagno. "Electoral Systems and Public Spending." *The Quarterly Journal of Economics* 117, no. 2 (2002): 609–57.

Miller, Gary, and Norman Schofield. "The Transformation of the Republican and Democratic Party Coalitions in the US." *Perspectives on Politics* 6, no. 3 (2008): 433–50.

Milligan, Kevin, and Michael Smart. "Regional Grants as Pork Barrel Politics." CESifo Working Paper Series No. 1453. Available at SSRN: http://ssrn.com/abstract=710903 (2005).

Norton, Michael, and Dan Ariely. "Building a Better America—One Wealth Quintile at a Time." *Perspectives on Psychological Science* 6, no. 1 (2011): 9–12.

Obinger, Herbert, Stephan Leibfried, and Francis G Castles. *Federalism and the Welfare State: New World and European Experiences*. Cambridge University Press, 2005.

Persson, Torsten, and Guido Tabellini. "The Size and Scope of Government: Comparative Politics with Rational Politicians." *European Economic Review* 43, no. 4 (1999): 699–735.

Persson, Torsten, and Guido Tabellini. "Constitutional Rules and Fiscal Policy Outcomes." *American Economic Review* 94, no. 1 (2004): 25–45.

Persson, Torsten, Gerard Roland, and Guido Tabellini. "Towards Micropolitical Foundations of Public Finance." *European Economic Review* 42, no. 3 (1998): 685–94.

Pierson, Paul. "Fragmented Welfare States: Federal Institutions and the Development of Social Policy." *Governance* 8, no. 4 (1995): 449–78.

Powell Jr., G. Bingham. "Political Representation in Comparative Politics." *Annual Review of Political Science* 7 (2004): 273–96.

Powell, G. Bingham Jr., and Georg Vanberg. "Election Laws, Disproportionality and Median Correspondence: Implications for Two Visions of Democracy." *British Journal of Political Science* 30, no. 3 (2000): 383–411.

Przeworski, Adam. *Capitalism and Social Democracy*. Cambridge University Press, 1985.

Przeworski, Adam. "Institutions Matter?" *Government and Opposition* 39, no. 4 (2004): 527–40.

Rehfeld, Andrew. *The Concept of Constituency: Political Representation, Democratic Legitimacy, and Institutional Design*. Cambridge University Press, 2005.

Rickard, Stephanie J. "Electoral Systems, Voters' Interests and Geographic Dispersion." *British Journal of Political Science* 42, no. 4 (2012): 855–77.

Riker, William. "Federalism: Origin, Operation." *Significance* 145 (1964).

Riker, William. *Liberalism against Populism*. Waveland Press, Prospect Heights ILL, (1982).

Rodden, Jonathan. "The Dilemma of Fiscal Federalism: Grants and Fiscal Performance around the World." *American Journal of Political Science* 46, no. 3 (2002): 670–87.

Rodden, Jonathan. "The Geographic Distribution of Political Preferences." *Annual Review of Political Science* 13 (2010): 321–40.

Roemer, John. "Why the Poor Do Not Expropriate the Rich: An Old Argument in New Garb." *Journal of Public Economics* 70, no. 3 (1998): 399–424.

Rogers, Melissa Ziegler, and Nicholas Weller. "Income Taxation and the Validity of State Capacity Indicators." *Journal of Public Policy* 34, no. 1 (2013): 1–24.

Rogowski, Ronald, and Mark Andreas Kayser. "Majoritarian Electoral Systems and Consumer Power: Price-Level Evidence from the OECD Countries." *American Journal of Political Science* 46, no. 3 (2002): 526–39.

Romer, Thomas. "Individual Welfare, Majority Voting, and the Properties of a Linear Income Tax." *Journal of Public Economics* 4, no. 2 (1975): 163–85.

Rosenstone, Steven, and John Mark Hansen. *Mobilization, Participation, and Democracy in America (Longman Classics Edition)*. Longman Publishing Group, New York, 2002.

Saalfeld, Thomas. "The German Party System: Continuity and Change." *German Politics* 11, no. 3 (2002): 99–130.

Samuels, David. "Presidentialism and Accountability for the Economy in Comparative Perspective." *American Political Science Review* 98, no. 3 (2004): 425–36.

Samuels, David, and Richard Snyder. "The Value of a Vote: Malapportionment in Comparative Perspective." *British Journal of Political Science* 31, no. 4 (2001): 651–71.

Shugart, Matthew Soberg. "Presidentialism, Parliamentarism, and the Provision of Collective Goods in Less-Developed Countries." *Constitutional Political Economy* 10, no. 1 (1999): 53–88.

Shugart, Matthew Soberg, and John M. Carey. *Presidents and Assemblies: Constitutional Design and Electoral Dynamics*. Cambridge University Press, 1992.

Skocpol, Theda, and Edwin Amenta. "States and Social Policies." *Annual Review of Sociology* (1986): 131–57.

Soifer, Hillel David. "State Power and the Economic Origins of Democracy." *Studies in Comparative International Development* 48, no. 1 (2013): 1–22.

Sokoloff, Kenneth L., and Stanley L. Engerman. "History Lessons: Institutions, Factors Endowments, and Paths of Development in the New World." *The Journal of Economic Perspectives* 14, no. 3 (2000): 217–32.

Solt, Frederick. "Economic Inequality and Democratic Political Engagement." *American Journal of Political Science* 52, no. 1 (2008): 48–60.

Stepan, Alfred. "Toward a New Comparative Politics of Federalism, Multinationalism, and Democracy: Beyond Rikerian Federalism." in *Federalism and Democracy in Latin America*, edited by Edward Gibson. Johns Hopkins University Press, Baltimore MD, (2004): 29–84.

Strøm, Kaare. "A Behavioral Theory of Competitive Political Parties." *American Journal of Political Science* 34, no. 2 (1990): 565–98.

Strøm, Kaare. "Delegation and Accountability in Parliamentary Democracies." *European Journal of Political Research* 37, no. 3 (2000): 261–90.

Tavits, Margit, and Joshua D Potter. "The Effect of Inequality and Social Identity on Party Strategies." *American Journal of Political Science* 2 (2014). DOI: 10.1111/ajps.12144.

Tsebelis, George. *Veto Players: How Political Institutions Work*. Princeton University Press, Princeton NJ, 2011.

Tuschhoff, Christian. "The Compounding Effect: The Impact of Federalism on the Concept of Representation." *West European Politics* 22, no. 2 (1999): 16–33.

Weingast, Barry, Kenneth Shepsle, and Christopher Johnsen. "The Political Economy of Benefits and Costs: A Neoclassical Approach to Distributive Politics." *The Journal of Political Economy* 89, no. 4 (1981): 642–64.

Zechmeister, Elizabeth. "What's Left and Who's Right? A Q-Method Study of Individual and Contextual Influences on the Meaning of Ideological Labels." *Political Behavior* 28, no. 2 (2006).

4 Federalism and Redistribution

Introduction

Federalism is widely viewed as an institutional barrier to redistribution (Castles 1999; Huber, Ragin, and Stephens 1993). In empirical studies, federalism is associated with lower government spending, lower tax collection, lower fiscal redistribution and lower social spending (Cameron 1978; Brennan and Buchanan 1980; Grossman 1989). With smaller government comes, often but not always, more limited efforts to reduce income disparities. Figure 4.1 provides descriptive evidence of the differences in redistributive efforts between federal and unitary

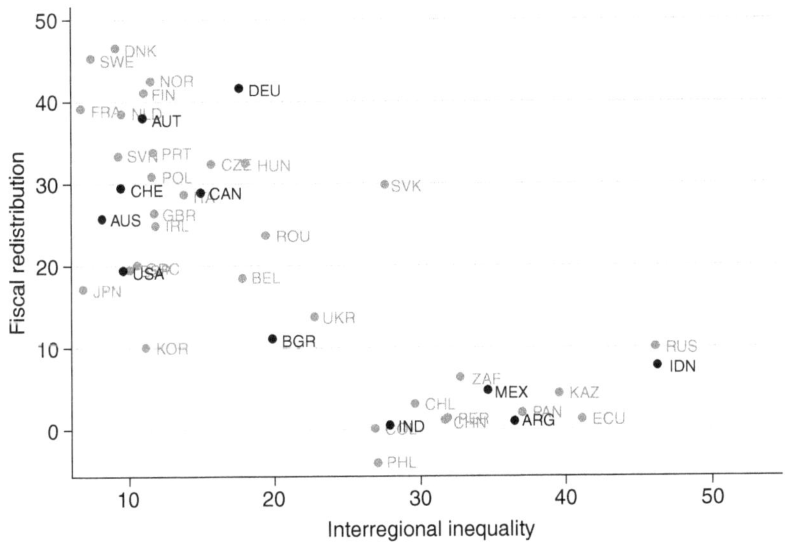

Figure 4.1 Fiscal Redistribution and Regional Inequality in Federations (sources: Fiscal redistribution (Solt 2014); interregional inequality (Lee and Rogers 2015); federalism (Persson and Tabellini 1999)).

Note
Federal nations are in black, unitary states are in gray. Data are from 2005. Fiscal redistribution is measured by the percentage difference in the national Gini coefficient between pre- and post-tax and transfer inequality. Interregional inequality is the adjusted Gini coefficient of regional GDP per capita.

states. In this sample of 50 developed and developing nations, federations redistribute at lower levels than unitary federations at similar levels of inequality.[1] This is true both of developed and developing nations. However, the variation in welfare states among federal states is so large as to point to heterogeneous effects of federalism (Obinger et al. 2005; Beramendi et al. 2015). The effects of federalism on redistribution may in fact be conditional on other political or economic factors.

Three primary characteristics of federalism appear to limit equalizing initiatives. First, federalism increases the number of veto actors involved in decision-making at the national level. Because redistribution may be against the short-term economic interests of well-off individuals and regions, introducing veto points into distributive policymaking increases the potential opportunities for blocking egalitarian reform. Federalism should thus be a conservative institution that preserves the status quo. Second, federalism fragments power, including that of the majority coalition that would benefit from fiscal redistribution (Persson and Tabellini 1994; Pierson 1995). When the national coalition in favor of redistribution is segmented across territories, its organizational challenges are greater. Third, federalism limits the policy scope of the national government. This may limit redistribution to citizens in regions with political elites opposed to reform and may stymie broader reform efforts (Stepan 2004). These features of federalism, and especially increased veto points, are frequently recognized as limiting political responses to economic inequality.

Less recognized are politicians' divergent incentives to deliver transformative social policy due to the nature of political competition and distribution. Federalism also affects the career incentives of politicians (both national and subnational) by incentivizing the provision of national resources to local districts. Because territorial distributions are visible to constituents and clearly linked to politicians' efforts, politicians may rationally prioritize delivery of locally targeted benefits above national social policy. Federalism, therefore, may lead to the underprovision of national social policy reform for lack of motivated politicians (Milesi-Ferretti et al. 2002).

Federalism introduces a territorial dimension to politics that increases the salience of spatial economic endowments and political distribution. Once individuals and social groups are divided into political units, their political identity and preferences can be affected. Regional differentiation creates important regional competition for goods, and makes relevant relative regional wealth and inequality that are diminished in a national conception of inequality. While the national income distribution is most salient to the national coalition in favor of central redistributive reform, with federalism inter- and intra-regional distributions of income also shape constituents' interests. The coalition in favor of national efforts for redistribution can thus be divided in federal systems, both in organizational terms (as is frequently recognized) but also in terms of the preferences of the ostensible coalition (Beramendi 2007).

In this chapter I argue that federalism affects redistribution by incentivizing territorial distribution of national goods, by providing tools for anti-redistributive regional actors to shape and block national policy, and by fragmenting the national redistributive coalition ideologically and organizationally. Federalism highlights regions in national representation and incentivizes politicians to please constituents by advancing their regions' interests. If regions are uniform in economic endowments and ideology, federalism should not matter for redistributive outcomes because the deciding actors will have common preferences. However, regional actors may have distinct preferences for redistribution informed by their regions' political economy (Beramendi 2012). Countries' regions vary considerably in these endowments, as demonstrated in Chapter 2, and they should be important for politicians that answer to regional constituencies. Moreover, regional inequality changes the nature of federalism and, consequently, national representation in federal countries. Federalism operating under the distributive tensions of divergent regions should face different distributive dilemmas than those faced in homogenous federations.

After defining federalism and examining the theoretical links between federalism and redistribution, I will then elaborate the logic using the three country examples. Federalism in the USA, Germany, and Argentina varies dramatically on nearly every dimension. US federalism emphasizes competition among subunits and shows strong policy decentralization on both the tax and expenditure side of redistribution. National actors representing the states have several points in the policy process at which to veto or shape legislation, and they often take that opportunity. Germany's federalism, on the other hand, is based predominantly on cooperative risk-sharing among the Länder. The territorial Bundesrat has weaker powers than the US Senate but does play an important role in legislation affecting the Länder, including on budgets. However, the Länder have limited say in most social policy because their funding is semi-autonomous from the national legislature. As regional inequality has grown in the German Federation, the Bundesrat has exercised increasing authority in the budget processes under its domain to limit already expansive redistributive programs (Gunlicks 2002). The rich Länder have tried to limit redistribution across regions, but have had limited success. Argentina's federalism shares many of the constitutional features of US and German federalism, but differs significantly in its fiscal federalism and in the role provincial actors play within the parties. As in Germany, Argentina's political parties rely on interregional transfers to build national political coalitions. As in the USA, many redistributive programs are administered at the sub-national level. Argentina's uneven development shows the strongest effect on both the natures of federalism and redistribution, as provinces with starkly different interests must negotiate with the center for their preferred redistributive policy. In all three nations, distributive concerns that stem from divergence in regional income and economic endowments play out strongly in national politics through the institutions of federalism.

Defining Federalism

The definition of federalism is controversial due to the enormous variation in policy decentralization around the world. In Riker's (1964) seminal definition, federalism is present when states and their central government each have policy areas upon which they hold ultimate authority. In practice, there are many varieties of federalism, with considerable mixing of government responsibilities. There is also variance in the relevance of federalism across different policy areas.

In a more inclusive and detailed definition, Obinger et al. (2005, p. 9) describe federalism as:

1 A set of institutional arrangements and decision rules at central government level for incorporating territorially based interests; these arrangements vary in the degree to which they provide veto powers to subordinate branches of government.
2 A set of territorially based actors with ideas and interests who vary greatly in number and heterogeneity.
3 A set of jurisdictional arrangements for allocating policy responsibilities between different levels of government; this refers to both policy-making and policy implementation.
4 A set of intergovernmental fiscal transfer arrangements.
5 A set of informal arrangements—both vertical and horizontal—between governments.

Obinger et al.'s definition highlights several important facets of federalism related to the discussion at hand. First, they emphasize the centrality of territorially based interests and of politicians empowered to act on the basis of those interests. This is a crucial mechanism that potentially divides preferences in the latent national majority redistributive coalition. Second, they point out the veto powers available to politicians with sub-national constituencies, which vary in both number and force. Federal countries have secondary institutions (bicameralism, supreme courts) to support the vertical separation of power that creates these veto points. All federal nations have difficult-to-amend written constitutions that demarcate powers between the center and the regions. Supreme courts adjudicate disputes between the center and the regions, and disputes among regions that relate to constitutionality. In all federal systems, constituent units serve as the basis for representation in some part of the national policy process. This includes most often territorial upper chambers, sometimes with strong policy powers, and in some cases regional referenda with the power to veto or create national law.[2] In many nations, inter-governmental bargaining between executives of the national and sub-national levels is a very important arena of policymaking as well. In these forums, politicians with regional constituencies have some degree of influence over the content and eventual passage of national legislation.

Third, like Riker, they emphasize the importance of jurisdictions of policy-making and policy implementation, and their partition between the central and national governments. Federalism is clearly in place where a policy is exclusively controlled by a sub-national government. The distinction between policy making and policy implementation is likewise critical. The USA is strongly federal on both counts—a large number of policies are both made and implemented at the state level. In Germany, the Länder implement policy that is made by the national government. Argentina is a mix between the two—much of the provinces' resources come from national transfers, but they also maintain policy authority in potentially redistributive policy areas (e.g, health, education). Importantly, unlike in the USA and Germany, the ultimate authority in Argentina on all policy matters may in fact be the central government.[3]

For analysis of redistributive policies, it is essential to note that in many unequivocally federal countries some welfare policies are administered exclusively by the central government. Accordingly, it is reasonable to ask whether that nation is federal on these matters (Obinger et al. 2005). At a fundamental level, federalism influences national policymaking and the cascade of politicians (including senators, regional parties, etc.) engaged in decision-making. In this sense, federalism will matter for redistribution even when it is under the exclusive control of the national government. These actors are highlighted for their role in redistributive policymaking in the examples below. Moreover, in nearly all federal nations, some policies that can be redistributive, but that are not considered part of the welfare state, are handled at the sub-national level. This includes, among other things, education policy and spending, as well as subsidized housing.

Finally, Obinger et al. highlight fiscal federalism, which is composed of taxation, expenditure, and transfers among levels of government. Fiscal federalism is crucial for policy autonomy of the national and sub-national governments because whoever controls the money can shape the policy. For example, in the USA, the central government transfers money to the states, earmarked for a large number of policy areas. The federal government sometimes tries to shape the character of policy at the sub-national level by making transfers contingent on policy change in the states (Rosen 2004).[4] The three countries analyzed in this book have distinct fiscal federalisms that incentivize very different behaviors in national and sub-national politicians (Rodden and Wibbels 2011).

All of these features show that federal systems vary substantially in how they are designed. Their design likely reflects the reason for adopting federalism in the first place, as well as the characteristics of the constituent units. Riker (1964) attributes the adoption of federalism to a response to territorial threats. When threatened by an external force, leaders of regional subunits recognize that they can more effectively defend their interests by joining together. More recently, with the example of the European Union, federalism has also been seen as a response to economic threat.[5] Nations with disparate but complementary endowments may be better able to utilize resources if they can coordinate. Federation is thus a bargain to maximize some good, whether territorial integrity or economic productivity. The design of federations, at the same time, should reflect the interests and endowments of the constituent parts. Weaker regions look to protect their authority so that they are not dominated by more powerful regions. Wealthy regions look to place limits on regional redistribution in order to avoid paying beyond the benefits of the union (Bolton and Roland 1997). In this way, federal institutions should be at least partially endogenous to initial distributions of regional income, and their terms subject to revision with transformations in regional income distributions.

Theoretical Foundations: Why Federalism Matters for Redistribution?

At the foundational level, federalism and redistributive policies may seem to be in great conflict (Linz 1997). Federalism is an institutional device that allows for diversity among territories, while still preserving the benefits of national unity. Redistributive policies, and the welfare state specifically, often seek to create uniformity among the population. The prominent arguments for why federalism may limit redistribution are: (1) federalism fragments the national coalition that would benefit from the welfare state (Pierson 1995; Skocpol and Amenta 1986); (2) federalism increases the number of actors necessary to pass legislation, thus vetoes of redistributive legislation are more likely (Huber et al. 1993); and (3) federalism limits the policy scope of the national government to govern according to the interests of the majority of the population (Stepan 2004).

As a starting point, redistributive policy is considered popular with a majority of citizens, but very unpopular with those that would fund it. Despite their latent numerical advantage, those that would benefit from redistribution always face considerable resistance to its passage (Aysan 2005). Federalism, and its associated institutions, may challenge the unity and coherence of the majority coalition that would benefit from redistribution (Swank 2001). The problems of organization stem from variations within decentralized systems. Many federal nations have decentralized party organizations with loose association across regions. The left, therefore, must overcome this organizational heterogeneity to engage in collective action. If organizations seek to change policy at the regional level, moreover, they may face distinct policy environments in each region, which may create both redundancies in effort and additional work to tailor the reform to the laws of each region. Federalism also challenges the organization of the majority coalition because it "is founded on and generates diversity, encouraging the emergences of territorially diverse political economies, each with its own set of deeply rooted political interests and values" (Obinger et al. 2005, p. 35). Thus, federalism is associated with the greater preference heterogeneity within the majority coalition that stems from territorial (and perhaps other) differences.

Federalism, like presidentialism, increases the number of actors needed to make redistributive (or any other) policy change. If the anti-redistributive coalition is able to capture any of the veto points in the federal secondary institutions discussed above, power can be used to limit or undermine redistribution. These veto points are sometimes available to a minority of actors that may create "blocking win sets" able to derail reform efforts of the majority.

Related to this, federal systems are also, to varying extents, "demos constraining" (Stepan 2004). The entire national citizenry comprises the demos. National legislative institutions are intended principally to enact the preferred policies of the demos. Federal nations diverge from the "one man, one vote" principle by including institutions that use territories as the basis for representation, such as bicameral legislatures. At their extreme, federal nations give powers to Senates equivalent to those of the demos (represented in the popular chamber). If the national majority is crucial to the adoption of redistributive reforms, federal constraints on the demos may stand in its way.

Federalism thus matters for national policy and national outcomes, and not just for differences across regions. Clearly, federalism can result in regional differences in decentralized redistributive policy. Federalism entails policy arenas that are the exclusive purview of sub-national regions. This policy decentralization may matter specifically to redistribution if welfare policies, in addition to tax and spending policies more broadly, occur at the level of the region. If regions have different tax bases, policies dependent on those bases will show variation across regions in terms of generosity and quality (Prud'homme 1995; Oates 1999). These differences may affect the government's overall contribution to redistribution and may also affect the national government indirectly by limiting its policy scope and its tools to reduce income inequality (Stepan 2004).

It is important to note that federal systems vary considerably in how they operate and their likely effects on redistribution (Obinger et al. 2005). The combinations of institutions as well as their socio-demographic and economic features help to explain some of these differences. Certain policies may operate very differently in some federal systems. For example, in Canada, most welfare programs operate as if it were a unitary state (Banting 2005). Others, such as US unemployment insurance and General Assistance (aid to adults without dependents) are strongly decentralized in management and administration. Moreover, redistribution and the welfare state may themselves shape federalism. Banting (1987) argues this is the case for Canada, whereby shared welfare programs dampen its ethno-linguistic cleavages.

Obinger et al. (2005) distinguish between two broad classes of federalism in the OECD—competitive and cooperative. Federalism in the English tradition (USA, Canada, Australia) focuses on inter-state competition. The German and Austrian federal systems emphasize coordination across sub-units. Competitive federalism is lauded for constraining the central government from imposing policies thought to hinder economic activity, especially high taxes and spending (Weingast 1995). According to this logic, competitive federalism should make redistribution less likely because it constrains the taxation and spending needed to fund it. Cooperative federalism, on the other hand, may encourage redistribution because regions can come together in systems of mutually beneficial risk pooling (Manow 2005).

According to some scholars, federalism may in some cases encourage redistribution when the national government is resistant to reform. To begin, states favorable to redistribution can introduce policies within their districts, providing welfare that might not exist otherwise. Federalism is also thought to encourage redistribution through policy experimentation in the states that can serve as a feasible model for the national government (Finegold 2005). A successful state project can ease concerns of worried national constituents. The USA provides many examples of successful state redistributive projects broadened to a national scale. Most prominently, Wisconsin adopted an unemployment insurance system that was the model for the Social Security Act of 1935 and Massachusetts' health care exchange served as the basis for the Affordable

Care Act of 2010. Finegold's (2005) argument suggests that the existence of a viable state model may explain, in part, why the Affordable Care Act passed under President Barack Obama but why a similar measure failed in 1993 under Bill Clinton. The centralization of policymaking in Germany makes the "states as laboratories of innovation" argument less plausible in cases of cooperative federalism.

The connection between federalism and redistribution may also work in the other direction (i.e., redistribution might impact federalism). Social policy might change a nation's federalism by increasing the scope of national policy over time as citizens seek common levels of protection and regional development, in order to avoid a "race to the bottom" on welfare provision. The provision of social policy also changes the nature of intergovernmental cooperation, and federal fiscal arrangements in every nation. These changes, in turn, have the potential to substantially alter the nature of a nation's federal system and its relative powers. This has been argued for Australia (Castles and Uhr 2007) and Canada (Banting 2005), but also for the growing power of the US national government after the initiation of the New Deal.

Federalism may also encourage regionalization of the party system (Brancati 2007; Chhibber and Kollman 2004). Regional legislatures provide an opportunity for region-specific parties to govern that would not be otherwise available at the national level. Regional parties might also gain national representation through indirect elections in territorial upper chambers, as in Germany. In some cases, regional parties run in national elections to improve their chances in regional races (Brancati 2007). The role that regionalism plays in party systems is directly addressed in Chapter 5.

Once in place, moreover, federalism appears to favor continued redistribution (Pierson 2001). Just as it is more difficult to pass initial reforms in federal systems, it is also more difficult to pull back those reforms down the line under federalism. Redistributive reforms tend to be popular, meaning that politicians will find it difficult to vote to eliminate them under federalism. With more actors influencing the ultimate policy outcome, it is likely that one of those actors will block passage to retrenchment.

Federalism, Regional Disparity, and the Welfare State

Theories of the virtues and follies of federalism typically assume regions at comparable levels of development. Regions are thought to have heterogeneous endowments and preferences but rough parity in wealth and unified goals of economic growth and material improvement. Accordingly, regions can compete to maximize national growth or cooperate to achieve economies of scale and efficient risk pools. However, most nations of the world are characterized by interregional inequalities in wealth and divergent political economies, especially in the developing world. These disparities may render theories of decentralization questionable if heterogeneity of interests and endowments drive divergent development.

Recent literature on the actual functioning of federalism, rather than its optimal design, suggests some revisions in our expectations about the role of federalism in policy outcomes. Rather than competition resulting in efficiencies, states may be in a race to the bottom on tax rates that undermines needed social safety nets (Oates 1999). Rather than cooperation allowing for shared risks, it may encourage profligacy as citizens have a difficult time assigning blame for ballooning debts (Rodden and Wibbels 2002; Rodden 2003). Importantly, in the developing world in particular, federalism usually exists under conditions of high interregional inequality that render both competitive and cooperate federalism unlikely.

With high levels of regional inequality, this implies differences in regional productivity and tax bases. If regions differ widely in productivity, as well as in their supporting physical and human capital of development, many regions will not be able to entice business or voters to "vote with their feet" to their localities with attractive tax rates or policy environments (Tiebout 1956). In the USA the Tiebout theory is plausible—isolated South Dakota was able to attract a very large portion of the credit card industry to move to Sioux Falls with a favorable regulatory environment. Now South Dakota has the largest bank assets of any state. The Tiebout effect thus assumes several factors that cannot be taken for granted in highly unequal federations—i.e., equivalent infrastructure across regions, easy transportation of goods and services across regional lines, and either relatively uniform human capital or high labor mobility to fill jobs in less dynamic regions. These assumptions are somewhat questionable even in the USA for many industries and they are undeniably dubious in regionally disparate Argentina.

Differences in regional tax bases also call into question the foundations of cooperative federalism. On the one hand, regional economic heterogeneity is a very positive foundation for federalism because it diversifies a nation's portfolio. When one industry, say financial services, is depressed, a commodities boom can support central revenues, and vice versa (Cox 2008). This fosters regional cooperation through risk pooling. However, regional disparity typically suggests that a handful of regions are producing the bulk of the tax revenues. In this case, productive regions may object to subsidization of poorer regions. Decentralization of policy under federalism, moreover, is likely to lead to disparate outcomes as poor regions cannot provide equivalent public services to those provided by rich regions, even when subsidized (Prud'homme 1995). At the same time, a strong motivation for cooperative federalism from the rich regions is to limit the poor's mobility to the productive regions. In short, high levels of regional inequality may be a primary reason why federalism operates differently in developed and developing federations (Rodden and Wibbels 2011).

Regional disparities may also stand in the way of efficient institutional adaptation. As Beramendi (2012, p. 29) describes,

> distributive conflicts associated with the geography of inequality drive elites' preferences apart through their impact on the electoral constraints they face. As these tensions exacerbate, the probability that either level of government responds favorably to the possibility of institutional change diminishes.

While the motivation for federalism may include risk-sharing, reducing externalities, and providing for necessary common goods, cooperation on these tasks may be strained by differences in regional wealth. The German example shows this over time. When regional inequalities were small (1960s–1980) party interests subsumed territorial interests (Lehmbruch 1976) but as regional inequality has grown, territorial concerns have grown in salience (1980s) and come to the forefront with reunification (Jeffery 1999). In response, the territorial Bundesrat has grown more active in budget affairs (Gunlicks 2002).

Decentralization of all kinds has the effect of rendering local interests salient and it thus highlights the effects of regional disparity in wealth. Territorial electoral districts at the national and local level give strong incentives for politicians to care about local rather than national concerns by pressing the interests of constituents in their districts. This is true both of politicians elected locally for local office (such as governors and regional legislators) and for politicians elected from local districts for national office. Given that regional income inequality promotes heterogeneity of interests across localities and within the national body elected by localities, electoral federalism should strongly impact how these preferences turn into policy outcomes in a nation.

Redistribution in Federations

Most research on redistribution examines interpersonal redistribution from rich to poor individuals. Federalism highlights the redistribution of resources across regions. Nearly all federal nations have a formal mechanism to redistribute income among regions. In Germany, this is the Law of Fiscal Equalization, or the Länderfinanzausgleich. The interregional transfer system is known as Federal Co-Participation in Argentina. The USA does not have a formal system of regional redistribution, but a large web of programs that provide (earmarked) federal resources to regions. In principle, these regional redistributive schemes should operate much like interpersonal redistribution—rich regions subsidize poor regions to encourage development in the latter, or discourage mobility from the latter to the former.

In practice, regional transfers are part of a national economic and political distributive game (Rodden and Wibbels 2002; Gordín 2006). From the economic perspective, transfers equilibrate resources (whether income, jobs, or productivity) across regions. This is important for the principle of equity, but also for the limiting of externalities and the sharing of risks across regions. For example, if some regions are very productive, they can expect a significant influx of labor from the less productive regions. An obvious example is the German case, in which reunification was expected to bring a major inflow of labor from the poor Eastern Länder with high unemployment rates to the economically dynamic Western Länder. In order to limit this internal migration, rich regions that would otherwise oppose redistributive regional transfers support transfers to poor regions. Moreover, regions have different economic risks and fluctuations. Transfer systems across regions can provide insurance for all regions in cases of economic hardship.

From the political perspective, regional transfers are very useful for building coalitions to overcome preference heterogeneity in territorial political systems (Diaz-Cayeros 2006). Said more coarsely, transfers are used to "buy" support of politicians who have territorial constituencies, including on policies of interpersonal redistribution. Because territorial constituencies increase the preference heterogeneity within party systems, representatives need to be compensated for compromising their preferred ideological position. These dynamics are explored in detail in the three case examples.

Among the many concerns that come with regional redistribution are the encouragement of profligacy and the discouragement of economic development. These critiques are analogous to those on the incentive effects of the welfare state. If regions do not need to raise their own resources, they will not internalize the costs of policy and will tend to overspend (Rodden and Wibbels 2002; Treisman 2006). The central pot of resources is a commons that is overgrazed by the regions. This argument has been made for Federal Co-Participation in Argentina (Saiegh and Tommasi 1999), and for the welfare state as a whole in Germany (Manow 2005). Regional redistributive schemes also tend to base their generosity on regional income. Thus regions have incentives to stay or appear poor in order to keep resources flowing to them, and few incentives to improve their financial status.

A somewhat different question is whether regional redistribution is in fact progressive. For a regional redistributive system to be progressive, it must see resources allocated to poor provinces, whether measured by economic productivity, the income level of its citizens, or likely both. The Länderfinanzausgleich is highly redistributive and progressive from relatively rich Western Länder to poorer Eastern Länder (Beramendi 2012). Regional transfers in other nations, notably Argentina and Brazil, are not predominantly progressive. Rather, distribution formulae appear to be shaped principally by representation and overrepresentation in the national legislature (Gervasoni 2010). In these countries, transfers could be redistributive but they are not progressive, and do not appear to reduce inequality (Beramendi, Rogers, and Diaz-Cayeros 2015).

Argentina's fiscal federation is also vertically imbalanced, which creates an additional challenge to fiscal soundness and cooperative budgeting. This means that the national government collects most of the revenue while the provinces spend most of it. Vertical fiscal imbalance has many negative consequences for the national and provincial budgets that are well discussed in other places (Saiegh and Tommasi 1999; Jones, Sanguinetti and Tommasi 2000; Tommasi et al. 2001; Rodden 2002). For the purposes of examining redistributive outcomes, it is important to know that provinces get the majority of their money from the central government. In Argentina, 18 of 24 provinces get more than 60 percent of their revenue from the national government and the average is 72 percent. Five provinces get around 90 percent of their revenue from the national government. Again, it is important to remember that the provinces do the majority of the spending. The provinces that are most dependent on national resources are the least developed.

Regional Incidence of National Redistributive Programs

While intergovernmental transfers and fiscal equalization schemes may be the most obvious ways that central governments redistribute to regions, national welfare policies also have different regional effects. Affluent regions will be net contributors and poor regions net recipients in these programs through a progressive income tax. This brings two important factors to light. One involves the deciding criteria for redistributive distributions. Differences in urban versus non-urban costs of living, for example, are important criteria for whether affluent regions are likely to see significant benefits to their poor populations from redistributive programs. Second is the fact that affluent regions, including the poor within those regions, may oppose national redistributive efforts. These regions may be better off providing their preferred level of distribution at the regional level.[6]

In Table 4.1, the regional incidence of national redistribution is demonstrated for Germany and the United States using data from the LIS. Unfortunately, comparable data are not available for Argentina. For each case, I show the "fiscal power" of the states and the level of redistribution. Fiscal power refers to their level of tax collection. In the German case, this refers to tax collection before fiscal equalization and for the USA the taxes collected exclusively by the states. Redistribution is the change in the Gini coefficient that results from government taxation and spending.

Redistributive welfare programs have uneven regional effects in Germany. The automatic formula of the redistributive programs indirectly transfers income from rich to poor Länder. The redistributive effects of national policy show strong progressivity toward the East. Very evident in Table 4.2 is that fiscally powerful (affluent) Länder governments benefit much less from national redistributive programs. The higher, on average, the level of Länder tax collection, reflecting the overall economy size, the lower the effects of government redistribution. For example, in 2010 government policy reduced income inequality by around 28 percent in Western Länder. In Eastern Länder, however, this figure was closer to 37 percent.

The USA also shows considerable differences in the redistributive incidence across states. What is apparent in Table 4.1 is that the effects of redistributive policy are not apparently stronger in poorer places than in richer places, as is evident in Germany. In the USA, relatively poor states are spread throughout the list. For example, South Carolina and Arkansas, both comparatively lower income, fiscally weak states, benefit very differently from redistributive policies. South Carolina benefits the least of all from redistributive policy and Arkansas benefits the second most of all states. Redistributive social policies in the USA do not appear to be uniformly progressive from richer to poorer states. Clearly, redistributive policies of all stripes differ among federations. This variation is explored in detail in the following case analysis.

Federalism and Redistribution in Argentina, Germany, and the USA

In the theoretical discussion in Chapter 3, I discussed the primary mechanisms whereby political institutions may lead to divergences in redistributive policy. Unlike in most research supportive of this thesis, I suggest that one major reason why certain institutions are associated with lower redistribution is that they bring territorial interests to the fore. In the following section, I provide texture to these dynamics in the discussion of the three federal case studies. First, I introduce the three federalisms, and then I discuss them all according to the mechanisms that link territorial politics to redistribution.

Germany—Cooperative Federalism and Redistribution

When scholars argue that federalism undermines redistribution, the most potent counter case is Germany. Despite its federal structure, Germany is one of the most redistributive nations in the world, including high transfers from rich to poor individuals, and from rich to poor regions. Why does federalism appear consistent with redistribution in Germany and inimical in so many other cases?

The most straightforward reason is that federal systems vary tremendously across the world, with the operation of German federalism looking quite distinct from US federalism on nearly every dimension. Much of this distinction depends on the interacting institutions (especially electoral rules and parliamentarism) in Germany that defuse the territorial cleavage. Within the operation of federalism itself, the policymaking process in Germany is strongly national while the implementation and administration is in the purview of the Länder. This type of federalism is based on a principle of cooperation and risk-sharing, and not competition between subunits. Thus, even the operation of federalism favors a national orientation that defuses to some extent the territorial cleavage.

Germany is a particularly important federal case to examine with regard to the regional cleavage because the nation's income distribution faced a major exogenous shock with reunification (Beramendi 2012). The nation experienced a very different distributive scenario in 1990 than in 1989—one in which the income differences coincided very strongly with regional lines. Under these circumstances, the federal institutions could not be said to be endogenous to the existing structure of inequality because the rules were designed before East Germany merged with the West.

Germany's federal system has very different effects on redistribution than that seen in the USA in particular. First, Germany's welfare system is strongly nationalized and the bulk of its taxes shared to reduce regional income disparities. The "para-state" financing of social welfare through an automatic, largely autonomous income stream limits the "politics" around increasing or reducing taxes to fund changes in program generosity. While the territorial Bundesrat has a very strong position in (blocking) national government expansion in general, this role is limited in the redistributive programs that are funded by direct contributions by workers (Mares 2003).

Table 4.1 Regional Incidence of Redistribution, the United States and Germany

(1)	*(2)*	*(3)*	*(4)*	*(5)*	*(6)*
German Länder	*Taxes of the Länder*	*Redistribution*	*United States*	*Tax Collection per capita*	*Redistribution*
Hamburg	147.6	0.984	Alaska	210.2	0.817
Bavaria	128.3	0.871	District of Columbia	202.2	0.844
Hesse	121.6	0.813	New York	171.0	1.020
Baden-Württemberg	116.8	0.827	Wyoming	152.1	0.935
North Rhine-Westphalia	99.3	0.754	Connecticut	145.2	0.943
Rhineland-Palatinate	95.6	1.193	New Jersey	140.9	0.925
Schlweswg-Holstein	93.8	0.817	North Dakota	125.5	1.175
Berlin	91.8	0.886	Massachusetts	123.7	0.915
Bremen	88	1.307	Maryland	118.1	0.833
Lower Saxony	87.9	1.007	Hawaii	117.7	0.969
Saarland	79.4	1.194	Vermont	114.8	0.992
Brandenburg	65.8	1.077	California	112.2	0.997
Saxony-Anhalt	54.1	1.026	Minnesota	111.6	0.907
Mecklen-W Pomerania	54.1	1.100	Rhode Island	111.3	1.005
Saxony	53.8	1.129	Maine	106.5	1.113
Thuringia	53.3	1.010	Wisconsin	105.1	1.077
			Illinois	103.7	0.988
			Pennsylvania	101.1	1.002
			Colorado	98.5	0.890
			Kansas	97.1	1.071
			Nebraska	97.0	0.956
			Delaware	96.6	1.027
			Washington	96.5	0.957
			New Hampshire	95.4	0.821
			Iowa	95.3	0.985
			Virginia	94.1	0.874

Nevada	91.3	0.911
Ohio	91.3	1.067
Michigan	87.9	1.135
Indiana	87.4	1.057
Louisiana	86.6	1.002
West Virginia	85.3	1.262
Oregon	85.0	1.020
Florida	84.9	0.919
Texas	83.4	0.892
North Carolina	83.1	0.908
Montana	79.0	1.001
Arkansas	78.9	1.147
Kentucky	77.0	1.036
Missouri	76.9	1.115
South Dakota	76.8	1.113
Arizona	76.6	0.946
Georgia	75.3	0.963
Oklahoma	73.7	1.011
Mississippi	73.2	1.126
Utah	73.1	0.989
Tennessee	69.7	1.062
South Carlonia	69.4	0.827
Alabama	68.5	0.990
Idaho	67.2	1.190

Sources: Länder VAT tax collection (Federal Ministry of Finance); state tax collection per capita (Tax Policy Center); redistribution by Länder/state (LIS).

Notes
Länder are ordered based on tax collection before VAT apportionment (% of national average). States are ordered according to tax collection per capita (% of national average). Redistribution is measured as the percentage difference in the regional Gini coefficient before and after government tax and expenditures, in percentage.

Germany's central government spending is heavily weighted toward broad social goods. Germany spent 26 percent of its GDP on social spending in 2014 (OECD Social Expenditure Statistics 2014). In Figure 2.6 in Chapter 2, Germany is shown to allocate more of its spending toward broad social categories than any other government in the OECD. Importantly, Figure 2.6 also shows what Germany is not spending as much on in relative terms—categories that are more easily targeted to localities. Germany spends considerably less on defense (not surprisingly given its demilitarization after World War II), public order, education, and even general public service (which includes intergovernmental transfers) than on social spending categories.[7] Why does a federal government spend (relatively) so much in social categories, and (relatively) so little on pork? If veto power and pork incentives in the Senate lead federalism to limit redistribution in the USA, why does this same dynamic not occur in the German case? Why does federalism not have the same effect of fragmenting the majority coalition favorable to redistribution in Germany? The difference depends on the nature of federalism in the German case, the funding of the welfare state, and the variation in electoral dynamics across the cases.

The United States—Federalism and Fragmented Redistribution

The USA is the landmark case for the argument that federalism limits the development of a redistributive welfare state. Despite great wealth and latent societal demand for redistribution, the USA is a "laggard" on nearly every dimension of social provision. Federalism is the most frequently cited reason for this position (Pierson 1995; Skocpol and Amenta 1986). In particular, authors in this tradition cite the fragmentation of the redistributive coalition under the fragmented political and administrative system, the constitutional restrictions that keep redistribution out of the policy scope of the federal government, and the opportunities to veto redistribution by anti-redistributive state representatives in the Senate (Douglas 2000).

On the other hand, many researchers question whether federalism has an unequivocally negative effect on redistributive efforts in the USA. For one point, Finegold (2005) argues that it is difficult to assess the counterfactual result if the USA were not federal. In his attempt to assess the counterfactual of the pivotal moments in the development of the US welfare state, Finegold argues that in many ways federalism made redistribution more likely by restricting the scope of national authority (and thus protecting states' redistributive policies) and by allowing for policy innovation at the sub-national level that served as a model for the nation.

Argentina—Federal Transfers and the Failures of Redistribution

Although federalism is a central topic in the political economy of inequality and redistribution, very few studies examine its effects in the developing world (Beramendi, Rogers and Diaz-Cayeros 2015). Much is written about Argentina's federal system, but very little links its inefficient design and negative outcomes to effects on the redistributive state. Argentina's federalism creates a strong subnational pull in its politics and high levels of horizontal redistribution through intergovernmental transfers. This federal design, however, stands in the way of a highly redistributive national state.

The extent of the welfare state is well documented in the advanced industrial countries. It is easy to say, then, that Germany is a leader in redistributive reforms and the USA is a laggard. Studies of the welfare state in developing nations, including the relatively well-studied Latin American region, are rare and typically suffer from lack of data (Segura-Ubiergo 2007). It is thus not straightforward to classify Argentina as a laggard or a leader in redistributive efforts according to a comparable group of federal countries. While Argentina certainly redistributes less than Germany and even the United States, it may provide a much greater social safety net than most developing nations.

Available data show a mixed picture, but on the whole Argentina redistributes very little from rich to poor individuals. On the one hand, Argentina was an early adopter (in Latin America) of unemployment insurance and pensions (Segura-Ubiergo 2007). However, these labor protections were very narrow, only benefiting relatively high-income formal workers. The welfare state itself in Argentina is on the whole regressive (Mesa-Lago 1978). In comparative federalist perspective, Argentina redistributes on a similar level to that of Mexico, but less than that of Brazil (Beramendi et al. 2015). Even if we can say that Argentina is hardly redistributive, despite relatively high levels of development, a strong labor movement, and an educated and politically active population, can we attribute these outcomes to federalism?

In the following section, I argue that federalism does indeed contribute to weak redistribution in Argentina. In line with the three mechanisms emphasized in the book, federalism encourages distribution of territorially targeted goods (intergovernmental transfers), it fundamentally fractures the national redistributive coalition though the federally structured party system, and it offers strong veto points for territories in highly malapportioned legislatures.

Pork and Federalism

Territorial politics incentivizes territorial distribution, which is best accomplished through pork or interregional transfers rather than social spending (Dixit and Londregan 1996). In this section, I discuss how pork is related to federalism specifically. For federalism to matter for pork, it needs to be linked to the institutional representation of regions at the national level. Accordingly, I look for the effects of territorial bicameralism for their role in pushing spending toward geographic distributions.

The primary mechanisms whereby federalism should encourage territorial spending are through coalition building between the popular and territorial house, and by senators providing goods to their constituencies for reelection. The first mechanism is clear in all three cases, but to different degrees and using different dynamics. The USA and Germany stand in contrast via the different mechanisms used to build coalitions in the territorial house (national pork versus interregional transfers). Argentina resembles Germany in its use of transfers as bargaining chips for coalition building. In both cases, sub-national politicians control the career paths of national politicians in territorial houses, but through different institutional mechanisms—indirect elections in the German case and party nomination in the Argentine case.

The political institutions that support federal separation of power, most notably territorial bicameralism, by definition highlight geographic representation. For senators, their constituency is their state and the exigencies of reelection suggest that they should focus on representing the interests of that state. From that perspective, the territorial upper house should be a big driver of geographically targeted spending in nations. In the USA, both houses have institutional incentives to deliver targeted goods. In the Argentine and German cases, where the popular houses have lower incentives to target goods geographically, senates should be a primary driver of pork in these systems.[8]

Coalition Building with Senators

Territorial upper chambers encourage territorial distribution through coalition building dynamics. Recall that territorial constituencies induce location-specific preferences. Senators, by this logic, should have preferences that reflect their region-specific interests. With the heterogeneity of interests that these region-specific interests imply, national political parties must find ways to overcome these differences. One straightforward way to do this in territorial bicameral systems is to target resources to regions.

In the USA, Senators are brought into legislative coalitions that provide specific benefits to the states. To understand the context under which this happens, it is important to distinguish the operation of the US House versus the US Senate and also to recall that they share co-equal power on nearly all legislation. The US House is a more partisan body, with votes more effectively whipped by party leadership on the basis of targeted rewards and punishments to members (Cox and McCubbins 2005). Managing the Senate, on the other hand, is like "herding cats" (Lott 2005). One of the reasons for this is senators' lower pressure for reelection. Senators face reelection every six years rather than every two. This provides opportunities to exercise more autonomy from the party in periods away from their reelection, and focus more on their policy goals (Lazarus and Steigerwalt 2009). The Senate operates on the basis of norms and seniority, and party effects, while certainly present, are weaker than those found in the House (Gailmard and Jenkins 2007). To herd the cats of the Senate, therefore, parties in the US have strong incentives to target resources at particular states to buy their support (Lee and Oppenheimer 1999).

In Germany, members of the Bundesrat are Cabinet ministers of the Länder governments that also represent their Land in the national legislature. Unlike direct elections of the senates in the USA and Argentina, therefore, the partisan composition of the sub-national government has a direct effect on the composition of the Bundesrat.[9] This interlinking of electoral fates creates strong incentives for the national party organization to coordinate with Länder party organizations (Lancaster and Patterson 1990). This coordination contributes to organizational and platform coherence of the parties, reducing to some extent the pork and fragmentation effects otherwise expected with federalism. At the same time, the difficult task of convincing the Länder delegations in the Bundesrat to support the party positions in the Bundestag incentivizes geographic distributions (Breunig 2008). The most obvious tool to build this coalition is through the use of transfers. However, pork and social transfers are also viable tools. Länder delegations, which must vote as a block, are brought into coalitions through geographically oriented spending from the national government (ibid.)

Argentina's Senate shows altogether different coalition-building dynamics from those of USA and Germany. As in the other two cases, the Argentine Senate is a crucial veto player for all bills related to redistribution. Strong federalism in the party system has made the province the locus of political careers (Jones et al. 2002). Nearly all politicians, including senators, see their careers as focused in their home provinces and see the strings of their future career pulled by the provincial governor.[10] Senate elections in Argentina are conducted using a three-member electoral district for each province, regardless of population. The party that wins the majority of the vote gains two provincial seats, and the second placed party gains the third. These rules have the effect of overrepresenting the majority party in the province and strongly overrepresenting the less populated provinces. Transfers are used, particularly in the Senate, to cobble together a coherent national policy coalition (Gibson and Calvo 2000). However, this national policy coalition disproportionately weights the interests of less populated states in the interior, many of which oppose redistribution (Porto and Sanguinetti 2001).

Senators Bringing Home the Bacon

Senators may thus be awarded with resources for their regions in exchange for joining a party coalition to support legislation. Senators value these resources because their electoral fates depend, to some extent, on "bringing home the bacon" to their regions. What is important to remember about geographic distributions in federal systems is that it likely takes resources away from redistributive social spending. These three cases vary, again, on the extent to which senators have incentives to pursue pork for their own electoral interests.

Based on their territorial constituencies, US senators have strong incentives to bring home the bacon. Research on the American case suggests that pork incentives are perhaps lower in the Senate than in the House because senators face reelection less frequently (Lazarus and Steigerwalt 2009). At the same time, Senate elections are, on average, more competitive, so pork may be more useful to incumbents endeavoring to protect their jobs. Pork is unequivocally important to US Senators in securing reelection. From a comparative perspective, we need to see whether pork substitutes for redistributive spending in the US case. One way in which it does is by the fact that pork is more useful to Senators than are intergovernmental transfers (Lee 1998). Senators can claim credit for pork more easily than they can for their states' share of federal transfers (Lee 2000). While

Senators spend considerable time constructing the formulae by which states gain federal resources, transfers are a much less important part of the reelection portfolio of US Senators than they are for members of the German or Argentine territorial houses. Whether the US Senate's emphasis on pork results in more or less redistribution than Germany and Argentina's emphasis on transfers depends on the progressive nature of the transfers, discussed in detail below.

German Länder blocs in the Bundesrat have strong incentives to deliver pork and influence interregional transfers in their interests, but these desires are muted by centripetal party incentives (Beramendi 2012). If Bundesrat members pursue reelection, they must consider their constituency. For these members, the constituencies are not only the Länder but specifically the elected representatives of the Länder assemblies. To this end, how can Bundesrat members please Länder politicians? Two possible resources stand out—transfers and pork. Transfers are most valuable for Länder assemblies because they allow for greater discretion in how to use the funds, and members gain credit from constituents for the policy outcomes that result from transfers. While pork is also valued, because it brings valued goods to their region, it lacks the flexibility and the credit-claiming opportunities of transfers for Länder-level politicians. In the Argentine case, there are few obvious incentives for Senators to pursue pork. Because senators are elected in closed-list multimember districts, their "personal vote" is low.[11] However, those party lists are determined by sub-national party leaders, usually governors. Governors that control the party lists and members' future career paths prefer transfers above pork because they have more discretion over the former (Remmer and Wibbels 2000).

The effects on redistribution of senators bringing home the bacon, as in the US case, or bringing home the transfers, as in the German and Argentine cases, will depend on the redistributive content of both. As I argued in detail in Chapters 2 and 3, it is not obvious that pork is inimical to redistribution, except in that it takes away resources from social spending. If a senate's pork brings schools that build human capital, and roads that link towns to markets, it produces an egalitarian result. The result depends, then on the redistributive effects of the particular geographic distribution. Similarly, interregional transfers may or may not reduce income inequality. In the German case, interregional transfers do indeed redistribute income to poor regions and to poor individuals to a very large degree. In the Argentine case, however, transfer allocation primarily reflects population levels, and transfer spending in the provinces has not resulted in reductions in interregional inequality (Gervasoni 2010; Delgado and Russo 2000).

Veto Power of Regions

Institutions of federalism increase veto powers within the political system. This has been well recognized in supporting literature. The argument demonstrated through these cases is that regions are a particular type of veto actor, one more likely to limit redistribution than other types of veto actors. Regions have particular, constitutionally supported mechanisms to reject changes to government policy. These tools are not available to the majority of poor individuals except through partisan majorities. Federalism also limits the policy options of a majority coalition that favors redistribution because it limits the scope of policymaking at the national level, and because it provides regions with constitutional powers to block policy change. Federal democracies, including the ones considered here, vary considerably along these dimensions.

Constitutional Powers of Regions

From the perspective of redistribution, for federal institutions to affect outcomes, they must be involved in the policies that address inequality. In particular, this means that territorial upper chambers, sub-national politicians, and supreme courts are decision-makers in taxing and spending policy. This is true in all of the cases considered here, but again the variance is dramatic. Particularly important in the German case is the separate fiscal structure of social policy (Mares 2003). Politicians linked to Länder thus have very little control over these policies. In the USA, the Senate has co-equal power with the House to initiate and pass budget legislation. Thus we should expect strong regional dynamics reflecting the state veto power in the US case. In Argentina, the president is the agenda-setter on the budget and parties strongly control the process through the legislature. The veto role of provinces occurs within the party structure as provincial members side with their governors over the president, as well as in intergovernmental bargaining between presidents and governors.

What is important about the federalist institutions in most national contexts is that they provide veto powers. These are useful primarily for protecting the status quo, and not for changing it (Lee and Rogers 2015). With regard to redistribution, therefore, regions have particular powers to protect the status quo. This gives rich regions the upper hand because they often have tools to block expansionary efforts that do not benefit them directly. In other words, rich regions tend to be privileged under the status quo. Of course, this depends critically on whether the status quo is redistributive and progressive, as the German case demonstrates. Federalism thus may affect redistribution by giving regional actors the ability to block egalitarian reforms.

The role of the US Senate and Supreme Court in protecting the powers of states, and in limiting redistributive policies in that country have been well documented (Katznelson et al. 1993). Beramendi (2012) describes how senators from Southern states, seeking to protect their regional political economy, effectively blocked centralized redistribution in the New Deal policies. Similarly, Southern senators tried to use their minority veto power through the filibuster to block redistributive reforms in the 1960s “Great Society” legislation. The Supreme Court has frequently rejected efforts by the federal government to centralize the provision of redistribution (Finegold 2005). In the USA, federal institutions have created structural conditions that limit redistribution and have provided specific veto points for regional actors to block redistributive reform.

Again, this depends in part on the nature of the status quo for the US case as well. In the historical examples, the status quo policy was, essentially, no redistribution. Thus, exercising the Senate veto or having the Supreme Court override redistributive legislation preserved the low redistribution equilibrium. In other cases, however, the Senate has used its veto to protect existing redistributive legislation. Frequent attempts by the Republican House to strike down the Affordable Care Act from 2010 to 2014 have been struck down (by failure to bring up the bill) in the Democratic Senate. In the current period, in which Republicans hold both the House and the Senate, it is still not expected that the Affordable Care Act will be eliminated. This is because of both the Democratic senators' threat of filibuster and the likelihood of veto by the Democratic president. Nonetheless, the Supreme Court could, on the basis of federal principles, strike down the law in the future.

The Bundesrat has strong veto powers in most areas of legislation, most prominently in decisions on taxation and spending. On this dimension, German federalism should thus limit redistribution due to the powers of the Bundesrat to veto policy. This case has been made for German health care—rich regions in the Bundesrat have blocked efforts to increase spending by the national government (Webber 1988). Similarly, the national government has strong control over the tax and expenditure powers of the states. Strong interrelations between the national government and the Länder thus place these actors in a "joint decision trap," in which they are forced to cooperate (Scharpf 1988). This interconnectedness provides incentives for the actors to work together for mutual advantage.

What is important to recall about the specific funding structure of social spending in the German case is that it is quasi-autonomous. This means that the effective veto available to the Bundesrat on many policy areas is not present for most welfare policies. Thus the welfare state in particular has not been subject to Bundesrat veto. The status quo whereby most redistributive social spending is outside the policy domain of the Bundesrat shows the important restrictions on the ability of the affluent to affect reform. The status quo is more favorable in many regards to the poor than to the rich regions. Even if a fundamental change in the redistributive system were on the table, rich regions only have veto powers to block change from the status quo, not the powers to fundamentally alter it.

This dynamic came into focus through the reform efforts of the period 1990–1994 following reunification. Because reunification so dramatically altered the economic geography of Germany by adding five regions that were all poorer than every Western Land, the rich regions in the South in particular called for a restructuring of the transfer system to limit the mass outflow of their resources to the East. However, they were largely unsuccessful in changing this arrangement because they did not have the votes for proactive change. This is not to say they did not try. Theo Weigel, the finance minister from (rich) Bavaria's (regional) CSU party, introduced legislation that included a reduction of intergovernmental transfers over time (Lehmbruch 1996). However, this proposal was rejected by relatively poor Länder in the North that would lose out financially from the proposal and even from affluent Länder (including the CSU delegation) who thought it increased the power of the national government vis-à-vis the Länder (Sally and Webber 1994). Instead, as veto powers theory would suggest, the fiscal structure stayed very close to the status quo (Beramendi 2012). From this perspective, the tools of regions are limited to protecting existing arrangements.

Argentina's federal institutions create veto points at several crucial parts of the budget process, and also take important redistributive policy areas outside of the hands of the central government. Like the popular Chamber of Deputies, the Senate has the power to reject budgets from the president that include redistributive spending. Significant policy areas, such as taxation and some aspects of interregional transfers, are directly negotiated by the president and governors. For example, the governors negotiated a "floor" to interregional transfers in 1992 with the president to eliminate fluctuations in their resources.[12] The president uses such direct intergovernmental negotiations with governors when the legislative route appears to be blocked (Spiller and Tommasi 2003).

The Argentine case of regional vetoes brings up several important institutional concerns that relate to all three cases. First, what happens to these institutions when interregional inequality is high? In a similar vein, how is the structure of representation associated with regional representation, and how is it related to redistributive outcomes?

The veto powers of regions are particularly important in conditions of high inequality, as the cases of Argentina and Germany in particular demonstrate. The German case shows a dramatic, exogenous shift in regional inequality with reunification that prompted policymakers to question existing institutional arrangements. The Argentine case shows an institutional system endogenously structured in reaction to high levels of interregional and interpersonal inequality (Ardanaz and Scartascini 2013; Eaton 2001). Overrepresentation of conservative regions in the legislature serves to protect, via the veto, existing low levels of interpersonal inequality and high levels of interregional transfers (Beramendi et al. 2015).

With increasing regional inequality, politics within the German Bundesrat have become more contentious, especially on matters of interregional sharing of taxes. This has resulted in greater polarization within the Bundesrat and between the Bundestag and Bundesrat on matters of regional differences (Jeffrey 1999).[13] This has also led the Bundesrat to take a more active role in policymaking following reunification, especially on budget matters (Gunlicks 2002). Reunification accelerated existing trends of regional inequality between the northern and southern parts of West Germany. The growing importance of the Bundesrat may not have direct effects on most social welfare policies, but it affects redistribution through its role in tax and spending categories within its domain.

Federalism is linked to malapportionment, in theory, due to the representation of territories in national politics. The representation of territories can result in violations of the "one person, one vote" principles of democracy. For example, in the USA, equal representation of all states (two senators per state) dramatically overrepresents sparsely populated states such as Wyoming and Montana, and dramatically underrepresents populated states such as California or New York. In Argentina, the malapportionment in the Senate is even greater than it is in the USA and the lower house is also substantially malapportioned (Samuels and Snyder 2001). Germany's Bundesrat is more evenly apportioned because

Länder seats are calculated based on population, but it is malapportioned nonetheless (Homburg 1997). The role of malapportionment in the three countries is discussed in detail in the next chapter on electoral rules and representation.

Fragmenting the Coalition

Federalism complicates the efforts of the majority of individuals that would benefit from the redistribution that would come from organizing for coherent policy reforms at the national level. Federalism is important in this regard for several interrelated reasons. Federalism is "demos constraining" because it limits the scope of the national government to make policy in some areas, including ones that affect incomes and inequality. From an organizational perspective, the majority coalition must spread resources across regions and tailor reform efforts to different political and institutional environments. Regional inequality within federations creates tension among rich and poor regions regarding the level and nature of the central government. This can divide the interests and preferences of the poor in rich and poor regions alike. Regional inequality in some cases also overlaps with ethnic, religious, and linguistic tensions that are regionally concentrated. In some cases, such as Canada, Belgium, or Switzerland, federalism was designed to address concerns with centralization from different demographic groups (Lijphart 2012).

US federalism is a quagmire for the majority redistributive coalition (Pierson 1995). For theorists concerned about populism, this is a very positive feature of US democracy. Territorial representation, by this estimation, is positive because the separate constituencies keep the interests of the rulers separate, and limit the possibility of major shifts in policy. Riker (1964) argues that federalism matters mostly because it fragments parties, and thus potential majority coalitions. He says: "this is the famous American federalism, copied over half the world. The constitutional restraint is not, however, the legal division of duties between central and local governments but rather the resultant localization of political parties that renders national leadership of them impossible" (1982, p. 250).

To consider how the majority might advance redistribution *at the national level*, and how this is affected by federalism, we again need to look at the US Senate. As discussed earlier, parties in the US Senate have weaker tools to impose discipline than they do in the popular house. If the majority coalition (represented by a leftist party) favors redistribution, this may not translate into significant reform in the face of somewhat autonomous, and territorially oriented, senators. Given that their constituencies are states, and states have distinct preferences for redistribution based on their own regional economies, senators have a wide range of policy preferences. Thus the Senate serves as a specific roadblock, based on regional interests, for a redistributively oriented leftist party.

In the US case, national redistribution is nearly always framed in terms of the states.[14] This is so because of the Senate's veto power, the interests of the House in gaining Senate support, and the existing state organization of redistributive schemes. Significant social policies are also enacted at the state level, or in a mixed federal–state system that integrates rules and shares funding. This not only creates veto points at several steps in the policy process, but also complicates the efforts of pro-redistributive actors to organize for their promulgation.

Differences in the nature of federalism between the US case and that of Argentina or Germany can be seen in how interpersonal and interregional resources are funded. While Argentina redistributes little from the national level to individuals, it redistributes considerable resources interregionally through flexible intergovernmental transfers.[15] Germany redistributes large amounts through both interpersonal and interregional transfers. In both countries the intention of interregional transfers is to equilibrate resources across regions. The USA redistributes relatively little interpersonally and interregional redistribution occurs almost exclusively through conditional grants to states. This means that states have little discretion on how this money is spent. At the same time, this system is also the result of the Supreme Court strongly limiting the federal government from attempts to redistribute resources directly to individuals (Finegold 2005). In the USA, the focus of intergovernmental grants is instead on providing specific services. This allows for more direct targeting of constituencies in the US system, especially that based on geographic criteria. Senators expend particular effort to affect the formula for block grants that go to states (Lee 2004). Thus the US redistributive system reflects both federal design and also the tension between the center and the states on redistributive policies.

In contrast, the design and operation of German federalism, at least with regard to redistributive policy, does not have the fragmenting effect on the redistributive coalition that it does in the USA and many other federal systems. The reasons for this are related to the financing of the welfare state, and to the party system.

In a decentralized tax and spending system, federalism complicates the organizational power and policy preferences of the majority coalition that is in favor of redistribution. This does not occur to the same degree in Germany because its tax and spending system is not decentralized, at least with regard to social welfare. The welfare system operates as a separate, national entity with uniform standards that makes coordination of the coalition for and against redistribution organizationally simplified. The welfare system also operates according to automatic, individual standards for benefits. This means that, unlike in the USA, politicians are not bargaining over the relative distribution of resources to their states. This limits incentives to organize along regional lines, and limits the zero-sum character of the social spending distribution. Moreover, given strong provisions to block interstate competition in welfare provision, constituents across state lines have fewer reasons to evaluate their interests in social policy on the basis of Länder identity.

The system of intergovernmental transfers in Germany, while obfuscating fiscal accountability, does share the same role in political bargaining that it does in the USA. In the USA, earmarked intergovernmental transfers act as pork targeted to particular states in the Senate and encourage members of the House of Representatives to organize as state delegations for the same purpose (Lee 2000).

In Germany, transfer levels are also used to entice regional representatives into the bargain. In the example provided above in which CSU's Theo Weigel proposed to reduce interregional transfer over the long run, he also included large short-run transfer increases to Eastern Länder. The goal was to build a coalition between rich Western Länder and poor Eastern Länder (both generally under CDU–CSU control at the time) to lay the costs of transition more on the (SDP-controlled) Northern Länder (Lehmbruch 1996).

While the effects of federalism on redistribution in the German case are clearly muted, the looming question is why should this be? Why have the rich Länder not sought a change in German federalism to limit the outflow of their resources? The answers are at least two. First, affluent Länder have sought changes to the fiscal structure to limit overspending, to reduce the shared percentage of taxes, and to encourage interstate competition (Münch 1998; Pitschas 1994). Second, the addition of the Eastern Länder has changed the party dynamics and bargaining position within both the Bundestag and Bundesrat. Both major parties, including the conservative CDU–CSU, have sought to incorporate the voters in the East. Interregional transfers have served as a powerful tool in the post-reunification period to cobble together these mixed (regional) income coalitions.

At the same time, the nature of political competition is shaped by the party system that strongly encourages cooperation across regions in Germany. Strong party discipline mutes regional interests in the name of platform coherence. Also important is that the major parties in Germany are both programmatically in favor of social welfare (Manow 2005; Kitschelt 2001). This party cohesion works across the Bundestag and Bundesrat as co-partisans with tied electoral fates work together to agree on a common set of policies. These dynamics are discussed in greater detail in Chapter 5.

The Argentine case strongly reflects the tensions between national and regional coalitions. Gibson (1996) argues that differences in regional economic preferences have thwarted attempts by conservative elites to form a rightist party. In response to these tensions, coalitions in Argentina are heavily fragmented along regional (center, interior) and, most importantly, provincial lines. At the same time, parties on the left have bridged these regional differences through interregional transfers and clientelistic exchange.

Governors and all of the politicians in Argentina under the command of the governors care primarily about provincial revenue for their political survival and that revenue comes largely from the national government. Provincial revenue is the source of political power in the provinces (Remmer and Gélineau 2003). Provincial revenue is used to shore up votes through the provision of public services of value to constituents (Gordín 2006). It is also the source of political patronage and clientelism that keep governors in office, especially in the least populated and least developed provinces (Gibson and Calvo 2000). Incumbency advantage, gained through the strategic distribution of provincial revenues, is particularly strong in the least populated provinces (Stokes 2005; Behrend 2011).

Importantly, because most spending in Argentina occurs at the provincial level, funded through central transfers, politics at the national level becomes a zero-sum game among provinces. Constituencies seeking resources should rationally pursue them through the governor, both because the governor controls central transfers and because the governor controls national politicians in the legislature. This fragments the majority coalition in favor of reform along provincial lines.

The picture of Argentina thus presented is one in which all elected politicians but the president care about the province more than the national government. However, all ultimately depend on the national government for central transfers, economic development and growth, or both. The provinces vary considerably in their population, wealth, political and economic development, and economic dynamism. Those provinces with the lowest populations and lowest levels of development have a large voting bloc on national policy and the greatest influence within national parties but these are precisely the provinces that are inimical to interpersonal redistribution (Ardanaz and Scartascini 2013).

Conclusion

This chapter has explored the role of federalism in redistributive outcomes, with particular attention to how it plays out in the USA, Germany, and Argentina. The three mechanisms that link institutions to lower redistribution via territorial politics are: pork, regional vetoes, and fragmented majority coalitions. These are all shown to be theoretically and practically linked to federalism. Importantly, the three federal countries analyzed show very different effects on redistribution that reflect their own political dynamics, their particular regional inequalities, and institutional settings.

It is important to emphasize how this account of federalism's link to redistribution is different from previous studies. Existing research on US politics recognizes that federalism may have particular effects on the design (state-oriented) and nature (pork-heavy) of national spending. This research has also shown that the Senate is a special blocking point for redistributive legislation. I extend these arguments to a comparative context to show how territorial bicameralism in particular could impact redistribution through pork and transfers, regional vetoes, and malapportionment. Moreover, I emphasize the fragmentation of redistributive coalitions within the party system due to the nature of federalism in Argentina and the USA. The German case shows a strong contrast due to its centrifugal party system that is able to overcome to some degree these fragmenting tendencies.

In the next chapter, I explore the role of electoral rules—both the nature of constituencies and ballot structure—and how they affect redistributive outcomes. Many of the themes in the US, German, and Argentine cases introduced in this chapter carry over to the dynamics seen in their party systems due to electoral rules.

Notes

1 The statistical association between federalism and lower redistribution has been demonstrated (see Cameron 1978; Lee and Rogers 2015).
2 The referendum is central to Switzerland's federal system.
3 The federal government's history of intervention into the provinces to replace governors and wrest policy control makes its federal status somewhat questionable according to Riker's definition (Gibson and Falleti 2004).
4 An example of this is legislation making federal highway grants contingent on states adopting an over-age 21 drinking limit.
5 The European Union was certainly formed in part in response to military threat as well.
6 For a detailed examination of regional redistribution by interregional transfers and regional incidence of national redistributive programs, see Rogers and Lee (2015).
7 Much of the redistribution across regions occurs through the regional incidence of the national social security system (Manow 2005).
8 Germany's SMDs and their pork incentives are discussed in the next chapters.
9 Senates in the USA and Argentina were also elected by sub-national governments in the past. On this reform in the USA, see Schiller (2006) and Argentina, see Micozzi (2013).
10 In some cases national members' principals are opposition parties within the province and not the governor. Even in this case the members' incentives are to please provincial party leaders. This may take a different form if the party leader is the governor. However, this is relatively uncommon, with about 20 percent of legislators coming from parties different than the provincial governor (Jones and Hwang 2005).
11 Senators' personal vote is higher than it is for members of the Chamber of Deputies. The personal vote in closed-list PR declines as district magnitude increases (Carey and Shugart 1995).
12 This floor was eliminated in 2001 with the series of reforms to recover from the economic collapse of 1999–2001. The governors agreed to eliminate the floor because the booming economy in the post-2001 period promised higher transfers for the years to come (Saiegh 2004).
13 For instance, the governments of Bavaria and Baden-Württemberg brought a case before the constitutional court in 1998 to argue that they were being unfairly burdened. This is not surprising given they are highly populated and affluent and thus in a weak bargaining position for transfers (Gunlicks 2002).
14 Social security pensions and disability subsidies are the notable exceptions.
15 Argentina's pension system, for example, has historically been run by the provinces. Neoliberal reform in 1994 privatized most pensions, taking these resources away from the provinces. In 2008 the government nationalized pensions and has used these resources for debt financing (*The Economist* "Now or Never" February 16, 2013). See Bonvecchi and Lodola (2011) on variation in federal and provincial control across different transfers in Argentina.

References

Ardanaz, Martin, and Carlos Scartascini. "Inequality and Personal Income Taxation the Origins and Effects of Legislative Malapportionment." *Comparative Political Studies* 46, no. 12 (2013): 1636–63.

Aysan, Ahmet Faruk. "Inequality, Institutions and Redistribution." Ph.D. Economics, University of Maryland College Park (2005).

Banting, Keith. *Welfare State and Canadian Federalism*. McGill-Queen's University Press, Montreal, 1987.

Banting, Keith. "Canada: Nation-Building in a Federal Welfare State." In *Federalism and the Welfare State*, edited by Herbert Obinger, Stephan Leibfried and Francis G Castles. Oxford University Press, 2005.

Behrend, Jacqueline. "The Unevenness of Democracy at the Subnational Level: Provincial Closed Games in Argentina." *Latin American Research Review* 46, no. 1 (2011): 150–76.

Beramendi, Pablo. "Inequality and the Territorial Fragmentation of Solidarity." *International Organization* 61, no. 4 (2007): 783.

Beramendi, Pablo. *The Political Geography of Inequality: Regions and Redistribution*. Cambridge University Press, 2012.

Beramendi, Pablo, Melissa Rogers, and Alberto Diaz-Cayeros. *Barriers to the Left Turn: Distributive Tensions in Developing Federations*. Manuscript, Duke University, Claremont Graduate University, and Stanford University, 2015.

Bolton, Patrick, and Gerard Roland. "The Breakup of Nations: A Political Economy Analysis." *The Quarterly Journal of Economics* 112, no. 4 (1997): 1057–90.

Bonvecchi, Alejandro, and Germán Lodola. "The Dual Logic of Intergovernmental Transfers: Presidents, Governors, and the Politics of Coalition-Building in Argentina." *Publius: The Journal of Federalism* 41, no. 2 (2011): 179–206.

Brancati, Dawn. "The Origins and Strengths of Regional Parties." *British Journal of Political Science* 38, no. 1 (2008): 135–59.

Brennan, Geoffrey, and James M. Buchanan. *The Power to Tax: Analytic Foundations of a Fiscal Constitution*. Cambridge University Press, 1980.

Breunig, Christian. "Legislative Politics in Germany: Some Lessons and Challenges." *German Politics* 17, no. 3 (2008): 381–92.

Cameron, David R. "The Expansion of the Public Economy: A Comparative Analysis." *American Political Science Review* 72, no. 4 (1978): 1243–61.

Carey, John M., and Matthew Soberg Shugart. "Incentives to Cultivate a Personal Vote: A Rank Ordering of Electoral Formulas." *Electoral Studies* 14, no. 4 (1995): 417–39.

Castles, Francis Geoffrey. *Comparative Public Policy: Patterns of Post-War Transformation*. Edward Elgar Publishing, Cheltenham UK, 1998.

Castles, Francis G., and John Uhr. "The Australian Welfare State: Has Federalism Made a Difference?" *Australian Journal of Politics and History* 53, no. 1 (2007): 96–117.

Chhibber, Pradeep, and Ken Kollman. *The Formation of National Party Systems: Federalism and Party Competition in Canada, Great Britain, India, and the United States*. Princeton University Press, Princeton NJ, 2004.

Cox, Gary W., and Mathew D. McCubbins. *Setting the Agenda: Responsible Party Government in the US House of Representatives*. Cambridge University Press, 2005.

Cox, Kevin R. *The Territorialization of Politics and What Happened in Western Europe*. Paper presented at the International Political Geography Colloquium, Reims, France, 2008.

Delgado, Felisa Ceña, and José Luis Russo. "Evolución De La Convergencia Y Disparidades Provinciales En Argentina." *Revista de Estudios Regionales*, no. 57 (2000): 151–75.

Dixit, Avinash, and John Londregan. "The Determinants of Success of Special Interests in Redistributive Politics." *Journal of Politics* 58 (1996): 1132–55.

Douglas, Paul H. *Social Security in the United States: An Analysis and Appraisal of the Federal Social Security Act*. Beard Books, Washington DC, 2000.

Eaton, Kent. "Decentralisation, Democratisation and Liberalisation: The History of Revenue Sharing in Argentina, 1934–1999." *Journal of Latin American Studies* 33, no. 1 (2001): 1–28.

Finegold, Kenneth. "The United States Federalism and Its Counter-Factuals." in *Federalism and the Welfare State. New World and European Experiences. Cambridge.* edited by Herbert Obinger, Stephan Leibfried and Francis G. Castles, Cambridge University Press (2005): 138–79.

Gailmard, Sean, and Jeffery A. Jenkins. "Negative Agenda Control in the Senate and House: Fingerprints of Majority Party Power." *Journal of Politics* 69, no. 3 (2007): 689–700.

Gervasoni, Carlos. "A Rentier Theory of Subnational Regimes." *World Politics* 62, no. 2 (2010): 302–40.

Gibson, Edward L. *Class and Conservative Parties: Argentina in Comparative Perspective*. Johns Hopkins University Press, Baltimore MD, 1996.

Gibson, Edward L., and Ernesto Calvo. "Federalism and Low-Maintenance Constituencies: Territorial Dimensions of Economic Reform in Argentina." *Studies in Comparative International Development* 35, no. 3 (2000): 32–55.

Gibson, Edward L., and Tulia G. Falleti. "Unity by the Stick." *Federalism and Democracy in Latin America* Johns Hopkins University Press, Baltimore MD, (2004): 226–54.

Gordin, Jorge. "The Politics of Intergovernmental Fiscal Relations in Argentina." IBEI Working Paper No. 2006/2. Available at SSRN: http://ssrn.com/abstract=960752 (2006).

Grossman, Philip J. "Fiscal Decentralization and Government Size: An Extension." *Public Choice* 62, no. 1 (1989): 63–9.

Gunlicks, Arthur B. "The Impact of Unification on German Federalism." *German Politics* 11, no. 3 (2002): 131–52.

Homburg, Stefan. "Ursachen Und Wirkungen Eines Zwischenstaatlichen Finanzausgleichs." In *Fiskalföderalismus in Europa*, edited by Alois Oberhauer. Duncker & Humblot, Berlin, (1997): 61–95.

Huber, Evelyne, Charles Ragin, and John D. Stephens. "Social Democracy, Christian Democracy, Constitutional Structure, and the Welfare State." *American Journal of Sociology* 99, no. 3 (1993): 711–49.

Jeffery, Charlie. "Party Politics and Territorial Representation in the Federal Republic of Germany." *West European Politics* 22, no. 2 (1999): 130–66.

Jones, Mark P., and Wonjae Hwang. "Party Government in Presidential Democracies: Extending Cartel Theory Beyond the US Congress." *American Journal of Political Science* 49, no. 2 (2005): 267–82.

Jones, Mark P., Pablo Sanguinetti, and Mariano Tommasi. "Politics, Institutions, and Fiscal Performance in a Federal System: An Analysis of the Argentine Provinces." *Journal of Development Economics* 61, no. 2 (2000): 305–33.

Jones, Mark P., Sebastián Saiegh, Pablo T. Spiller, and Mariano Tommasi. "Amateur Legislators–Professional Politicians: The Consequences of Party-Centered Electoral Rules in a Federal System." *American Journal of Political Science* 46, no. 3 (2002): 656–69.

Katznelson, Ira, Kim Geiger, and Daniel Kryder. "Limiting Liberalism: The Southern Veto in Congress, 1933–1950." *Political Science Quarterly* 108, no. 2 (1993): 283–306.

Kitschelt, Herbert. "Partisan Competition and Welfare State Retrenchment: When Do Politicians Choose Unpopular Policies." in *The New Politics of the Welfare State*, edited by Paul Pierson. Oxford University Press (2001): 265–302.

Lancaster, Thomas D., and W. David Patterson. "Comparative Pork Barrel Politics Perceptions from the West German Bundestag." *Comparative Political Studies* 22, no. 4 (1990): 458–77.

Lazarus, Jeffrey, and Amy Steigerwalt. "Different Houses: The Distribution of Earmarks in the US House and Senate." *Legislative Studies Quarterly* 34, no. 3 (2009): 347–73.

Lee, Dong-wook, and Melissa Rogers. *Comparing Inequalities: Regional and Interpersonal Income Disparity, Institutions, and Government Spending*. Manuscript, Claremont Graduate University CA, 2015.

Lee, Frances E. "Senate Representation and Coalition Building in Distributive Politics." *American Political Science Review* 94, no. 1 (2000): 59–72.

Lee, Frances E., and Bruce I. Oppenheimer. *Sizing up the Senate: The Unequal Consequences of Equal Representation*. University of Chicago Press, 1999.

Lehmbruch, Gerhard. *Parteienwettbewerb Im Bundesstaat*. Kohlhammer, Stuttgart, 1976.

Lehmbruch, Gerhard. "German Federalism and the Challenge of Unification." in *Federalizing Europe?*, edited by V. Wright and J. J. Hesse. Oxford University Press (1996): 169–203.

Lijphart, Arend. *Patterns of Democracy: Government Forms and Performance in Thirty-Six Countries*. Yale University Press, New Haven CT, 2012.

Linz, Juan José. "Democracy, Multinationalism, and Federalism." *Estudios/Working Papers (Centro de Estudios Avanzados en Ciencias Sociales)*, no. 103 (1997).

Lott, Trent. *Herding Cats: A Life in Politics*. ReganBooks, New York, 2005.

Manow, Philip. "Germany: Cooperative Federalism and the Overgrazing of the Fiscal Commons." in *Federalism and the Welfare State*, edited by Herbert Obinger, Stephan Liebfried and Frances Castles. Cambridge University Press (2005): 222–62.

Mares, Isabela. *The Politics of Social Risk: Business and Welfare State Development*. Cambridge University Press, 2003.

Mesa-Lago, Carmelo. *Social Security in Latin America: Pressure Groups, Stratification, and Inequality*. University of Pittsburgh Press, 1978.

Micozzi, Juan Pablo. "Does Electoral Accountability Make a Difference? Direct Elections, Career Ambition, and Legislative Performance in the Argentine Senate." *The Journal of Politics* 75, no. 1 (2013): 137–49.

Milesi-Ferretti, Gian Maria, Roberto Perotti, and Massimo Rostagno. "Electoral Systems and Public Spending." *The Quarterly Journal of Economics* 117, no. 2 (2002): 609–57.

Münch, Ursula. "Entflechtungsmöglichkeiten Im Bereich Der Sozialpolitik. Zur Diskussion Um Eine Föderalisierung Der Sozialversicherung." *Ursula Männle (Hg.), Föderalismus zwischen Konsens und Konkurrenz. Baden-Baden: Nomos* (1998): 73–91.

Oates, Wallace E. "An Essay on Fiscal Federalism." *Journal of Economic Literature* 37, no. 3 (1999): 1120–49.

Obinger, Herbert, Stephan Leibfried, and Francis G. Castles. *Federalism and the Welfare State: New World and European Experiences*. Cambridge University Press, 2005.

Persson, Torsten, and Guido Tabellini. "Does Centralization Increase the Size of Government?" *European Economic Review* 38, no. 3 (1994): 765–73.

Persson, Torsten, and Guido Tabellini. "The Size and Scope of Government:: Comparative Politics with Rational Politicians." *European Economic Review* 43, no. 4 (1999): 699–735.

Pierson, Paul. "Fragmented Welfare States: Federal Institutions and the Development of Social Policy." *Governance* 8, no. 4 (1995): 449–78.

Pierson, Paul. *The New Politics of the Welfare State*. Oxford University Press (2001).

Pitschas, Rainer. "Regionalisierung Der Rentenversicherung Aus Verwaltungswissenschaftlicher Sicht." *Neue Zeitschrift für Sozialrecht* 3 (1994): 289–96.

Porto, Alberto, and Pablo Sanguinetti. "Political Determinants of Intergovernmental Grants: Evidence from Argentina." *Economics and Politics* 13, no. 3 (2001): 237–56.

Prud'Homme, Remy. "The Dangers of Decentralization." *The World Bank Research Observer* 10, no. 2 (1995): 201–20.

Remmer, Karen L., and François Gélineau. "Subnational Electoral Choice Economic and Referendum Voting in Argentina, 1983–1999." *Comparative Political Studies* 36, no. 7 (2003): 801–21.

Remmer, Karen L., and Erik Wibbels. "The Subnational Politics of Economic Adjustment Provincial Politics and Fiscal Performance in Argentina." *Comparative Political Studies* 33, no. 4 (2000): 419–51.

Riker, William H. *Federalism: Origin, Operation, Significance*. Little, Brown and Co, Boston, 1964.

Rodden, Jonathan. "The Dilemma of Fiscal Federalism: Grants and Fiscal Performance around the World." *American Journal of Political Science* 46, no. 3 (2002): 670–87.

Rodden, Jonathan. "Reviving Leviathan: Fiscal Federalism and the Growth of Government." *International Organization* 57, no. 4 (2003): 695–729.

Rodden, Jonathan, and Erik Wibbels. "Beyond the Fiction of Federalism." *World Politics* 54, no. 4 (2002): 494–531.

Rodden, Jonathan, and Erik Wibbels. "Dual Accountability and the Nationalization of Party Competition: Evidence from Four Federations." *Party Politics* 17, no. 5 (2011): 629–53.

Rogers, Melissa, and Dong-wook Lee. *Electoral Geography, Inequality, and Representation*. Manuscript, Claremont Graduate University CA, 2015.

Rosen, Harvey S. *Public Finance*. Springer, New York, 2004.

Saiegh, Sebastián. "The 'Sub-National'connection: Legislative Coalitions, Cross-Voting and Policymaking in Argentina." *The Argentine Crisis at the Turn of the Millennium: Causes, Consequences, and Explanations*, edited by Flavia Fiorucci and Marcus Klein. Aksant Academic Publishers, Amsterdam (2004).

Saiegh, Sebastián, and Mariano Tommasi. "Why Is Argentina's Fiscal Federalism So Inefficient? Entering the Labyrinth." *Journal of Applied Economics* 2, no. 1 (1999): 169–209.

Sally, Razeen, and Douglas Webber. "The German Solidarity Pact: A Case Study in the Politics of the Unified Germany." *German Politics* 3, no. 1 (1994): 18–46.

Samuels, David, and Richard Snyder. "The Value of a Vote: Malapportionment in Comparative Perspective." *British Journal of Political Science* 31, no. 4 (2001): 651–71.

Scharpf, Fritz W. "The Joint-Decision Trap: Lessons from German Federalism and European Integration." *Public Administration* 66, no. 3 (1988): 239–78.

Schiller, Wendy J. "Building Careers and Courting Constituents: US Senate Representation 1889–1924." *Studies in American Political Development* 20, no. 2 (2006): 185–97.

Segura-Ubiergo, Alex. *The Political Economy of the Welfare State in Latin America: Globalization, Democracy, and Development*. Cambridge University Press, 2007.

Skocpol, Theda, and Edwin Amenta. "States and Social Policies." *Annual Review of Sociology* (1986): 131–57.

Solt, Frederick. *The Standardized World Income Inequality Database*. Working paper. SWIID Version 5.0, October 2014.

Spiller, Pablo T., and Mariano Tommasi. "The Institutional Foundations of Public Policy: A Transactions Approach with Application to Argentina." *Journal of Law, Economics, and Organization* 19, no. 2 (2003): 281–306.

Stepan, Alfred. "Toward a New Comparative Politics of Federalism, Multinationalism, and Democracy: Beyond Rikerian Federalism." In *Federalism and Democracy in Latin America*, edited by Edward Gibson. Johns Hopkins University Press, Baltimore MD, (2004): 29–84.

Stokes, Susan C. "Perverse Accountability: A Formal Model of Machine Politics with Evidence from Argentina." *American Political Science Review* 99, no. 3 (2005): 315–25.

Swank, Duane. "Political Institutions and Welfare State Restructuring: The Impact of Institutions on Social Policy Change in Developed Democracies." in *The New Politics of the Welfare State*, edited by Paul Pierson. Oxford University Press (2001): 197–237.

Tiebout, Charles M. "A Pure Theory of Local Expenditures." *The Journal of Political Economy* 64, no. 5 (1956): 416–24.

Tommasi, Mariano, Sebastián Saiegh, Pablo Sanguinetti, Ernesto Stein, and Mauricio Cárdenas. "Fiscal Federalism in Argentina: Policies, Politics, and Institutional Reform [with Comments]." *Economia* 1, no. 2 (2001): 157–211.

Treisman, Daniel. "Fiscal Decentralization, Governance, and Economic Performance: A Reconsideration." *Economics and Politics* 18, no. 2 (2006): 219–35.

Webber, Douglas. "Krankheit, Geld Und Politik: Zur Geschichte Der Gesundheitsreformen in Deutschland." *Leviathan* 16, no. 2 (1988): 156–203.

Weingast, Barry R. "The Economic Role of Political Institutions: Market-Preserving Federalism and Economic Development." *Journal of Law Economics and Organization* 11, no 1. (1995): 1–31.

5 Territorial Elections and Redistribution

> Vote your conscience. Vote your district. Just don't surprise me.
>
> (US House Majority Whip Frank Underwood in *House of Cards*)

Introduction

Constituencies are central to democratic representation. Responsive politicians target their ideological appeals and public policies to their voting public (Downs 1957). Importantly, political institutions determine the universe of politicians' constituencies, influencing how voters view their interests, organize, and hold politicians accountable for high quality representation (Carey 2007).

Geographic electoral constituencies are the norm in democratic polities (Rehfeld 2005). However, nations differ substantially in whether their electoral constituencies are strongly territorial due not only to whether districts are drawn based on geography but also due to incentives for nationalizing politics encouraged by institutions such as PR, the size of districts, parliamentarism, and unitarism (Caramani 2004; Gerring et al. 2005).

From the perspective of the politics of economic inequality, territorial electoral constituencies strongly engage the mechanisms of focus in this analysis. By making targeted local goods visible to constituents interested in local outcomes, territorial constituencies lead decision-makers to oversupply local goods and undersupply national goods, including centralized redistributive outlays (Milesi-Ferretti et al. 2002; Lee and Rogers 2015). By segmenting the playing field, territorial constituencies and district-centered voting rules, through their effect on the organization of political parties, divide the national coalition in favor of redistributive policies and highlight distinct preferences related to regional interests. Accordingly, territorial representation also increases heterogeneity within parties and party systems, as coalitions must manage policy concerns due to the interpersonal and interregional dynamics of inequality.

Electoral rules have the potential to influence redistributive outcomes through two different pathways: the nature of constituency (territorial or not) and the incentives voting rules provide to politicians and voters. Electoral rules, such as whether voters cast votes for parties or individuals, have strong effects on party cohesion and constituency orientation. Ultimately, these factors may influence the nature (targeted to national groups or geographic districts) and generosity of government allocation.

In this chapter, I first define electoral constituencies and voting rules. These are separate, but interacting, features of election structure that influence party behavior and politicians' reelection incentives. Next, I discuss the theoretical links between constituency structure and redistribution, and between voting rules and redistribution. I address preference heterogeneity within parties that comes from different regional economic endowments. Finally, I apply these theoretical insights to the contrasting cases of Argentina, Germany and the USA.

Defining Electoral Rules

Before exploring the theoretical mechanics underlying the ways in which electoral rules may influence the politics of inequality and redistribution, it is useful to define them for these purposes. Electoral rules capture a wide range of institutions that determine the rules by which voters cast ballots in elections. Following Rehfeld (2005), these institutions may be usefully divided into two categories: constituencies and voting rules.

Constituencies

Constituencies are the basis for grouping voters for electoral purposes. These may be formal groupings established by law or voluntary mergers of like-minded individuals. Formal constituencies are established by governments to sub-divide large populations. Of course, the government need not establish constituencies beyond the national one. Most nations, however, divide their populations into smaller fragments. In theory, these fragments could reflect many different principles of group identity, including geography, ethnicity, language, race, occupational grouping, among others. In practice, nearly all nations sub-divide their electoral constituencies according to geographic boundaries.

In my sample of 50 democracies, all except the Netherlands and Slovakia determine electoral districts through geographic sub-divisions of the nation. Outside of my sample, Israel's Knesset and Serbia's National Assembly also maintain one national electoral district. In a full exploration of all voting constituencies, the Electoral Knowledge Network shows that 96 percent of nations use territorial electoral districts, whether drawn for electoral purposes or by using existing regional borders (aceproject.org). Territorial constituencies are thus the overwhelming standard for determining the unit of representation around the world.

Rehfeld (2005, p. 8) discusses the concept of constituency and the role of territory in defining constituency in detail. He describes territorial constituency as a default mechanism of representation, which is chosen without consideration for alternative notions of constituency in nearly all nations. He argues,

> Territorial constituencies have become such a habit of mind that it may seem "natural" for political representation to be defined by where people

> live. If, by nature, all politics were local, this naturalness might be a good justification for territorial representation. But the truth of Tip O'Neill's aphorism, that all politics is local, depends not on the nature of politics per se but on the institutional incentives that lead politicians to serve local interests over nonlocal interests, incentives that arise only because electoral constituencies are defined territorially. The localness of politics is thus epiphenomenal, nothing more than a byproduct of territorial electoral constituencies. If electoral constituencies were defined by profession (and not by residency at all), all politics would be "vocational." If constituencies were defined by political party (again, without regard to where members lived), all politics would be "ideological."

Territorial constituencies thus serve as a basis for political identity and politicians' constituency service. Rehfeld argues that territorial constituencies fundamentally shape politics by making, to varying extents, all or some politics local in most nations.[1]

Constituencies are also formed on a voluntary basis. Political parties may be said to have constituencies that are not established by formal rules but by attachment of voters and interest groups. These can include representation of subsections of the population based on ascriptive characteristics, such as race, ethnicity, religion, or language. The most common policy area upon which voters form voluntary constituencies to support parties is preferences for government redistribution (Bobbio 1996). Along these lines, leftist parties draw support primarily from voters interested in higher levels of government redistribution, and conservative parties are predominately supported by voters that seek limited government intervention into economic affairs. Accordingly, party constituencies are strongly shaped in most nations by both income level and ideological views on government's role in addressing income inequality.

Voting Rules and Party Organization

Voting rules delimit the way that voters (however grouped) cast their ballots and how votes are tabulated. The varieties and combinations of voting rules are enormous, but may be simplified into the extent to which they give strong incentives for parties to organize their members at the national level. Ballot structure, in particular, influences party control through the control of access and ordering of politicians (Carey and Shugart 1995).[2] Ballot structure determines how voters cast their ballots (whether they vote for individuals or parties, or both) and, related to this, how politicians gain seats (whether through direct choice by voters, or selection by party members). Ballots thus vary considerably in the relative power they give to parties and individual politicians in deciding politicians' career paths.

Party control of ballot access means that parties determine who represents them on the ballot and, often, which of those politicians is likely to get a seat in the legislature. Whether parties have the option of ordering their politicians on ballots is a function of district magnitude and list structure. In multimember districts, parties may have the ability to determine the ranking of a slate of candidates, whereby the higher on the list, the more likely they will serve in office. In closed-list representation (the most common PR system) parties control both access to the ballot and the ordering of candidates within the party slate. This ballot structure encourages strong party cohesion (and stifles party heterogeneity) because individual politicians that diverge from the party platform and voting line can be denied the opportunity to run or be placed at the end of the list, making them unlikely to return to office. In the most open list systems, such as in Finland, parties control access to the ballot, but voters may select individual candidates within those lists to determine the ranking of the list. At the other extreme, some systems do not allow parties to control either access or ordering. In such a system (Brazil offers an example), politicians may claim affiliation with any party they choose, and they can gain access to a seat based on their individual vote total in open lists. Politicians have low incentives to follow party mandates in this institutional setting and they will in fact have strong impetus to highlight their personal characteristics and distinct policy preferences to attract followers. This electoral structure in the Brazilian case contributes to a highly fragmented, low discipline party system and policy focus away from national policy concerns (Ames 1995).

In SMD elections only one politician represents each party in each district election. Nations vary in how the politicians get the party nomination in SMD, whether through parties or direct appeals to voters. In the USA, the party's representative is chosen directly by voters through a primary contest. Thus ballot access is controlled by voters (who may or may not be constituents of that party) and not directly by party leaders.[3] In Germany's SMD seats, local party offices select their candidate. This variation strongly affects who is the principal of the politicians, whether local voters, local party organizations, or national parties (Carey 2007).

Electoral rules, by demarking constituencies and by providing parties with varying incentives to encourage ideological homogeneity, influence how political systems address income inequality. The necessary conditions for high levels of government redistribution, laid out in Chapter 3, require that politicians have incentives to deliver policies that benefit the lower income spectrum of their societies. Where politics is local, the incentives of politicians on both the left and the right are largely to deliver goods home, rather than targeting a social group that spans districts. Nationalized politics encouraged by closed-list PR give legislative parties incentives to support the interests of their reelection constituencies, which are not typically geographically based (Blais and Massicotte 1996). Class is the largest national constituency group in most countries, which leads to strong, class-based national representation in most PR countries. Where parties lack mechanisms to unify their message and to discipline the behavior of members, a national coalition favorable to income redistribution will find large-scale policy change difficult because parties are organizationally and ideologically fragmented.

Constituency Targeting and Redistribution

Electoral systems—comprised of both constituency structure and voting rules—should influence redistributive outcomes primarily through their sway on the delivery of goods to constituencies and their effects on the organization of the majority coalition in favor of redistribution. For politicians with different constituencies to vote with a party, they must be compensated for their loss of ideological coherence (Scharpf et al. 1976). That is, if a politician's district has a specific preference, and if the compromise position of his party that aggregates preferences across many districts diverges from that preference, that politician can demand returns for these conformity costs (Kernell et al. 2011). This compensation will depend on which benefits are most useful to politician's career goals. In territorial elections, the most useful benefit is most often district-targeted goods (Cain et al. 1987). Territorial constituencies thus affect the nature of government distribution based on the reelection incentives of politicians and the bargaining chips parties use to encourage cohesive coalitions.

From the perspective of redistribution, territorial allocation of resources may be important because it reduces incentives (and available resources) to provide non-territorial goods, including centralized social policy. As Rehfeld (2005, p. 10) describes,

> Because the allocation of territorially specific goods such as highways, medical centers, and schools is important for the good of any nation, it may even be possible to justify territorial constituencies because they create what would purportedly be the right kind of incentives for representatives to secure territorially designed goods for their constituents. In this account, the process of logrolling—"if you vote for my project, I'll vote for yours"—purportedly produces the national good through a series of trade-offs between representatives within the legislature. The problem, though, is that the incentives to allocate goods territorially must be justified against the other kinds of incentives that would be created if constituencies were defined along nonterritorially based dimensions such as race, gender, or profession. So we need a prior argument that logrolling between advocates of this particularity—whether territory, race, profession, or so on—is what will most likely produce good outcomes that aim at the national interest. We cannot simply say that logrolling ensures the national good without considering what kinds of logs are being rolled.

Rehfeld thus argues that territorial delineation of electoral constituencies reduces attentiveness to the "national good" in politics. As the diversity of redistributive outcomes across the 50 nations in my sample reveals, however, defining elections by geography alone cannot explain policy to reduce income inequality. The extent to which territorial constituencies are likely to encourage targeted goods, or fragment national coalitions, depends in large part on whether voting rules dilute or reinforce the territorial cleavage.

Ballot and voting structure can influence national redistributive outcomes through their influence on party cohesiveness and their incentives for individual politicians to adhere to national party mandates.[4] Voting rules, in addition to the executive selection and constitutional structure discussed in other chapters, reinforce or dilute the role of territory as a constituency principle.

PR should dilute the salience of territorial constituencies on national politics. PR allots multiple seats to each district, depending on the district magnitude. District magnitude refers to the number of seats allotted to each district. SMD voting rules designate one seat per electoral constituency (district magnitude equals one), defined almost exclusively as a geographic territory. With a district magnitude greater than one, politicians will have less incentive to deliver goods to a local constituency or to represent specific territorial interests. Two electoral mechanisms explain why. With multiple politicians representing one territorial district, it is difficult for a single politician to claim credit for delivering targeted goods to that locality. If there are multiple party members representing the same district, a common occurrence in nearly all proportional electoral systems, voters cannot easily distinguish the origin of these goods and therefore cannot reward the politician reciprocally.

The distinction between open- and closed-list selection highlights the second mechanism that leads proportional systems to be decoupled from territorial representation. In closed-list PR, politicians are selected by party leaders to represent particular territories. There is no "personal vote" in this type of system because voters cast ballots for parties and not for individuals. Parties have strong incentives, accordingly, to provide coherent platforms that appeal across the nation and voters use this as their selection device. For nationalized parties, the delivery of policies that span the nation are more efficient for gaining votes than are targeted appeals to each district (Cox 1987). Such appeals are more efficient from an ideological and logistical perspective—parties can target their prospective voters across each district (such as welfare programs to win low-income voters, or income tax breaks to entice high-income voters). Pork or regional transfers, in contrast, would have the negative properties of being inefficiently targeted (because all voters can benefit from local public goods) and overly expensive, as pork would need to go to all districts. National policy delivery, rather than pork, makes more sense from an ideological, party unity, and likely fiscal perspective for parties in proportional systems. Thus, closed-list PR dilutes the territorial constituency effect and should strengthen the national constituencies for and against redistribution.

In open-list PR, on the other hand, the link to territorial constituency is more ambiguous than it is in closed-list PR or in SMD. In open-list PR, territorial districts have multiple members competing, but whether politicians will represent their party in the legislature is determined by popular vote rather than party leaders' selection. Party members are listed on the ballot and voters are able to select among them. This selection mechanism encourages the personal vote because co-partisans must compete to win seats (Carey and Shugart 1995). Politicians cannot primarily use their party label to appeal to voters because it is shared with their closest competitors. Accordingly, to distinguish themselves among co-partisans, in particular, politicians cultivate voters through appeals other than party label.

These alternative appeals by open-list PR politicians can take many forms, including territorial. Appeals can also be based on personality; fame, charisma, expertise, experience, and personal appearance are all possible characteristics that attract votes. These may create an independence of politicians that weakens a coherent majority party pursuit of redistributive policy and may in some cases encourage pork. Politicians can also appeal based on alternative policy agendas to those of their co-partisans. Similar to primary contests in the USA, members of the same party can express more extreme or moderate views to appeal to different constituencies within the party. Again, this should encourage ideological fragmentation within national parties, which should, in turn, make a redistribution coalition less likely.

Politicians may also appeal on a territorial basis in open-list PR. Take the example of Brazil, in which districts are allotted according to state boundaries. Within the state of Amazonas, eight seats are available. A party member could direct her appeal toward a particular sub-division within Amazonas, say the capital of Manaus. This politician could try to convince voters that she would be the best choice for this territorial constituency that, she could argue, has distinct preferences from the rest of the Amazonas state. The problem of credit-claiming for policies directed to the capital, however, remains (Samuels 2002). Moreover, territory is only one logical basis for appeals among others, including ideology and personality described above. Variance in district magnitude in Brazil, from eight in Amazonas to seventy in São Paolo, also affects both fragmentation of parties and the means by which politicians can appeal to voters.

Where PR, or at least closed-list PR, should reduce the incentives to appeal upon and deliver goods to territorial constituencies, SMD rules should reinforce the salience of electoral geography.[5] Recall that in SMD systems, such as the US House of Representatives or the UK House of Commons, one politician is chosen from each (territorial) district. SMD provides strong incentives to highlight geography in electoral appeals and in the delivery of goods. Members can most easily claim credit for geographically targeted public goods delivered to their constituency (Rae 1971). Moreover, because voters select members directly and policy preferences differ across constituencies, members have incentives to highlight their own policy ideas and district-specific ideology, distinct from national policy platforms. SMD is linked to increased pork, personal vote appeals, and party ideological heterogeneity in the USA and also in the UK where the parliamentary system and unitary structure dilute territorial incentives (Cain et al. 1987). This logic also has an empirical basis—every type of federal spending appears to help the reelection chances of legislative incumbents in the US House except for targeted spending to individuals (not districts) (Levitt and Snyder 1997).

SMD is not straightforwardly inimical to redistribution in theory, however. SMD electoral rules are thought to enhance the majority power within the specified districts by encouraging two-party competition (Duverger 1959). If that local bipartism links up to a national two-party competition, then the majority of the nation can decide policy without concession to the national minority (Cox 1997). Assuming that the poor are the majority in every district, SMD could allow the poor to capture all districts and dominate national policy. Whether SMD districts result in nationally oriented parties, depends on the ideological coherences of those parties. For example, Keefer and Khemani (2009) show that ideologically coherent parties in India deliver less pork within the context of SMD elections. They argue this is so because those parties' voters evaluate candidates based on party ideology; effort spent on delivering targeted goods is not as valuable for parties with weaker platforms. The ideological coherence of parties in the UK versus the more ideologically fragmented USA helps to explain why pork is lower in the UK than USA. Ideological coherence is a function of both political institutions and social heterogeneity (Crisp et al. 2013).

There are nonetheless several reasons to be skeptical that SMD will empower the majority poor in the fashion described and thus lead to massive fiscal redistribution. First, as explained above, SMD should encourage territorial distribution of goods since it is nearly always based on geographic constituencies. Second, as emphasized below, SMD rules may fragment the coalition in favor of redistribution as they must coordinate across districts. Third, and related to this, territorialization of constituencies will highlight heterogeneity of regional wealth and in the aggregation of incomes within districts.[6] More plainly, some districts are rich, some poor, some equal, some unequal, and living within those districts will shape one's preferences for national policy independent of national majority income distributions.

Territorial Preference Heterogeneity and Party Cohesion

In the previous section, I argued that constituencies and voting rules influence how politicians are incentivized to target resources to their constituents. Territorial constituencies, especially when reinforced by SMD, encourage politicians to deliver pork to their districts. If social spending, especially centralized social spending, is the most effective way to reduce inequality in a nation, territorial constituencies and SMD (and to a lesser extent open-list PR) may be a barrier to redistribution.

Constituencies and voting rules not only structure incentives for resource delivery but also affect the heterogeneity of parties. As described above, nationalizing institutions, such as (rare) non-geographic constituencies, and voting structures that give stronger leverage to parties vis-à-vis politicians allow parties to increase platform coherence. If advancing redistributive legislation is more likely if a unified majority coalition is able to press those demands, then electoral systems that encourage party cohesion should be favorable to redistribution.

Why would territorial politics increase party heterogeneity? Or, on the other side of the coin, why do party-centric rules reduce party heterogeneity. Societies may be said to have a latent level of heterogeneity that is informed by many different properties, including differences in income, race, religion, ethnicity, occupation, language, and geography, among many other things (Lipset and Rokkan 1967). Political institutions can have strong effects on the number of cleavages that are actively represented, as well as in incentivizing groups to compromise for the purposes of electoral coordination (Amorim-Neto and Cox

1997). In particular, parties that can maximize their power by eliminating intra-party heterogeneity, such as in closed-list PR and parliamentary systems, have strong incentives to do so. However, in territorialized systems, parties may be better off allowing for territorial heterogeneity to maximize vote share. Politicians' tailored district appeals in the USA, for example, are thought to increase party vote share over broad national appeals (Crisp et al. 2013).

Socioeconomic Sources of Territorial Party Heterogeneity

Latent territorial heterogeneity will depend on differences in the regional spread of social groups (income groups, ethnic minorities, etc.), economic geography, and the interconnection of regional and national fates. The regional spread of social groups, such as linguistic group geographic concentration in Canada, Belgium, or Switzerland, encourages party system heterogeneity in those nations. In Canada, specific Quebecois parties represent Franco-phone interests in the national legislature. In Belgium, regional linguistic parties duplicate the left–right spectrum within the linguistic territories. That is, there are Flemish-specific socialist and conservative parties and Walloon-specific socialist and conservative parties. Where minority groups are more evenly spread across territories, as may be said for African-Americans in the USA, these groups are less likely to establish specific regional parties, and are more likely to be integrated within nationalized parties. Of course, voting rules strongly influence whether groups form their own parties or coordinate within larger parties (Cox 1997).

Also little recognized in the nationalization of parties is the role of economic geography. Parties are more likely to be nationalized if regions' economies are strongly interconnected. If regions' prosperity is linked, whether through economic interdependence or migration of labor, this should encourage coordination of voters across district lines on the basis of common national interests (Beramendi 2012). If, on the other hand, regions' fates are largely distinct from national economic tides, the efforts of parties to dampen territorial preferences should be challenged.

Regions' economic fates are tied to some extent in all nations. Common monetary policy, for example, affects all citizens dealing in that currency. One way to measure the interconnectedness of regional economies is to see if regional GDP growth is correlated with national GDP growth. In Table 5.1, I show the correlations of regional and national GDP growth for a sample of federal nations to provide comparability with the three country case examples in bold. The regions within those nations with the highest and lowest correlations are also listed. Some nations have highly interconnected regions, such as Spain, whereby changes in national economic tides track extremely closely with changes in regional tides. Germany's regional growth is also strongly correlated with national growth—they correlate at $p=0.87$. On the opposite spectrum, India's ($p=0.39$) and Argentina's ($p=0.43$) regional growth are largely disconnected in comparison. US states are an intermediate case, with reasonably high association between national and state economic tides, but fair variance within. Notably, the economically dynamic states of Illinois and California swing most

Table 5.1 Correlation between Changes in National GDP and Provincial GDP, Decentralized Sample

Country	*Correlation–National GDP and Region GDP growth*	*Most Connected Regions (Highest Correlation)*	*Least Connected Regions (Lowest Correlation)*	*Years Included*
Argentina	**0.43**	**Buenos Aires City, Buenos Aires Province**	**Tierra del Fuego, Santa Cruz**	**1970–2005**
Austria	0.71	Salzburg, Vorarlberg	Burgenland, Wien	2000–08
Belgium	0.82	Limburg, West Vlaanderen	Luxembourg, Vlaams-Brabant	2000–09
Bolivia	0.74	Santa Cruz, Cochabamba	Tarija, Pando	1988–2010
Brazil	0.55	São Paulo, Minas Gerais	Mato Grosso do Sul, Tocantins	1995–2010
Canada	0.68	Ontario, Quebec	Saskatchewan, Yukon	1981–2010
China	0.79	Jiangsu, Hebei	Tibet, Hainan	1980–2010
Germany	**0.87**	**Baden-Württemberg, Nordrhein-Westfalen**	**Berlin, Hamburg**	**2000–09**
India	0.39	Uttarakhand, Chandigarh	West Bengal, Meghalaya*	1980–2010
Italy	0.88	Lombardia, Tuscany	Calabria, Sicily	2001–09
Mexico	0.78	Jalisco, Federal District	Zacatecas, Tabasco	1993–2010
Russia	0.61	Chechen Republic, Samara Region	Nenets Autonomous Region, Kamchatka	2002–09
Spain	0.96	Cataluña, Valencia	Cueta, Melilla	2001–09
USA	**0.71**	**Illinois, California**	**North Dakota, Wyoming**	**1997–2009**

Source: Rogers and Lee (2015) from national accounts.

Note

* In India and Russia, some provincial GDP values have significant negative correlations with national GDP (e.g., Puducherry). This table includes those with the lowest absolute correlation.

closely to national tides and the natural resources states of North Dakota and Wyoming grow on a relatively independent trajectory.

Regardless of institutions, unified incentives to improve national economic growth should reduce party preference heterogeneity based on regional economic interests. From this perspective, Germany's parties should have somewhat limited territorial preference heterogeneity, the USA somewhat more, and the Argentine parties very high divergence at the national level. These differences are further diluted by political institutions in the German case but magnified in the US and Argentine cases.

Regional Parties

Regional parties, and party system nationalization, are of clear relevance to territorially informed heterogeneity of the party system. Regional parties are defined as parties that compete in only one region (Brancati 2008). This can include regional parties competing at the regional level, or representation of region-specific parties at the national level. Full party system nationalization exists when the same political parties compete across all districts in a nation (i.e., no regional parties compete at the national level). In previous research, regionalism and party system nationalization in the party system have not been explicitly linked to the likelihood of redistributive policy at the national level.[7] However, consistent with the three mechanisms argued throughout, regional parties might matter for redistributive policy if they are able to shift policy more toward geographically targeted goods, if they hold veto power, or if they ideologically fragment the party coalitions in the legislature.

Regional parties enter the legislature with a somewhat different mandate from that of the national parties. While the national parties are ostensibly representatives of their constituency across the entire nation, regional parties are clearly sent to office to represent the interests of their region. Because regional parties are unlikely to gain majorities on their own, they must compromise ideologically to be part of the governing or majority voting coalition. To stay within their regional mandate, ideological compromise may press them to seek regionally targeted goods if they hold a position in the government (Ziegfeld 2012). Regional parties are linked to pork and ideological fragmentation. According to Crisp et al. (2013), "low levels of nationalization are always 'bad' in the sense that they lead to regionalized politicking and particularistic budgeting" (p. 7). Regionalized targeting of policies should, accordingly, be a less useful strategy in nationalized party systems with ideological coherence.

Ziegfeld (2012) shows that regional parties are more likely to hold cabinet portfolios in committees that specialize in geographically targeted goods. Keefer and Khemani (2009) also demonstrate that ideologically coherent parties are less likely to deliver pork. While regional parties may desire pork disproportionately, it is not obvious that their role in national government will necessarily hurt the chances of the redistributive coalition. In fact, regional parties could be a reasonable coalition partner for redistributively oriented leftist parties that cannot form a simple majority. This is a possible interpretation of the current party alignments (national populists plus regional parties) in Argentina, for example.

Regional parties may hold veto power at the national level if they are pivotal in some regard. If they are part of a minimum majority coalition, for example, regions could block policy change. This is plausible in the Argentine and German cases discussed below. The Christian Democratic Union (CDU) in Germany has formed a permanent coalition with the Christian Social Union (CSU), a party that only competes in Bavaria. CSU seats are required for CDU majorities, thus the CSU holds potential veto power in CDU–CSU coalitions. Other regional parties also have representation in the (territorial) Bundesrat. If the interests of regional parties that hold veto power are substantially different from the redistributive coalitions' preferences, this may undermine redistributive efforts.

Regional parties certainly suggest that the territorial cleavage is relevant in national politics and this may signal inequality in regional income and ideological fragmentation of the majority coalition in favor of redistribution. However, regional party participation in national politics appears to be more a function of political and economic decentralization than the strength of the regional cleavage per se (Brancati 2008; Chhibber and Kollman 2004). Many countries that have clear regional cleavages, such as Indonesia or Sri Lanka, do not have regional parties, while some nations, such as the Czech Republic, have regional parties and no strong regional conflict.

If regional parties are synonymous with the ideological fragmentation of national coalitions, including those of the left, then national social spending will be less likely. In this sense, party nationalization, with the same ideologically coherent parties competing throughout the nation and at the national level, should be linked to nationalized policy, including broadly targeted social allocation. Yet, Morgenstern et al. (2009) emphasize there are two routes to party system nationalization. One occurs when national parties offer the same policies across all districts and the other is when national parties tailor their appeals to each district. The latter case characterizes the USA, which has two ideologically heterogeneous national parties competing in elections at every level of government. Stokes (1967) emphasized the importance of localized politics in the USA because it required pork expenditures to pacify local constituents, which thus takes away resources for national based spending. Importantly, Crisp et al. (2013) show that the type of nationalization a party system takes—whether coherent or regional—is dependent on the heterogeneity of the regions themselves. An important source of this heterogeneity is the income levels of the regions, as discussed throughout this book. These dynamics are addressed in the case studies below.

Electoral Rules and Redistribution in the USA, Germany, and Argentina

Having laid out theoretical links between electoral systems—both territorial constituencies and voting rules—and redistribution, I now explore these dynamics in the three focus cases. The USA, Germany, and Argentina span the entire spectrum of personally oriented to mixed to party-oriented systems. These electoral systems provide very different incentives for parties to coalesce, to deliver targeted local goods, and to conceptualize political interests in either broader or more local terms. Accordingly, the party dynamics related to redistribution diverge sharply across the three cases.

The US party system, as with its federalism, presents the extreme case for territorially oriented politics, which thereby weakens the majority coalition pressing for income redistribution. The strong personal vote in SMD systems both encourages targeted pork to districts (whether states or congressional districts), and "allows" for considerable preference heterogeneity within the same party as members represent very diverse districts. Pork, in turn, is a solution to the preference heterogeneity in the two mass parties, as members are encouraged to vote along party lines in exchange for particular benefits for their district (Stokes 1967).

Germany's electoral system in the Bundestag (popular house) was designed after World War II to achieve particular party system dynamics. Specifically, designers hoped to avoid the extreme fragmentation and polarization of the party system during the Weimar period that preceded National Socialism. At the same time, designers also prioritized direct mandates from localities to the national government. The result is a mixed-member electoral system with both nationalizing closed-list PR elections and localizing SMD, both organized according to Länder. Thus the German system is a middle ground between nationalizing and localizing incentives, with only a subset of politicians incentivized to deliver pork to their districts (Lancaster and Patterson 1990). Territorial constituencies in the SMD, significant malapportionment in both houses, and regional parties introduce regional heterogeneity into the German parties in the Bundestag.

Argentina's electoral system in both its popular Chamber of Deputies and its Senate are organized on the basis of closed-list representation. This institution should encourage strong nationalization and cohesion of national parties. On the basis of voting patterns, closed-list PR has this effect in Argentina (Benton 2003). However, territorial interests are strong in Argentina's parties due to the geographic organization of elections, and to the selection of party lists by provincial party leaders. The result is not pork as traditionally characterized, but rather a bargaining through discretionary transfers to provinces. The mixture of strongly cohesive institutions and highly diverse constituencies also encourages clientelistic exchange (Gibson and Calvo 2000). Clientelism is a mechanism to hold parties together once the collective action problem (on the part of parties) has been solved, but managing the social choice problem (the establishment of coherent platforms despite heterogeneous preferences) remains elusive (Kitschelt 2000).

Targeted Spending to Localities

US electoral institutions encourage provision of pork. The ways that Senate elections encourage this result was discussed in detail in the previous chapter. In this section, I focus on these dynamics in the popular chamber, the House of Representatives. Like senators, members of the House represent territorial districts according to SMD.[8] Differences in the district size, electoral calendar, and the size of the chamber have led parties to organize differently across the two chambers, with possible implications for redistribution and pork provision.

The US House of Representatives has 435 members chosen by SMD from districts that are sub-divisions of states. The precise ways that these district lines are drawn is determined by the states, but all are territorially contiguous.[9] In comparison with the US Senate, the House is more partisan (Gailmard and Jenkins 2007). Parties have tools to encourage party discipline in the House, including selection of leadership positions and committees and campaign resources (Kernell et al. 2011). Frequent elections make House members particularly reliant on the resources of parties to maintain their jobs. The majority party controls the flow of legislation (both what is voted upon and how) and has majority representation on all committees (Cox and McCubbins 2005). Despite clear ties to local constituents, individual politicians in the House sacrifice their autonomy to some extent to align with political parties that overcome collective action problems in the legislature and in the electorate (Aldrich 1995).

Cohesion in legislative voting is encouraged by selective rewards and punishments to members. One particularly important class of rewards is district-specific appropriations (Levitt and Snyder 1997). At the same time, the pull of local districts is strong enough that parties rationally allow members to stray on certain votes if the party line conflicts with the preferences of their district (Fenno 1978). Even still, the majority party only allows for defections up to the point in which the majority of the majority party it is still able to win (Cox and McCubbins 2005). District-targeted rewards are often the price the party pays to "buy" the vote of pivotal legislators (Engstrom and Vanberg 2010).

In the House, parties manage the heterogeneity of members' preferences that diverge due, in part, to differences in their districts and the exigencies of reelection. Pork is a primary tool used to convince members to toe the party line. The Senate, on the other hand, is less partisan and individual members are more autonomous due to their numbers (1 of 100 rather than 1 of 435), their larger constituencies, their distance from reelection (six years instead of two), and their particular powers (e.g., the filibuster). From this perspective, senators are more expensive to buy with pork than are members of the House.[10] Furthermore, divided government—in this case, split partisanship between the House and the Senate—makes coming to agreement on policy change more difficult. Pork is expected to increase in divided government, as members across parties (which are even less ideologically aligned than the diverse party caucus) can charge a high price for compromising their ideological preferences (Schwarz 2006).

In summary, in the USA pork is a means of increasing party cohesion and changing the status quo policy and is thus the most efficient resource for gathering votes (Huber and Ting 2013). Legislators can claim specific credit for district-targeted goods, and voters reward pork over broadly targeted goods (Grimmer 2013). Snyder and Levitt (1997) also show that voters do not electorally reward individual social spending by US legislators. While many voters certainly use the partisan cue to select candidates in SMD, members are not highly incentivized to contribute to broad national social policy. National social policy represents a common pool problem in which every party member benefits from (or could be hurt by) its effects regardless of whether they helped pass the legislation or not. Accordingly, national social policy is expected to be underprovided even though parties make substantial efforts to increase party cooperation and discipline. This is also because one of same tools that parties use to encourage cohesion, pork, takes resources away from common national social policy.

Argentina's electoral system does not strongly encourage pork barrel politics. Closed-list representation in the Chamber of Deputies and the Senate incentivizes loyalty to party leaders and not credit claiming on the basis of specific service delivery to local populations (Micozzi 2013). At the same time, the organization of Argentina's party system and the career paths of politicians incentivize the delivery of resources to the province, especially in the form of intergovernmental transfers. In comparison with US institutions, we see very different electoral rules achieving somewhat similar outcomes: targeted goods to localities, but through different funding mechanisms (pork versus transfers).

Argentina's party lists in the Chamber of Deputies and the Senate are determined by local party chiefs, most often the governor. To gain reelection, therefore, legislators need to stay in the good graces of their local boss. It is also worth considering how the reelection rates of legislators in the US compare with Argentina and how this could affect distribution of resources. In the US House and to a slightly lesser extent the Senate, nearly all members are reelected if they run for an additional term. In the US House, the reelection rate is in the 90–99 percent range; in the Senate it is in the 85–90 percent range (Abramowitz et al. 2006; Squire 1989). In Argentina, on the other hand, renomination on the party list is somewhat rare. Reelection rates in the Argentine Chamber of Deputies are around 15–20 percent (Jones et al. 2002). The career paths of US and Argentine legislators thus look very different. While House members can expect to keep their jobs for a while and perhaps advance to higher offices in the national government (static ambition), Argentine legislators must prepare for a career outside of the legislature (progressive ambition) (Rohde 1979). Most will return to their home province and take jobs allocated by the governor (Micozzi 2014). According to both list structure and reelection rates, therefore, legislators have incentivizes to target resources preferred by their local party leader, usually the governor.

Argentine legislators can focus their efforts among three categories of distributive goods: broad national policy, targeted pork, or interregional transfers. If their career paths are controlled by governors, they have a very strong incentive to focus their efforts on interregional transfers (Eaton 2002). Governors prefer transfers, as opposed to pork, because they have more discretion over the allocation. For governors, national policy is less important than their region-specific interests, especially the resources available to make preferred policy and buy electoral support (Remmer and Gélineau 2003).

The redistributive effects of these different systems are not altogether clear. While the USA "oversupplies" pork to the detriment of broad social spending, Argentina "oversupplies" regional transfers instead of centralized social policy.

Ultimately, the effects on redistribution depend on whether pork or interregional transfers reduce income inequality. In neither the USA nor Argentina are these resources thought to have a major redistributive effect (Gervasoni 2010).

Germany provides an interesting contrast to both Argentina and the USA. Unlike Argentina, Germany's parties are more nationalized and cohesive. Unlike the USA, Germany's parties are generally incentivized to deliver social goods over pork. The pork incentives exist in Germany's SMD "direct mandate" seats, but the funding structure of social policy and the nationalizing effects of closed-list PR shift spending toward social policy. The autonomous funding structure of social policy in Germany, as discussed in the previous chapter, encourages politicians at all levels to overspend on social policy due to murky accountability for the costs associated with the programs.

German party orientation toward social policy is driven by the relative absence of personal vote incentives. Germany's parties are nationalized and centralized, they span regions and are broadly programmatic on a left–right dimension, and voters are ideologically aligned to the parties. For these parties, it is more efficient to deliver goods to their particular constituents (rich, poor, old, young, etc.) on the basis of social criteria (Milesi-Ferretti et al. 2002; Huber and Ting 2013). The politicians in closed-list elections need to be loyal to their party and they do not gain significantly from targeted pork to their Länder-based constituencies.[11] From these politicians, we expect a provision of social goods that span the electorate.

At the same time, Germany also has SMD seats in its lower house. These seats are organized first by Länder and then subdivided within the Länder in a process similar to districting in the US House of Representatives. These members, because their constituencies are local and their election is direct, have some incentives to deliver constituency service and target resources to their districts. Lancaster and Patterson (1990) find that SMD members showed more interest in pork barrel projects than list members. Strattmann and Baur (2002) find systematic differences in committee membership between politicians with different mandates. The SMD members were much more likely to join committees with opportunities to target local constituencies, such as construction, traffic, and agriculture committees, than were closed-list members. The closed-list members were more likely to pursue committee memberships that were stepping stones to higher office within the party. Sieberer (2010) finds that SMD members vote more autonomously from the party than do closed-list members. Pork may therefore detract somewhat from social spending in the budgets controlled by the legislature.

The behavioral difference between SMD and PR members is in some ways surprising because of strong expectations that the PR system should "contaminate" the SMD seats and vice versa (Nohlen and Schultze 1978). Two features of the electoral system make convergence likely. First, the allocation of the SMD and PR seats are linked. Voters cast two votes, a direct mandate vote and a party vote. The party vote determines the overall apportionment of the Bundestag according to the vote percentage. For each direct mandate seat a party receives, they have one less seat to allocate in the proportional representation seats. Thus the SMD seats are compensatory for the PR seats. Second, party members running for the SMD seats are also typically included in the party list. If they are unsuccessful in attaining the SMD seat, they will likely join the Bundestag as part of the closed-list delegation. Crisp (2007) argues that contamination should reduce the localizing effect of the SMD seats because parties will implement a strong overall strategy that overcomes incentives from the SMD elections. For example, parties can strategically orient resources to loyal SMD members.[12] Due to dual candidacies, direct mandate candidates have incentives to adopt mixed strategies to optimize their chances in both contests (Bawn and Thies 2003). Both dynamics should reduce the likelihood that direct mandate members in multimember systems will pursue pork, relative to pure SMD systems.

The nomination process for SMD seats in the USA versus Germany also provides different incentives to target local goods. In the USA, nomination for SMD seats is decided by local voters in a primary contest between co-partisans. Primaries encourage the personal vote because politicians must distinguish themselves on a basis other than party identification (Adams and Merrill 2008). US primaries thus encourage narrow targeting of organized interests and pork provision (Bawn and Thies 2003). In Germany local party councils decide nominations for SMD seats. The reelection incentive is to please local constituents, not the Länder as a whole as in the PR seats. This local orientation and relative party autonomy of SMD members is reinforced by the high likelihood of renomination (Roberts 1988) and by the higher rates of reelection than that associated with PR seats (Manow 2007).

The mixed-member system also shows interesting interactions with the left–right dimensions and regional differences in income. Specifically, the (center right, partly regional) CDU–CSU regularly wins a large majority of its lower house seats through the SMD seats. For example, in the eighteenth Bundestag, 75 percent of the government CDU–CSU's seats came from "direct mandate" SMD seats and the rest from PR Land list seats. In contrast the center-left SPD gained 70 percent of its seats through the PR lists. Die Linke ("The Left") a leftist party concentrated in the Eastern regions, gained 94 percent of its seats through PR. By implication, the center-right should have both more incentive to deliver pork since so much of their membership is directly elected and they should have lower party cohesion. The different allocations of seats by the left and the right might reflect the relative geographic concentration of constituents of the right within specific parts the Länder (including affluent citizens) and the dispersion of the constituents of the socialist party within and across the Länder. This concentration versus dispersion of right and left voters reinforces the idea that leftist parties likely perform better in larger electoral districts, where they can better leverage their numerical majority (Rodden 2010).

So how does Germany's multimember system influence redistribution? Evidently, the multimember system is compatible with high levels of redistributive spending in the German case. The evidence in Chapter 2 also shows that Germany spends the majority of its resources in broad social categories. This is certainly due, in part, to the funding structure of social spending that obfuscates responsibility for budget deficit discussed in Chapter 4. At the same time, the strong closed-list PR system encourages broad constituency targeting that spans regions and dilutes the pork incentives of the SMD districts. Nonetheless, the electoral system that includes SMD politicians and the territorial Bundesrat leads the major parties to distribute some level of pork, and high levels of regional transfers, to these locally oriented politicians in order to encourage broad party agreement.

Blocking Power of Regions

Electoral systems do not directly provide veto power to any set of actors, as some of the constitutional powers of federalism or executive systems do. In that sense, electoral rules are not the source of blocking power to specific regional actors that may be used to impede redistributive policies. However, electoral rules shape who is elected and how they are elected. These rules vary considerably in which types of actors (majority vs. minority, regional vs. social class) are best able to attain representation to make policy.

While electoral rules may not provide blocking powers per se, they can favor some actors over others. In highly territorial political systems, the representation of place is common in territorial districts, but especially in region-specific representation. Territorial upper houses violate to some extent the one person, one vote principle in favor of one region, one vote. Lowers house representation can also be disproportionate, as the German and Argentine cases show. Electoral rules, including the allocation of seats across the different territories, can have strong effects on political outcomes, including redistribution. Importantly, malapportionment of seats (i.e, the overrepresentation of territories with lower populations) influences political bargaining and, ultimately, redistribution. Malapportionment may be particularly inimical to redistribution if it gives greater political weight to political elites opposed to centralized redistribution (Ardanaz and Scartascini 2013).

Malapportionment may be important for redistributive policy for several reasons. First, representation of regions nearly always favors the voice of rural regions above populated urban regions. On average, rural regions tend to have more equal income distributions, more conservative populations, and lower union density. All of these factors make support for redistribution likely to be lower in rural areas. Less populated regions in some cases are poorer, which may increase support for regional equalization. Not all unpopulated regions are poor, however. For example, sparsely populated areas rich in natural resources in both the USA and Argentina have a strong voice in their Senates. These regions might be particularly opposed to centralized welfare designs and may have a disproportionate voice to strike them down. Stepan (2004, p. 45) argues for this point:

> there might be a prolonged period in a country during which a strong majority of the political leaders, and a strong majority of the electorate in the country, believe that major changes are necessary. But, if the federation has been crafted to facilitate "win-sets" of blocking vetoes by small minorities, the efficacy and legitimacy of that democracy could be eroded.

The existence of such win sets points to the veto powers of regions.

Stepan (2004) and Gibson and Calvo (1998) raise the additional concern that malappointment encourages rent-seeking. According to this logic, votes of regions with small populations can be cheaply bought on a per capita basis. Votes from overrepresented, sparsely populated regions are thus particularly attractive for coalition building. These authors argue that malapportionment can stand in the way of reform desired by the majority, if politicians from overrepresented areas use their blocking win set position to extract rewards, or if they are bought off to block the majority preferences.

Malapportionment may be linked to lower redistribution, both on the taxation and expenditure side (Lee and Rogers 2015). On the taxation side, malapportionment appears to be an endogenous response by elites to limit the power of populated, urban provinces with more leftist voters (Beramendi and Rogers 2015). Ardanaz and Scartascini (2013) show that malapportionment is linked to lower progressive income tax collection. They argue that where overrepresented regions are aligned with elites who prefer lower levels of redistribution, malapportionment limits government responses to inequality. Malapportionment is therefore one very important mechanism by which regional representation can result in lower redistribution.

In Argentina, the provinces most dependent on national resources for provincial expenditures and those that are most clientelistic are the ones with the greatest voting weight in the national legislature (Calvo and Murillo 2004). Argentina's high regional inequality is, paradoxically, preserved to a some extent because of the considerable overrepresentation of less populated, politically conservative provinces. Many of these provinces would benefit, in theory, from increased redistribution to their poor, dependent populations. Elite preferences in those provinces, however, are opposed to centralized redistribution because of a loss in regional autonomy and concern that much of these benefits would flow to low-income populations in the urban areas (Beramendi et al. 2015).

Malapportionment also clearly shapes bargaining dynamics in the US Senate. Less populated states gain significantly larger appropriations on a per capita basis (Lee and Oppenheimer 1999; Lee 1998). Less populated states are more likely to be in the winning coalition. This occurs because these states are small, making their state projects cheap relative to the size of the federal budget. Less populated states also have a lower "shadow price." Shadow price refers to the amount necessary to convince politicians and their constituents to vote for a particular bill. With a lower population, the politician should have fewer constituents to distribute resources to, meaning their overall cost to "buy" is lower. Lazaras and Steigerwalt (2009) discuss the extreme example of Republican Senator Olympia Snowe, from the state of Maine. Snowe is an outlier for gaining extraordinarily high levels of appropriations for her state. This is possible for at least three reasons: she is from the overrepresented state of Maine, Maine is small and thus it is cheap to buy state projects, and she was the median member of the Senate. As median member, both parties could reasonably compete for her support.

Schneider et al. (2001) demonstrate that malapportionment plays a central role in bargaining in post-reunification Germany as well. They argue that

Germany's failure to adapt their political institutions to the new economic geography of Germany resulted in an informal change in the bargaining dynamics in the legislature. To cobble together coalitions in the current system, parties buy off less populated regions with discretionary elements of interregional transfers. To demonstrate their point, they analyze the predictors of transfers in the pre- and post-reunification periods. They find that the shadow price of Länder, based on their populations and representation, is a strong predictor of transfers after 1990 but not in the pre-reunification period. In other words, overrepresented regions receive more in interregional transfers now that regional inequality has grown higher.

Both houses of the legislature in Germany are substantially malapportioned. While malapportionment is expected to drive resources disproportionately to regions with greater representation, the effect is different across the two houses in Germany (Pitlik et al. 2006). Specifically, malapportionment leads to disproportionate allocations much more in the territorial Bundesrat than in the Bundestag. Importantly, the Bundestag is more malapportioned than the Bundesrat (Samuels and Snyder 2001). Pitlik et al. attribute these differences in allocation across houses to the stronger party discipline and the nationalizing incentives in the popular house.

One major change in Germany after reunification was in the seat allocations of the Bundesrat. Affluent, populated regions in the south of the country recognized that they could be a permanent minority in the territorial house under the representation system in place at the time of reunification. In this system, state representation was allocated according to population but not proportionally. Any Länder with a population above a specific threshold (seven million in the 1990 specification) receive a fixed number of seats (five prior to 1990). This ensures a certain level of proportionality not seen in the US Senate, but nonetheless underrepresents very populous regions. The more populated (and wealthy) Länder argued for a sixth seat in regions with populations exceeding seven million in 1990. This increased representation for the populated regions, and both reduced malapportionment and provided the minority of wealthy regions with potential blocking power in the Bundesrat (Beramendi 2012).

Territorial representation, through regional apportionment and malapportionment, thus affects redistribution by giving differential weight to regions with specific preferences that may be anti-redistributive. The majority coalition that favors redistribution, and its organizational mechanism typically supported by organized labor, has its strongholds in urban areas. Overrepresentation of rural areas in electoral system design thus weakens the regions with the strongest interest in redistributive reform.

Fragmenting the Coalition

The USA, Germany, and Argentina have very different party coalitions due, in part, to their constituency structure and their voting rules. Germany's closed-list system encourages cohesion of its multiple parties into nationalized bodies. The USA's SMD rules press politicians to target their appeals to localities, while at the same time they encourage local and national bipartism. Argentina's parties are strongly fragmented among regional interests.

Importantly, the extent and nature of fragmentation is different in these three nations. In Germany, fragmentation occurs in large part within the party system as a whole, resulting in multiple (including regional) parties, and not fragmentation within the parties themselves. In the USA, political institutions favor two heterogeneous parties, allowing for one-party majorities in each legislative house.[13] Argentina's fragmentation primarily takes place within the parties themselves, and particularly along regional lines within the Peronist party. Coalition formation in Argentina is frequently between the President's party (often Peronist) and regional parties with national representation (Gibson 1997).

Thus these three nations vary dramatically in whether and how we expect the majority coalition favorable to redistribution to emerge. In Germany party nationalization and cohesion favor redistributively oriented parties. The evidence that Germany's parties have encouraged high levels of social spending is unequivocal (Manow 2005). In fact, the left–right cleavage in Germany does not appear to play as clear a role in debates in social policy because both large parties—the CDU–CSU on the right and SPD on the left—broadly support redistributive spending (Kitschelt 2001).

Heterogeneity within the party system on regional and "second-dimension" politics may also impact party heterogeneity through coalition formation in the German case. As introduced above, regional parties are relevant to national legislative politics because at least two regional parties, the CSU and the South Schleswig Voters' Association (SSW) regularly hold seats. In the case of the CSU, they hold significant seats in the Bundestag and usually represent Bavaria in the Bundesrat. The SSW represents Danish and Frisian minorities in Schleswig-Holstein, and sometimes sends delegates to the Bundesrat through that Land. Unlike the CSU, the SSW has not competed in national elections since 1965. While not specific to any Länder, Die Linke, or The Left, is a party with origins and a primary support base in the former East Germany. The Left is a coalition party of the Party of Democratic Socialism, successor of the Socialist Unity Party that ruled East Germany until 1989, and a left-wing defector from the national SPD. Each of these parties increases, to different degrees, the heterogeneity of potential party coalitions for redistribution by bringing in region-specific preferences to the government and opposition.

Increasingly, German parties must also work in coalitions with parties that do not fit the traditional left–right party mold. In the last several decades, parties have formed in the interests of policies orthogonal to redistribution, such as the Alliance '90/The Greens, which advocates for environmental causes and peace. Alliance '90/The Greens is also a potential coalition partner for both right and left because its platform is not oriented around redistribution. Demographically, Green voters tend to be higher income, young, urban and educated.[14]

Multidimensional politics leads some low-income constituents to vote for parties based on non-economic issues, and some high-income constituents to vote with otherwise low-income parties. This ideological amalgamation within and across parties in multidimensional party systems reduces the likelihood of redistribution (Roemer 1998). The general intuition is that, with a mixture of low- and high-income constituents within party coalitions, none has strong incentives to tax the rich, which would include their own constituents. As with the case of the Greens, combining higher income voters in coalitions with leftist parties (the most frequent pairing) may dilute their redistributive goals. Moreover, anti-redistributive parties may specifically orient political conflict to the second (non-economic) dimension as income inequality grows in the nation (Tavits and Potter 2015).

In comparison with Germany, fragmentation of the US redistributive coalition emerges from within-party regional heterogeneity and from multidimensionality in the Democrat party. Both US national parties are regionally heterogeneous and multidimensional. It makes sense to focus on the Democratic Party in this case because it is the more leftist of the two and thus more programmatically oriented toward redistribution.

Historically, the Democratic Party has made limited efforts, in comparative perspective, to increase redistributive policy in part because of its regionally (and ideologically) heterogeneous base.[15] Specifically, between the New Deal (1933) and the Great Society legislation (1964–65), the Democrats were primarily a coalition of Southerners in the solidly Democratic (at all levels of government) South and of Northern labor and liberals (Poole and Rosenthal 2001). These politicians represented very different regional political economies and positions on redistribution, including interregional redistribution. The Southern Democrats acted as a veto within the party and in legislative voting—on labor policies in particular but also on redistributive policies more generally (Katznelson et al. 1993; Beramendi 2012). At the same time, Southern Democrats were keenly interested in bringing resources to the poor southern states (Olssen 1987; Burner 1968).

The divide between Northern and Southern Democrats limited efforts at redistribution. This regional marriage gradually faded after the Civil Rights Act of 1964. Southern Democrats were replaced by Republicans in most of the South in the 1970s–90s. Now the Democratic Party has a more homogenous ideological base, but a continued regional divide. The Democrats have their strongest bases in urban areas of every state, and more broadly in the Eastern and Western coastal states. This regional divide, in part, informs the continued ideological heterogeneity within the Democrats. For example, 39 of the 212 votes against the (Democratic-led) Affordable Care Act that established national health insurance requirements were from Democrats.[16] The majority of those 39 Democrats were from states that have predominately Republican leaders at both the local and national level. There was a clear regional, as well as partisan, trend in voting on this social policy.

The Democrats also have ideological heterogeneity from differences within the pro-redistribution coalition (from high- and low-income constituents) and from second-dimension politics. Demographically, the Democratic coalition is more varied (in income, education, race, etc.) than that of the Republicans (Weeden and Kurzban 2014). The Democrats have significant support from higher income groups that might be more traditionally considered likely constituents of the more conservative Republicans. As evidence, eight of the ten richest counties in the USA gave majority support for Democratic presidential candidate Barack Obama in 2012.[17] Two of the three richest counties (Westchester in New York, and Marin in California) supported Obama with 60 percent and 74 percent of vote share, respectively. All higher income constituents may not support the Democratic Party for exactly the same reasons. Some are drawn by its relatively pro-redistributive stance, others for its position on second dimension politics, including environmentalism and advocacy for rights for all genders and sexual orientations, racial and ethnic groups, and views on religion, and some for the combination. With high levels of heterogeneity within the Democratic Party, it is difficult for its members to come to broad agreements on significant changes to redistributive policy even when they are in the relatively rare position to advance it on their own.

Argentina's parties are more strongly fragmented on the basis of regional interests than on the left–right dimension. Provincial orientation is apparent in opinion polls of legislators. When asked "when there is a conflict between the needs of the province and the positions of your political party, how do you usually vote?" over 96 percent of respondents said their provinces always came first.[18] Despite party loyalty incentives under closed-list PR, for all politicians (except the President), provincial concerns trump national concerns. With parties' preferences divided along regional lines, agreement on national policy can be stunted, and thus organization at the national level to advance redistribution will be more difficult. This is additionally complicated because Argentine parties tailor appeals not only across regions but also across voters within regions (some with programmatic appeals, some with clientelism) (Weitz-Shapiro 2012).

The district magnitude in Argentina's PR system has important regional variation that is also related to party cohesion and regional weight in legislatures. Provinces serve as the first organizing principle of electoral constituencies. In populated areas, provinces are subdivided into several multimember districts for lower house elections, with district magnitudes averaging approximately ten. Less populated provinces are more often carved into multiple single member districts within the same province (Calvo and Murillo 2004). The effect of large multimember districts in populated areas is to fragment their parties substantially, and to limit the cohesion of the provincial bloc. With multiple SMDs, Peronists in particular do not need to compete against each other and can capture all districts (in theory) rather than capturing the percentage of seats linked to their vote share in a multimember district. The effect encourages single party dominance in the less populated (often conservative) regions with cohesive party blocs.

The cohesion of the interior party blocs and the fragmentation of the party blocs in more populated provinces are important for several reasons. First, their cohesion makes them attractive coalition partners. Convincing a provincial bloc as a unit may be cheaper and easier than attracting votes one by one from different territories. Second, if they desire, the less populated provinces can form a single bloc that can act as a "blocking win-set" against policy change. Third, it is reasonable to expect that many of the overrepresented provinces with tight party delegations are also opposed to centralized redistributive reforms but favorable to (non-progressive) interregional redistribution. In particular, affluent less populated regions such as Santa Cruz, Neuquén, and Chubut have relatively egalitarian income distributions and they also benefit disproportionally from the interregional transfers system (Beramendi et al. 2015).

Salience of national policy and the role of central transfers in legislative vote choice have been structured into Argentina's political party system. The Peronist and Radical parties have historically been built upon a "dual logic" of ideologically driven voters and politicians in the most populated provinces and secured by the votes of the less-populated, over-represented interior provinces (Gibson 1996; Gibson and Calvo 2000). The votes of the populated provinces are not easy to gain or keep, due to electoral rules and voter incentives, so parties rely on the less populated provinces to deliver victories at the polls (Calvo and Murillo 2004). This relationship between the populated and less populated provinces is made possible by central transfers (Gibson and Calvo 2000) and by the reality that vote choice in most of the interior provinces may be driven, directly or indirectly, by central transfers more than provincial or national policies (Remmer and Gélineau 2003). If national politicians know that central transfers are more important to their political fate (because they are more important to provincial party leaders than national economic policy) then national policy will be secondary to the interests of those able to deliver central transfers. National social policy should suffer accordingly.

In Argentina, parties are the mechanism by which politicians lobby for and secure those resources. The party system reduces the likely volatility of policymaking that would otherwise result from the extreme provincial heterogeneity informed by regional economic disparities. Parties are long-standing agreements that benefit members across regions. Politicians from provinces interested in affecting national policy are able to form relatively stable coalitions through national parties despite high regional inequality. Transfers are the glue that holds these disparate provinces together in party coalitions. Politicians interested in securing central transfers are useful in the party coalition because they reduce uncertainty in forming majorities for policy reform. Parties are widely known to reduce transaction costs to agreements over time—Argentine parties serve this purpose in securing votes in exchange for national resources (Spiller et al. 2003).

In Gibson's seminal 1996 book, he articulates the foundation for these political coalitions in Argentina—i.e., elites in the most developed provinces forming alliances with interior politicians keen on central resources above national policy. He argues in a different context,

> The provincial party leaders … were prone to fragmentation and political bickering. They were non-ideological. Their commitment to higher ideals began and ended with the protection of local political fiefs and regional economic interests. They could be easily bought by the central government with offers of patronage-laden provincial government posts.
>
> (Gibson 1996, p. 88)

Importantly, this suggests that fragmentation of interests upon which the party system is built in Argentina is largely non-ideological with respect to redistribution. By this account, the majority coalition of the poor and low income labor that would prefer redistribution has not had an effective party mechanism by which to advance its interests because of the dominance of the regional cleavage.

Gibson attributes challenges in national party building to regional factionalization and to intra-elite conflict that has precluded national policymaking based on ideology. This is no doubt true—the interests of the outward-oriented provinces (especially the capital and business interests in the province of Buenos Aires) have fundamentally conflicted with those provinces more in favor of protectionist policies and statism, including the relatively developed provinces in Córdoba and Santa Fe, among others. This regional chasm challenges every party in Argentina and results in dualism in the foundation of the mass parties in Argentina (Gibson and Calvo 2000; Gibson 1996). What is less often recognized has been a fragile solution to this challenge (central transfers) that has enabled party building and reasonably non-ideological legislative bodies (Diaz-Cayeros 2006).

Argentina's party system is fragmented, territorialized, and to some degree unrepresentative of its population. In particular, Gibson (1996) has noted that despite a notable constituency, there has not been a successful broad-based conservative party in Argentina since the advent of widespread suffrage in the early twentieth century.[19] Rather, parties compete to varying degrees on the left, often with populist rather than programmatic appeals. Regional ideological divides are at the center of this truncated party system, according to Gibson. He argues that conservative politicians have been unable to form a cohesive national party because the interests of the regions vary so widely. For example, while conservative politicians in Buenos Aires seek open markets for their export-oriented products and foreign investment, their counterparts in the interior seek protection. The center and left, primarily through the Peronist party, have overcome this challenge on the right by co-opting politicians in the interior (including regional parties) with the use of regional transfers and by appealing to voters with a combination of redistributive policy promises, patronage, and clientelist exchange.

Importantly, regional parties also play an important role in Argentine national politics. They regularly have significant representation in the Chamber of Deputies and in the Senate.[20] They are commonly part of the majority coalition in the legislature. Nearly every province has regional parties that have regional legislative representation and some also hold governorships. Governorships are important to politicians in the national legislature, even when they are from a different party, because governors provide jobs back in the province after they finish their terms in Congress. Regional parties further complicate and regionalize the already ideologically fragmented Argentine party system and limit coherent efforts to advance redistributive policy.

Conclusion

In this chapter I have emphasized how electoral constituencies and rules relate to redistributive policy through their role in coalition-building in the party system. In strongly territorial systems, coalition-building at the national level often places politicians with very different regional interests in the same parties. Overcoming regional vetoes and regionally informed ideological heterogeneity, where possible, must often be done with geographically targeted pork or regional transfers.

In the next chapter, I address the role of executives in redistributive policy. Executive system design is not as straightforwardly linked to redistributive policy except through its effects on party cohesion. However, executives, as visible representatives of their party, may also be important agenda setters on redistributive policy even apart from their legislative delegation. Again, Argentina, the USA, and Germany vary dramatically in the role of the executive in redistributive policy.

Notes

1 Somewhat outside the scope of this discussion is Rehfeld's critique of the often-espoused virtues of territorial representation. This includes, most commonly, that territorial representation allows for a close accountability between voters and politicians in smaller, geographically compact constituencies. The accountability mechanism is justified at the local level for local policies, but very limited for national legislative elections in which voters number in the hundreds of thousands. Importantly, for Rehfeld, representation should reflect the common good and territorial representation (or any other constituency grouping other than a national one) would not incentivize representation of the common good but a particular group.

2 This ignores the details by which voters may cast ballots that may also influence party-line voting, such as ballots organized by office or party (Engstrom and Kernell 2005).

3 Parties may affect the likelihood of one candidate or another winning the primary, however, through selective funding or endorsement. Interest groups certainly try to influence which of the parties' candidates end up on the ballot.

4 Rehfeld (2005) emphasizes that researchers need to be careful to distinguish the effects of territorial constituencies from the voting rule. Territorial constituencies are both independent of, and interact with, voting rules. He argues, for instance, "Conceptually, proportional systems should be understood as cases in which an electoral constituency is defined simultaneously at the moment one votes. By contrast, in territorial systems the electoral constituency is defined prior to an election" (p. 21).

5 Mixed-member systems, a combination of PR and SMD, are an intermediate case, discussed in detail in the German case example.

6 A fourth mechanism, not discussed extensively in this chapter, is the coalition formation across poor, middle, and rich groups. Iversen and Soskice (2006) argue that SMD (or majoritarian systems more broadly) result in lower redistribution because middle class voters cannot trust poor voters not to expropriate wealth at the highest levels if they capture a majority. Accordingly, in SMD systems the middle classes join with the rich for center right majorities. In PR systems, middle class groups can have sway in the government coalition to direct redistribution in their interests. Center-left coalitions of this type are common in PR systems.

7 I have no a priori expectation of whether region-based parties will have an effect on redistribution at the region level except where central policy affects regional policies.

8 Unlike in the House, however, every Senator shares the district with another politician that is elected at a different time.

9 See Cox and Katz (2002) on the electoral consequences of district manipulation, also known as gerrymandering.

10 Retiring Maryland Senator Barbara Mikulski described the independence that comes with not facing reelection. When considering running for reelection, she asked herself, "Do I spend my time raising money, or do I spend my time raising hell? Do I focus on my election, or do I focus on the next generation?" (www.npr.org/2015/03/02/390245024/sen-mikulski-ground-breaker-for-women-legislators-wont-seek-reelection)

11 See Shugart et al. (2005) on personal vote incentives in proportional systems.

12 This could also work to weaken the PR side if parties used PR members (through constituency service perhaps) to boost success in SMD seats. Running for SMD seats in hopeless districts is considered good service to the party that is rewarded in their future career (Ismayr 2001).

13 Strong fiscal power of the national government also increases the likelihood of two national parties in the US case (Chhibber and Kollman 2004).

14 www.infratest-dimap.de/?id=282.

15 Also historically speaking the US had some degree of multipartism at the national level, including two House seats held by the Socialist Party of America and a notable presidential candidate, Eugene V. Debs.

16 The Affordable Care Act is discussed in more detail in Chapter 6.

17 www.cnbc.com/id/49726054.

18 Elites survey, University of Salamanca. Questionnaire 51, 2003–07 legislative session. http://americo.usal.es/oir/elites.

19 In a comparative chapter, Gibson also shows the historic weakness of conservative parties in Brazil, Chile, Colombia, Mexico and Peru due to regionalism.

20 Examples include Neuquén People's Movement, Fueguino People's Movement (TDF), Frente Cívico por Santiago (Santiago del Estero), and Frente Cívico Córdoba.

References

Abramowitz, Alan, Brad Alexander, and Matthew Gunning. "Incumbency, Redistricting, and the Decline of Competition in US House Elections." *Journal of Politics* 68, no. 1 (2006): 75–88.

Adams, James, and Samuel Merrill. "Candidate and Party Strategies in Two-Stage Elections Beginning with a Primary." *American Journal of Political Science* 52, no. 2 (2008): 344–59.

Aldrich, John Herbert. *Why Parties?: The Origin and Transformation of Party Politics in America*. Cambridge University Press, 1995.

Ames, Barry. "Electoral Rules, Constituency Pressures, and Pork Barrel: Bases of Voting in the Brazilian Congress." *The Journal of Politics* 57, no. 2 (1995): 324–43.

Amorim Neto, Octavio, and Gary Cox. "Electoral Institutions, Cleavage Structures, and the Number of Parties." *American Journal of Political Science* 41, no. 1 (1997): 149–74.

Ardanaz, Martin, and Carlos Scartascini. "Inequality and Personal Income Taxation the Origins and Effects of Legislative Malapportionment." *Comparative Political Studies* 46, no. 12 (2013): 1636–63.

Bawn, Kathleen, and Michael Thies. "A Comparative Theory of Electoral Incentives Representing the Unorganized under PR, Plurality and Mixed-Member Electoral Systems." *Journal of Theoretical Politics* 15, no. 1 (2003): 5–32.

Benton, Allyson Lucinda. "Presidentes Fuertes, Provincias Poderosas: La Economía Política De La Construcción De Partidos En El Sistema Federal Argentino." *Política y Gobierno* 10, no. 1 (2003): 103–20.

Beramendi, Pablo. *The Political Geography of Inequality: Regions and Redistribution*. Cambridge University Press, 2012.

Beramendi, Pablo and Melissa Rogers. *Geography, Inequality, and Capacity*. Paper presented at the Conflict and Inequality workshop, ETH Zurich, April 16–18, 2015.

Beramendi, Pablo, Melissa Rogers, and Alberto Diaz-Cayeros. *Barriers to the Left Turn: Distributive Tensions in Developing Federations*. Duke University, Claremont Graduate University, and Stanford University, 2015.

Blais, André, and Louis Massicotte. "Electoral Systems." *Comparing Democracies: Elections and Voting in Global Perspective*, edited by Lawrence LeDuc, Richard Niemi and Pippa Norris. Sage Publications, New York, 1996.

Bobbio, Norberto. *Left and Right: The Significance of a Political Distinction*. University of Chicago Press, 1996.

Brancati, Dawn. "The Origins and Strengths of Regional Parties." *British Journal of Political Science* 38, no. 1 (2008): 135–59.

Burner, David. *The Politics of Provincialism: The Democratic Party in Transition, 1918–1932*. Knopf, New York, 1968.

Cain, Bruce, John Ferejohn, and Morris Fiorina. *The Personal Vote: Constituency Service and Electoral Independence*. Harvard University Press, 1987.

Calvo, Ernesto, and Maria Victoria Murillo. "Who Delivers? Partisan Clients in the Argentine Electoral Market." *American Journal of Political Science* 48, no. 4 (2004): 742–57.

Caramani, Daniele. *The Nationalization of Politics: The Formation of National Electorates and Party Systems in Western Europe*. Cambridge University Press, 2004.

Carey, John M. "Competing Principals, Political Institutions, and Party Unity in Legislative Voting." *American Journal of Political Science* 51, no. 1 (2007): 92–107.

Carey, John M., and Matthew Soberg Shugart. "Incentives to Cultivate a Personal Vote: A Rank Ordering of Electoral Formulas." *Electoral studies* 14, no. 4 (1995): 417–39.

Chhibber, Pradeep, and Ken Kollman. *The Formation of National Party Systems: Federalism and Party Competition in Canada, Great Britain, India, and the USA*. Princeton University Press, Princeton NJ, 2004.

Cox, Gary W. *The Efficient Secret: The Cabinet and the Development of Political Parties in Victorian England*. Cambridge University Press, 1987.

Cox, Gary W. *Making Votes Count: Strategic Coordination in the World's Electoral Systems*. Vol. 7: Cambridge University Press, 1997.

Cox, Gary W., and Jonathan N. Katz. *Elbridge Gerry's Salamander: The Electoral Consequences of the Reapportionment Revolution*. Cambridge University Press, 2002.

Cox, Gary W., and Mathew D. McCubbins. *Setting the Agenda: Responsible Party Government in the US House of Representatives*. Cambridge University Press, 2005.

Crisp, Brian F. "Incentives in Mixed-Member Electoral Systems General Election Laws, Candidate Selection Procedures, and Cameral Rules." *Comparative Political Studies* 40, no. 12 (2007): 1460–85.

Crisp, Brian F., Santiago Olivella, and Joshua D. Potter. "Party-System Nationalization and the Scope of Public Policy the Importance of Cross-District Constituency Similarity." *Comparative Political Studies* 46, no. 4 (2013): 431–56.

Diaz-Cayeros, Alberto. *Federalism, Fiscal Authority, and Centralization in Latin America*. Cambridge University Press, 2006.

Downs, Anthony. "An Economic Theory of Democracy." *The Journal of Political Economy* 65, no. 2 (1957): 135–50.

Duverger, Maurice. *Political Parties: Their Organization and Activity in the Modern State*. Methuen, London, 1959.

Eaton, Kent. "Fiscal Policy Making in the Argentine Legislature." In *Legislative Politics in Latin America*, edited by Scott Morgenstern and Benito Nacif. Cambridge University Press (2002): 287–314.

Engstrom, Erik J., and Samuel Kernell. "Manufactured Responsiveness: The Impact of State Electoral Laws on Unified Party Control of the Presidency and House of Representatives, 1840–1940." *American Journal of Political Science* 49, no. 3 (2005): 531–49.

Engstrom, Erik J., and Georg Vanberg. "Assessing the Allocation of Pork: Evidence from Congressional Earmarks." *American Politics Research* 38, no. 6 (2010): 959–85.

Fenno, Richard F. *Home Style: House Members in Their Districts*. Little, Brown and Co, Boston, 1978.

Gailmard, Sean, and Jeffery A. Jenkins. "Negative Agenda Control in the Senate and House: Fingerprints of Majority Party Power." *Journal of Politics* 69, no. 3 (2007): 689–700.

Gervasoni, Carlos. "A Rentier Theory of Subnational Regimes." *World Politics* 62, no. 2 (2010): 302–40.

Gerring, John, Strom C. Thacker, and Carola Moreno. "Centripetal Democratic Governance: A Theory and Global Inquiry." *American Political Science Review* 99, no. 4 (2005): 567–81.

Gibson, Edward L. *Class and Conservative Parties: Argentina in Comparative Perspective*. Johns Hopkins University Press, Baltimore MD, 1996.

Gibson, Edward L. "The Populist Road to Market Reform: Policy and Electoral Coalitions in Mexico and Argentina." *World Politics* 49, no. 3 (1997): 339–70.

Gibson, Edward L., and Ernesto Calvo. "Federalism and Low-Maintenance Constituencies: Territorial Dimensions of Economic Reform in Argentina." *Studies in Comparative International Development* 35, no. 3 (2000): 32–55.

Grimmer, Justin. "Appropriators Not Position Takers: The Distorting Effects of Electoral Incentives on Congressional Representation." *American Journal of Political Science* 57, no. 3 (2013): 624–42.

Huber, John, and Michael Ting. "Redistribution, Pork, and Elections." *Journal of the European Economic Association* 11, no. 6 (2013): 1382–403.

Ismayr, Wolfgang. *Der Deutsche Bundestag Im Politischen System Der Bundesrepublik Deutschland, 2*. Aufl, Opladen, 2001.

Iversen, Torben, and David Soskice. "Electoral Institutions and the Politics of Coalitions: Why Some Democracies Redistribute More Than Others." *American Political Science Review* 100, no. 2 (2006): 165–181.

Jones, Mark, Sebastián Saiegh, Pablo Spiller, and Mariano Tommasi. "Amateur Legislators–Professional Politicians: The Consequences of Party-Centered Electoral Rules in a Federal System." *American Journal of Political Science* 46, no. 3 (2002): 656–69.

Katznelson, Ira, Kim Geiger, and Daniel Kryder. "Limiting Liberalism: The Southern Veto in Congress, 1933–1950." *Political Science Quarterly* 108, no. 2 (1993): 283–306.

Keefer, Philip, and Stuti Khemani. "When Do Legislators Pass on Pork? The Role of Political Parties in Determining Legislator Effort." *American Political Science Review* 103, no. 1 (2009): 99–112.

Kernell, Samuel, Gary Jacobson, and Thad Kousser. *The Logic of American Politics*. CQ Press, Thosuand Oaks CA, 2011.

Kitschelt, Herbert. "Linkages between Citizens and Politicians in Democratic Polities." *Comparative Political Studies* 33, no. 6–7 (2000): 845–79.

Kitschelt, Herbert. "Partisan Competition and Welfare State Retrenchment: When Do Politicians Choose Unpopular Policies." *The New Politics of the Welfare State*, edited by Paul Pierson. Oxford University Press, 2001: 265–302.

Lancaster, Thomas, and W. David Patterson. "Comparative Pork Barrel Politics Perceptions from the West German Bundestag." *Comparative Political Studies* 22, no. 4 (1990): 458–77.

Lazarus, Jeffrey, and Amy Steigerwalt. "Different Houses: The Distribution of Earmarks in the US House and Senate." *Legislative Studies Quarterly* 34, no. 3 (2009): 347–73.

Lee, Frances E. "Representation and Public Policy: The Consequences of Senate Apportionment for the Geographic Distribution of Federal Funds." *The Journal of Politics* 60, no. 1 (1998): 34–62.

Lee, Frances E., and Bruce I. Oppenheimer. *Sizing up the Senate: The Unequal Consequences of Equal Representation*. University of Chicago Press, 1999.

Lee, Dong-wook, and Melissa Rogers. *Comparing Inequalities: Regional and Interpersonal Income Disparity, Institutions, and Government Spending*. Manuscript, Claremont Graduate University CA, 2015.

Lipset, Seymour, and Stein Rokkan. *Cleavage Structures, Party Systems, and Voter Alignments: An Introduction*. The Free Press, New York, 1967.

Manow, Philip. "Germany: Cooperative Federalism and the Overgrazing of the Fiscal Commons." In *Federalism and the Welfare State*, edited by Herbert Obinger, Stephan Liebfried and Frances Castles. Cambridge University Press (2005): 222–62.

Manow, Philip. "Electoral Rules and Legislative Turnover: Evidence from Germany's Mixed Electoral System." *West European Politics* 30, no. 1 (2007): 195–207.

Micozzi, Juan Pablo. "Does Electoral Accountability Make a Difference? Direct Elections, Career Ambition, and Legislative Performance in the Argentine Senate." *The Journal of Politics* 75, no. 1 (2013): 137–49.

Micozzi, Juan Pablo. "From House to Home: Strategic Bill Drafting in Multilevel Systems with Non-Static Ambition." *The Journal of Legislative Studies* 20, no. 3 (2014): 265–84.

Milesi-Ferretti, Gian Maria, Roberto Perotti, and Massimo Rostagno. "Electoral Systems and Public Spending." *The Quarterly Journal of Economics* 117, no. 2 (2002): 609–57.

Morgenstern, Scott, Stephen Swindle, and Andrea Castagnola. "Party Nationalization and Institutions." *The Journal of Politics* 71, no. 4 (2009): 1322–41.

Nohlen, Dieter, and Rainer-Olaf Schultze. *Wahlsysteme Der Welt*. Piper, 1978.

Olssen, Erik. "Southern Senators and Reform Issues in the 1920s: A Paradox Unraveled." In *The South Is Another Land: Essays on the Twentieth-Century South*, edited by Bruce Clayton and John A Salmond. Praeger Pub Text, Santa Barbara CA, 1987.

Pitlik, Hans, Friedrich Schneider, and Harald Strotmann. "Legislative Malapportionment and the Politicization of Germany's Intergovernmental Transfer System." *Public Finance Review* 34, no. 6 (2006): 637–62.

Poole, Keith and Howard Rosenthal. "D-Nominate after 10 Years: A Comparative Update to Congress: A Political-Economic History of Roll-Call Voting." *Legislative Studies Quarterly* 26, no. 1 (2001): 5–29.

Rae, Douglas. *The Political Consequences of Electoral Laws*. Yale University Press, New Haven CT, 1971.

Rehfeld, Andrew. *The Concept of Constituency: Political Representation, Democratic Legitimacy, and Institutional Design*. Cambridge University Press, 2005.

Remmer, Karen and François Gélineau. "Subnational Electoral Choice Economic and Referendum Voting in Argentina, 1983–1999." *Comparative Political Studies* 36, no. 7 (2003): 801–21.

Roberts, Geoffrey. "The German Federal Republic: The Two-Lane Route to Bonn" in *Candidate Selection in Comparative Perspective*, edited by M. Gallagher and M. Marsh: Sage Publications, London, 1988: 94–118.

Rodden, Jonathan. "The Geographic Distribution of Political Preferences." *Annual Review of Political Science* 13 (2010): 321–40.

Roemer, John. "Why the Poor Do Not Expropriate the Rich: An Old Argument in New Garb." *Journal of Public Economics* 70, no. 3 (1998): 399–424.

Rogers, Melissa, and Dong-wook Lee. *Electoral Geography, Inequality, and Representation*. Manuscript, Claremont Graduate University CA, 2015.

Rohde, David W. "Risk-Bearing and Progressive Ambition: The Case of Members of the United States House of Representatives." *American Journal of Political Science* 23, no. 1 (1979): 1–26.

Samuels, David. "Pork Barreling Is Not Credit Claiming or Advertising: Campaign Finance and the Sources of the Personal Vote in Brazil." *The Journal of Politics* 64, no. 3 (2002): 845–63.

Samuels, David, and Richard Snyder. "The Value of a Vote: Malapportionment in Comparative Perspective." *British Journal of Political Science* 31, no. 4 (2001): 651–71.

Scharpf, Fritz Wilhelm, Bernd Reissert, and Fritz Schnabel. *Politverflechtung: Theorie Und Empirie Des Kooperativen Föderalismus in Der Bundesrepublik*. Scriptor Verlag, 1976.

Schneider, Friedrich, Hans Pitlik, Harald Strotmann, and Günther Schmid. "On the Politicization of Intergovernmental Fiscal Relations in Germany after Unification." Working Paper, Department of Economics, Johannes Kepler University of Linz, 2001.

Schwarz, Peter. "Deficits and Divided Governments: The Case of the German 'Bundesrat'." *Constitutional Political Economy* 17, no. 2 (2006): 87–101.

Shugart, Matthew Søberg, Melody Ellis Valdini, and Kati Suominen. "Looking for Locals: Voter Information Demands and Personal Vote-Earning Attributes of Legislators under Proportional Representation." *American Journal of Political Science* 49, no. 2 (2005): 437–49.

Sieberer, Ulrich. "Behavioral Consequences of Mixed Electoral Systems: Deviating Voting Behavior of District and List Mps in the German Bundestag." *Electoral Studies* 29, no. 3 (2010): 484–96.

Snyder, J. M., and S. Levitt. "The Impact of Federal Spending on House Election Outcomes." *Journal of Political Economy* 105, no. 1 (1997): 30–53.

Spiller, Pablo, Ernesto Stein, and Mariano Tommasi. "Political Institutions, Policymaking Processes and Policy Outcomes: An Intertemporal Transactions Framework." *Design Paper* 1 (2003).

Squire, Peverill. "Challengers in US Senate Elections." *Legislative Studies Quarterly* 14, no. 4 (1989): 531–47.

Stepan, Alfred. "Toward a New Comparative Politics of Federalism, Multinationalism, and Democracy: Beyond Rikerian Federalism." In *Federalism and Democracy in Latin America*, edited by Edward Gibson. Johns Hopkins University Press, Baltimore MD, (2004): 29–84.

Stokes, Donald. "Parties and the Nationalization of Electoral Forces." in *The American Party Systems: Stages of Political* Development, edited by William Nisbet Chambers and Walter Dean Burnham. Oxford University Press (1967): 182–202.

Stratmann, Thomas, and Martin Baur. "Plurality Rule, Proportional Representation, and the German Bundestag: How Incentives to Pork-Barrel Differ across Electoral Systems." *American Journal of Political Science* 46, no. 3 (2002): 506–14.

Tavits, Margit, and Joshua D. Potter. "The Effect of Inequality and Social Identity on Party Strategies." *American Journal of Political Science* 59, no. 3 (2015): 744–58.

Weeden, Jason, and Robert Kurzban. *The Hidden Agenda of the Political Mind: How Self-Interest Shapes Our Opinions and Why We Won't Admit It*. Princeton University Press, Princeton NJ, 2014.

Weitz-Shapiro, Rebecca. "What Wins Votes: Why Some Politicians Opt out of Clientelism." *American Journal of Political Science* 56, no. 3 (2012): 568–83.

Ziegfeld, Adam. "Coalition Government and Party System Change: Explaining the Rise of Regional Political Parties in India." *Comparative Politics* 45, no. 1 (2012): 69–87.

6 Presidents and Redistribution

Introduction

Executive selection, unlike federalism and electoral rules, does not have an obvious territorial component. I have emphasized the role of territorial constituencies as an underlying causal mechanism linking certain political institutions to lower fiscal redistribution. However, presidents represent a national constituency and have long been believed to offset parochial concerns of legislators (Howell et al. 2013; Nzelibe 2006). Moreover, executive selection, including presidentialism, can contribute to the nationalization of otherwise localized party systems (Cox 1997). For their part, voters are most attentive to presidential races, based on levels of turnout, knowledge, and interest, thus indicating a nationalization effect of presidential elections (Claggett et al. 1984). Moreover, presidents may serve as "bridging" figures able to cobble together diverse constituencies in otherwise fragmented party systems (Shugart 1999).

Presidentialism has, nevertheless, been linked to lower levels of fiscal redistribution and apparent inattention to egalitarian reform (Huber et al. 1993).[1] The primary mechanism thought to discourage redistribution in presidential system is veto players. Presidential systems place more decision-makers at the table, reducing the likelihood of significant policy change. Associated gridlock that results from separation of powers and purpose hasten the advances of the majority coalition seeking national redistributive reform. Figure 6.1 shows that presidential systems do appear to be below the bar, at least among the most affluent nations, in redistributive outcomes for their levels of inequality.

The link between executives and redistribution is more complex than just added veto players, however. I argue that presidentialism, in particular, may influence redistributive outcomes according to all three mechanisms established in Chapter 3. First, where the race is territorialized, most notably in the US Electoral College, the majoritarian contest can encourage delivery of local goods to swing districts (Kriner and Reeves 2015). Even where the presidential contest is based on popular support, presidents have incentives to direct targeted geographic spending to specific districts to build a majority coalition within the legislature. This support is usually achieved in parliamentary systems through party discipline and national parties' control of politicians' career paths. Second, presidential systems are clearly endowed with more veto players, decreasing the

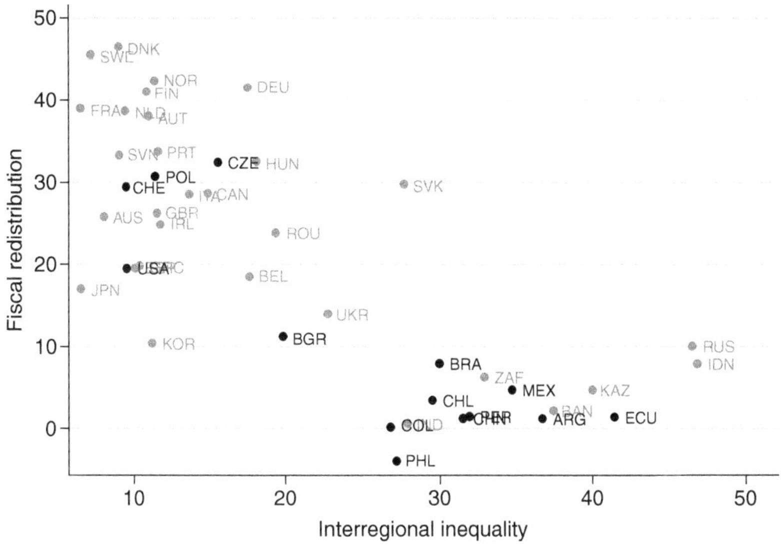

Figure 6.1 Fiscal Redistribution and Regional Inequality in Presidiential Systems (sources: fiscal redistribution (Solt 2014); interregional inequality (Rogers and Lee 2015); presidentialism (Persson and Tabellini 1999)).

Note

Presidential nations are in black, parliamentary states are in gray. Data from 2005. Fiscal redistribution is measured by the percentage difference in the national Gini coefficient between pre- and post-tax and transfer inequality. Interregional inequality is the adjusted gini coefficient of regional GDP per capita.

likelihood of policy reform of any type, including centralized redistribution. Legislators with district-specific interests are among those veto gates. Separation of powers also decreases the chances that a leftist majority can control all branches of government (Becher 2012). Third, presidentialism influences parties and party systems in important ways (Samuels 2002). Separate elections and survival decreases incentives to develop strong party organizations oriented primarily toward national issues. The ideological and regional fragmentation of many parties in presidential systems impedes efforts by pro-redistributive coalitions to advance reform.

Defining Executive Systems

Executive systems may be usefully grouped as parliamentary or presidential, although there is considerable variation within each group as well as hybrids between them.[2] Two primary features separate presidential and parliamentary systems—differences in origin and survival of the executive, on the one hand, and of legislative branches, on the other (Shugart and Carey 1992).

In parliamentary systems, the executive branch is selected from within the legislative branch. If the executive branch is dissolved, the legislature must also conduct new elections. Thus, the executive and legislative branches in parliamentary systems have fused origin and survival, rendering the two bodies interdependent and largely inseparable. In presidential systems, the legislative and executive branches are separately elected. In presidential systems, both bodies have finite terms in office, and there is no straightforward mechanism of dissolution to link their survival (Linz 1992).[3] Separate origin means presidents and legislators do not depend on each other to gain office. This allows for some degree of autonomy between parties in the different institutions and among individuals within the parties. Separation of survival means that legislators and presidents with different policy preferences have fewer reasons to compromise because legislative failure does not directly threaten their position. However, the fates of politicians are somewhat interlocked within the party system even in presidential systems, providing varying degrees of motivation to overcome preference heterogeneity (Hicken and Stoll 2011).

The origin and survival of the executive and legislative branches are relevant to policy change of any type (not just redistribution) because of their effects on party unity. Parliamentarism is expected to increase party unity because of the high costs of failure to coordinate in parliamentary systems (Diermeier and Feddersen 1998; Cox 1987). In parliamentary bodies, policymaking power is delegated to the executive branch comprised of the prime minister and cabinet. Attaining and holding the executive is crucial to policymaking. Legislative "back benchers" not part of the executive branch play a limited policymaking role and opposition members' policy relevance is even more limited (Lijphart 1999). The concentration of powers in the executive branch, and the threat of dissolution, motivates the cabinet members to enforce strict discipline so that they can retain their positions. It also motivates ambitious politicians to strive for the executive branch, which leads them to be goods agents of the party leadership since it allocates cabinet positions (Bowler et al. 1999). Both strong discipline and cabinet-seeking politicians thus encourage party homogeneity.

Parliamentary systems also encourage party homogenization through selection of politicians. Because party discipline is critical for attaining and maintaining the executive branch in parliamentary systems, parties have strong incentivizes to cultivate loyal members through the party organization. Parliamentary systems, moreover, have few ex post mechanisms to oversee the actions of politicians, so choosing party agents that will act in the interest of the leadership and its constituency is critical (Strom 2000). Parliamentary systems, in short, necessitate strong parties, both in government and opposition, and we see almost perfect party discipline in nearly all parliaments.[4]

At a fundamental level, parties in presidential systems have much weaker incentives to pay the "costs" of party unity. Party homogenization is costly to members who must conform to party edicts even where their own interests, or those of their regions, conflict. Coherent party platforms require that members all over the country and across different levels of government adopt similar stances. In parliamentary governments, these ideological differences are suppressed because they select loyal members. In a presidential system such as that of the USA, policy divergence is tolerated because of the importance of cultivating votes across heterogeneous constituencies that view their interests in regional terms (Rae 1971). Take, for example, the current debate over the Keystone Pipeline, a proposed pipeline that would ship crude oil from Canada to the Gulf port of New Orleans. (Rightist) Republicans generally support the pipeline as beneficial to the economy and reducing US dependence on foreign oil. In general, the Democrats oppose the Keystone on environmental grounds and prefer cultivation of "green" energy. However, for certain Democrats, notably Senator Mary Landrieu of Louisiana, the pipeline is strongly favored by constituents who view it as in the interest of their state.[5] These intraparty differences in ideology and policy preferences, particularly those that come from distinct regional economies, are common in presidential systems with strong territorial constituencies. Policymaking in presidential systems thus requires considerable bargaining to enact major reforms.

Unlike in parliamentary systems, the balance between legislative and executive powers varies considerably in presidential systems (Shugart and Carey 1992). If the presidential office is weak, party leaders have fewer incentives to impose strict party discipline either to win that office through elections, or to support the president in legislative matters.[6] The most well known presidential system, the USA, reserves the majority of powers for the legislative branch. In comparative perspective, the US president has rather weak and primarily reactive constitutional powers. In many other presidential systems, executives have much broader powers, including rights to initiate, revise, and veto policy, either unilaterally or with support of the legislature. Importantly, in many presidential systems, the executive branch is also the agenda-setter for budget policies. Redistributive policy often requires budget outlays, meaning the president will strongly shape the extent and nature of redistribution in these systems.

Presidential systems also do not rely so heavily on selection mechanisms to choose a chief executive. In parliamentary systems, the cultivation of a political career is a long-term project, requiring commitment over time to party activities. Parliamentary parties know their members well, and the individuals with a chance to become prime minister tend to be particularly entrenched within the party. Presidential candidates declare their own candidacy and in many cases openly compete with co partisans for the nomination of their party. With multiple decision-makers evaluating every policy, presidential systems and their parties rely more on ex post accountability mechanisms to weed out bad ideas and bad seeds (Strom 2000). The executive selection process is not as effectively controlled by the party in presidential as it is in parliamentary systems.

Related to this, the presidential contest is one strongly shaped by the dynamics of the personal vote. In addition to policy stances, presidential candidates attract support with personal characteristics, including charisma, career background, morality, and even physical appearance (Bartels 1996; Glass 1985). Not surprisingly, presidential systems, and the presidential office in particular, are notable for attracting outsider candidates and celebrities (Linz 1990). The autonomy of candidates in presidential systems contributes to ideological heterogeneity and lower levels of discipline in parties, relative to parliamentary systems.

Executive Systems and Redistribution: Existing Explanations

A broad consensus in the academic literature suggests that presidents are in the most suitable position within presidential systems to consider what is best for the nation as a whole (Nzelibe 2006). Parochial and short-sighted legislators do not have incentives to consider the interests of the majority of the nation's citizens. For example, Howell et al. (2013) argue that "presidents focus on the national implications of public policies while members of Congress monitor the effects of public policy on both the nation as a whole and their local constituencies" (p. 3132). This literature tends to focus on budget discipline as what is best for the nation, as discussed below in the case of Argentina. However, it might extend in theory to presidents responding to a national demand for government intervention to reduce inequality, such as Democratic presidents' efforts to reform health care in the USA.

Empirically, presidential systems are associated with lower government spending and lower redistribution (Persson and Tabellini 2003; Persson et al. 1997; Lizzeri and Persico 2001). While this relationship may have a theoretical basis, it is certainly plausible that presidential systems just happen to be in places in which redistribution is particularly unlikely. For example, presidential systems are most common in developing nations, including those with very high levels of land and income inequality, such as Latin America and Africa (Shugart and Carey 1992). While presidentialism may contribute to lower redistribution in those cases, it would be difficult to disentangle the structural conditions in those nations from the effects of institutions. Moreover, the design of presidential policymaking may be an endogenous response to concerns over distribution (Baldez and Carey 1999). If presidentialism is designed specifically to limit redistribution, then it will be particularly difficult to isolate the role of the executive from the power dynamics that lead to the design of presidentialism in the first place.

Unlike federal fiscal arrangements, which are very likely endogenous to interpersonal and interregional inequality, executive choice is not so straightforwardly linked to existing inequality. Adoption of parliamentary versus presidential forms appears primarily to reflect colonial history and regional trends (Shugart and Carey 1992; Gerring et al. 2009). However, the variation in powers of the executive and legislative branches may reflect concerns with societal heterogeneity, including regional and class cleavages. In this sense, presidents may be endowed with strong powers to overcome social divides that emerge in the party system (Shugart 1999).

As discussed above, the most frequent reason put forward for why presidential systems are linked to lower redistribution is separation of powers. Presidentialism has a strong status quo bias because reform must pass through multiple veto points (Tsebelis 2002). Presidentialism provides more points in the legislative process that representatives of the anti-redistributive coalition can capture to block reform (Huber et al. 1993). Persson et al. (1997) argue that competition between politicians in presidential systems limits collusion, and thus rent-seeking. Accordingly spending overall is lower in presidential than in parliamentary systems, including in redistributive categories. In all of these explanations, increased veto points is the reason why we expect lower redistribution in presidential systems.

Separation of powers is not the only theoretical connection between presidentialism and lower redistribution, however. Presidentialism is also linked to lower party discipline. As stressed throughout this analysis, strong parties are vital tools for redistributively oriented groups to advance their policy goals. By failing to inspire the same level of party coherence and discipline as demanded by the incentives of parliamentary systems, presidentialism may limit redistribution because of associated heterogeneity and fragmentation within the party system. Of particular relevance is the fact that parties in presidential systems have less motivation to quash regional divides (Brancati 2008).

Becher (2012) argues that government partisanship is a channel whereby the president's separate origin and survival lead to lower redistribution. His model demonstrates that unified leftist governments are more likely in parliamentary systems. Leftist governments are more often forced to share power under presidential systems due to the separation of survival between the legislative and executive branches. Leftist parties are typically more willing and able to implement redistribution, so parliamentary systems do more to reduce inequality because unified leftist control is more common. The separation of survival effect is also critical to prime ministers enacting redistributive reform. Chief executives in parliamentary systems can threaten dissolution, which gives the prime minister greater bargaining power vis-à-vis the legislature, compared to that in presidential systems. This control extends to all parties in the coalition, who face the risk of being shut out of government if they reject the government's redistributive policy proposal. Where redistribution requires policy change, therefore, presidential systems should have lower redistribution than that of parliamentary systems.

Existing theories thus explain the empirical link between presidentialism and lower redistribution as emerging from veto players and, by extension, to greater barriers to unified leftist control in these systems. In the following sections, I argue that executive selection relates to the likelihood of redistribution through the three mechanisms at the core of the book: geographically targeted distribution, territorial veto players, and fragmentation of the majority coalition along regional lines. In particular, I discuss ways in which territorial politics can play a role in presidential system dynamics, ones they are less likely to play in parliamentary systems, and how this can undermine efforts at interpersonal redistribution.

Presidents and Territorial Targeting

Presidentialism may be inimical to redistribution if scarce national resources are used on territorially allocated goods rather than social spending. Presidential elections and presidential–legislative bargaining are more likely than parliamentarism to result in the targeting of national resources to territorial constituencies, rather than spending that spans the nation, due to "election targeting" (distributing resources to affect electoral outcomes) and "legislative targeting" (distributing benefits to influence legislative outcomes) (Cox 2009). Presidential elections, as majoritarian contests, depend on the vote differential around 50 percent.[7] This provides incentives for candidates to target constituencies to pass the 50 percent threshold. Presidential–executive bargaining also incentivizes the targeting of resources to assist in the elections of co-partisan legislators that provide crucial support for presidents' legislative programs. For any given vote, moreover, presidents cannot count on the support of a majority in the legislature, unlike in parliamentarism. Presidents may need to distribute resources to targeted localities in order to win support of parochial legislators. These dynamics are less likely in parliamentary systems because of fused origin and survival of the government (executive) and the legislature.

It is important to recognize that most scholarly research assumes that presidents have strong incentives to limit targeted geographic spending relative to legislators. The reasoning behind these arguments is that presidents have a national constituency and thus do not value (inefficient) targeted geographic spending (Kiewiet and McCubbins 1988; Lizzeri and Persico 2001). According to these arguments, presidents can use the actual or threatened veto to encourage more nationally oriented spending (McCarty 2000). However, the case that presidents shy away from particularism has been seriously questioned in recent scholarship (Kriner and Reeves 2014; Stratmann and Wojnilower 2015).

Moreover, to say that the presidents prefer to limit pork is different from asserting that presidential systems will lead to lower pork. There is some theoretical justification for the former but little for the latter. There are good reasons to believe that presidential systems will spend less overall, because of increased veto players (Tsebelis 2002) or barriers to leftist power (Becher 2012). However, the composition of spending in presidential systems—due to the direct election of the president and to the necessity of building support among fragmented and, frequently, parochial legislators—should encourage targeted geographic spending in these systems relative to parliamentarism. This logic is supported by the results of the policy priority analysis in Chapter 2, which shows that presidential systems spend relatively more on spending categories particularly suitable for delivery of localized goods.

Election Targeting

Presidential systems may encourage targeted geographic spending to help the electoral chances of presidential candidates, and for the president and her party to target specific resources to help the electoral chances of co-partisans to build a legislative coalition.

Even though a president's constituency is the nation, presidential elections are sometimes territorial and this incentivizes targeting resources to districts. The most obvious example of a territorialized presidential election is the Electoral College in the USA described below. Winner-take-all elections in all but two states encourage candidates to concentrate time and resources on specific areas, especially swing states or swing electoral districts within states (Lizerri and Persico 2001). Kriner and Reeves (2012) show specifically that voters reward presidents for spending more time and resources in their districts. Reelection incentives, at least based on evidence in the USA, show that presidents have some reason to prioritize local public goods for electoral gain.

Even where the presidential contest is based exclusively on popular support, presidents may have incentives to direct targeted resources to mobilize core voters or persuade swing voters. Targeting constituencies may be more effective with local public goods where those constituents are geographically concentrated (Kriner and Reeves 2015). Engaged in contests that depend on crossing the majority threshold, parties need to mobilize or persuade a sufficient number of voters to show up and vote on their behalf. For core voters, this may be most efficiently achieved with national programmatic policies that span districts. However, ideologically moderate swing voters are more likely to respond to territorial allocations because they are indifferent between the parties' programs, and value district-specific goods (Dixit and Londregan 1996).

Presidents may target resources geographically not only for their own election, but also to increase the size of their coalition in the legislature (Alston and Mueller 2006). Parties interested in advancing their policy goals in separation of powers systems will have a much easier path if they can secure a unified government. The motivation to maximize votes, policy, and office lead all parties in presidential systems to pursue both the presidency and majorities in the legislature. A straightforward way to do the latter is to provide resources that will help co-partisans get elected. This may take the form of contributing direct resources to co-partisan legislators' campaigns or of directing geographically targeted policies at their districts. Recent scholarship that shows presidents reward districts that support them and their co-partisans suggests there is a strong motivation for presidents to build a supportive coalition (Cameron 2002; Wood 2009). Similarly, legislators are more likely to be reelected if their districts receive a higher share of federal funding (Levitt and Snyder 1995).

In parliamentary systems, the electoral logic favors winning the largest number of national seats. Because being in government is mandatory for policy relevance, party members have a collective goal to maximize national seat share. This limits the individual members' incentives to subtract from the national pie with pork to their districts. Maximizing national seats is most straightforwardly achieved with national programs that blanket the largest population (Austen-Smith and Banks 1988). Of course, if parties have geographically concentrated constituencies, it can make sense for them to target resources to those places (Rickard 2012). For example, this could be a reasonable option for Die Linke (The Left) in Germany with constituents concentrated in the East, if they joined the majority coalition.

Building Legislative Support

Even though both presidents and legislators understand the benefit of unified government, on any individual vote, locally tied legislators may choose their district over their party. Territorial heterogeneity of preferences and legislator autonomy in presidential systems mean that presidents and their parties will at times need to "buy" support from reluctant members. An effective way to do that is to target resources to their districts. Evidence that members of the president's party gain a disproportionate share of federal funding to their districts suggests that territorial allocations are used for coalition building (Berry et al. 2010; Albouy 2013).

Separation of powers systems encourage geographically targeted distribution even for social policies with national coverage. For example, national health and income support programs in the USA receive funding from the national government but are typically administered at the state level. Cox and McCubbins (2001, p. 28) explain why this might emerge from separation of powers systems:

> each veto player will be able to demand, and receive, side payments in the form of narrowly targeted policies. Thus, when the effective number of vetoes is great, even broad public policy will be packaged as a set of individual projects, or it will be packaged with narrowly targeted programs.

Cox and McCubbins also show that tension between the executive and legislative branches will encourage greater pork in order to overcome gridlock.[8]

In short, presidential systems provide greater incentives to target expenditures geographically. The logic of the winner-takes-all presidential contest makes directing policies at specific constituencies a viable strategy to push a candidate over the top. The separation of origin and survival requires presidents to work harder for support in the legislature. Some support, or defiance, comes courtesy of the electoral calendar with concurrent or non-concurrent races. Other support must be cobbled together with attractive policy platforms, and with targeted policies to supportive politicians' districts. These dynamics play out in Argentina and the USA in different ways, described in the cases below.

Presidents and Veto Players

Presidential systems are explicitly designed to slow down and moderate policy change. For those opposed to redistribution, the president is one more goalie standing in the way of undesirable reform. Veto power, like that held by the president, "may prevent a variety of pathologies, including the tyranny of the majority, populist-inspired legislation and socially inefficient redistributive coalitions" (Gerring et al. 2008, p. 335).

Presidential systems are less likely to pass major reforms to change the income distribution because they are biased toward the status quo (Huber et al. 2003). Assuming that the status quo policy is not highly redistributive, presidential systems should be associated with lower redistributive effort (Becher 2012). Of relevance here is whether territorial politics plays a role in the status quo bias of presidential systems. Also, can presidents initiate change in redistributive policy that might not otherwise be possible given regional fragmentation of the party system?

Policy change of all types (including redistributive policy) is more difficult in separation of powers systems because multiple actors must approve the change (Tsebelis 2002). Territorial separation of purpose contributes specifically to policy resoluteness. Politicians with different constituencies with different policy preferences will have a smaller range of policies that they will prefer relative to the status quo. This heterogeneity within parties means that even unified government cannot guarantee that the majority party will be able to change policy in its preferred direction.

On the other hand, research on parliamentarism shows these systems are dependent on strong, cohesive political parties (Bowler et al. 1999). Party fragmentation would be immobilizing to parliamentary systems because all policy action depends on a government composed of disciplined parties. Thus fused origin and survival motivate strong discipline in parliamentary systems that offsets incentives for party members to represent district-specific interests or, more generally, to defect from their party.[9]

At the same time, one could argue that presidents may make policy change more likely in societies with strong regional cleavages (Shugart 1999). Presidents can solve collective action problems and compensate for weak parties by setting the agenda in the legislature, or initiating policy on their own. Presidentialism may be a useful institution for overcoming immobilism driven by constituency pressures in the legislature. However, at a structural level, parties in heterogeneous societies might not be so weak if they existed within the institutional incentives to coalesce under parliamentarism (Gerring et al. 2008).[10]

Certainly, efforts at reducing income inequality qualify as policy areas that are likely to be highly salient and highly divisive in legislatures in any heterogeneous society. At the same time, political responses or lack of responses, to issues of income inequality may be important for democratic stability (Muller 1988; Oxhorn 2003). Accordingly, the president can be the actor that initiates change in divided societies. This idea is addressed for Argentina and the USA below, as both societies are divided in preferences for redistribution along regional lines. In both nations, the president has served as the catalyzing figure for redistributive reform as well as for retrenchment. The ability of presidents to do so depends on their policy goals, and on their formal and partisan powers.

Presidential systems also vary considerably in the powers allotted to the presidents and the legislature. These powers may come from formal sources (such as constitutions) or from informal sources (such as presidential leadership in the majority party) (Shugart and Carey 1992). When presidential powers are strong, presidentialism can behave much like parliamentarism with regard to speed and likelihood of policy change (Weldon 1997). That is, when the president has formal or informal tools to enact policy change, concerns that separation of powers limits reform are minimized (Cheibub 2002). Under these circumstances, leftist presidents may be able to advance redistributive policy. However, whether the sources of their powers are formal or informal may have implications for the lasting effects of redistributive reform, such as whether their decree powers can permanently change the status quo or whether a change in the party dynamics paves the way for retrenchment.

The constitutional role of particular interest to redistributive policies is the power of the president to control the budget. Assuming that party fragmentation and divided government are the reasons that policy change is more difficult in presidential systems, to the extent that presidents can control the legislative agenda and process, policy change may be more likely. Presidents do not face the collective action problems inherent in legislatures, so, if they can control the budget, the likelihood of change in redistributive (or retrenchment) policy should increase. Again, these powers dramatically vary across presidential systems (Alesina et al. 1999).

For the president to be a solution to policy immobilism in the area of redistribution, she needs policy tools to achieve those ends. In the USA, the president's role is limited to budget proposals (which can be amended by either legislative house), veto power (which reverts policy to the status quo), and partisan leadership (to rally co-partisans in the legislature and in the public) to affect reform. In other presidential systems, including most in Latin America, the executive branch has extensive budget powers.[11] In most presidential systems, the president has formal or de facto proposal power, and in many cases powers to restrict legislative amendments (Saiegh 2011; Cheibub 2006). In Chile, for example, presidents have exclusive budget proposal power, and the legislature is only able to revise those figures downward. Outgoing dictator Augusto Pinochet established this setup in the 1988 Constitution on the assumption that the president, as representative of the nation as a whole, would prefer smaller, balanced budgets (Baldez and Carey 1999). From the perspective of redistribution, it is unclear whether this implied that presidents would limit the pork tendencies of the legislature, or (more likely) limit expansionary welfare spending.

Importantly, for many presidents, even those on the left, balancing budgets is a more immediate policy goal than reducing income inequality. In recent decades in Latin America and the USA, presidents have been called upon to address budget imbalances during neo-liberal reforms. Where legislators have strong incentives to target resources to their personal constituencies (in SMD and open-list PR systems), strong presidential authority can override common pool resource problems in the legislature to enhance budget discipline (Hallerberg and Marier 2004). The dominant perspective in the literature has been that presidents can better internalize the national effect of budgets than can legislators, so this encourages less (redistributive) spending than more. Even if presidents have the power to pass redistributive reform, they may prioritize fiscal solvency.

Presidents and the Majority Coalition

A central theme in research on the politics of inequality is that a major change in redistributive policy requires a unified majority coalition to press legislation through the rigors of the legislative process. At a base level, parliamentary systems demand more unified parties, and more unified coalitions, than are incentivized by the institutional prerogatives of presidentialism (Persson et al. 1997). Forming and sustaining a majority coalition to advance redistributive reform will thus be more difficult in presidentialism because of coordination problems for leftist parties.[12] These include ideological coordination problems, such as heterogeneity within parties in legislative bargaining, or electoral coordination problems whereby the left is unable to gain a unified majority.

Presidential systems, however, vary in the extent to which they incentivize ideological coordination, electoral coordination, party discipline and national platform coherence. The mechanisms that distinguish incentives in presidential versus parliamentary systems may be usefully broken into the "separation of origin" and "separation of survival" effects (Becher 2012).

Separation of Origin

With presidents and legislators separately elected, divided government is much more likely in presidential than in parliamentary systems and partisan cooperation is less likely even among co-partisans.[13] Separation of powers also provides separation of purpose, meaning presidents have distinct constituencies from those of legislators and thus distinct mandates (Haggard and McCubbins 2001). The separation of purpose can reflect differences in partisan constituencies and differences in regional constituencies. Given that these distinct actors have active roles in the policy process, territorially motivated interests are more likely to fragment party interests in presidential than in parliamentary systems (Hutchcroft 2001). Fragmentation of parties and the greater likelihood of divided government linked to separation of origin should reduce the likelihood of redistributive reform in presidential systems (Becher 2012).

However, presidential and legislative origin is somewhat intertwined in many presidential systems. Of particular interest are the unifying incentives of executive "coattails," or "the ability of a candidate at the top of the ticket to carry into office ... his party's candidates on the same ticket" (Beck 1997, p. 251). In parliamentary systems, coattails are strong by definition—local elections choose the candidates from the executive branch. If voters evaluate locally elected politicians for national policy, local politicians have clear incentives to cooperate with presidents to improve national outcomes for their constituents (Rodden and Wibbels 2011; Shugart 1995; Samuels 2004). Presidential coattails are very different across nations and across elections, with important effects on party nationalization and coherence (Brancati 2008). In particular, if legislators are elected at a separate time from presidents (electoral non-concurrence), parties are expected to be more ideologically fragmented because voters do not so readily associate politicians with the president.[14] Non-concurrence provides incentives for legislators to distance themselves ideologically from unpopular presidents and their unpopular policies (Samuels 2004).[15] Where presidents are redistributively oriented, non-concurrence may limit their efforts to bring disparate legislators in line with their legislative programs.

At the same time, winning the presidency provides impetus for party system nationalization and harmonization of party platforms. If the office of the president is important for policymaking, and if the federal government has strong fiscal and political powers, parties will have strong incentives to coordinate to choose candidates, to pool campaign resources, and to organize electoral campaigns across regions (Cox 1997). Parties are "presidentialized," or organized to win the executive branch in presidential systems (Samuels 2002; Epstein 1989).

Critically, presidentialism may be more likely to encourage national party coordination across districts *without* party platform homogenization (Crisp et al. 2013). While the benefits of coordination to win the presidency are strong, the necessity of all politicians to adopt common policy stances is not so vital in presidentialism as in parliamentarism. Thus presidentialism may encourage nationalization, but not necessarily one that dampens the regional and ideological heterogeneity that may stand in the way of redistributive policy advancement at the national level.

Separation of Survival

Even when a leftist party holds the presidency and the legislature, its members might not agree to advance redistributive policy. Examples of this are described below for the USA in the first term of Bill Clinton. Separate survival allows legislators to reject presidential initiatives if they conflict with the preferences of their (different) constituents. The same does not hold for parliamentary systems. The threat of dissolution for individuals within government parties and parties that are members of the coalition is a serious concern because it means they will not necessarily be part of the next coalition (Becher 2012). Given that being part of government is essential for affecting policy, coalitions in parliamentary systems will have even greater cohesion across parties than presidential systems have within parties (Persson et al. 1997).[16] Dissolution (linked survival) gives executives power over backbenchers on fiscal policy issues, so governments can push their taxation and spending programs more easily in parliamentary systems (Becher and Christiansen 2014). If a leftist party wins government control and desires redistributive policy in parliamentary systems, therefore, it can more easily pass it, all else equal.

Executives and Redistribution in Argentina and the USA

In the three country cases under examination, the two presidential nations redistribute at relatively low levels and the parliamentary case is among the most redistributive in the world. While all of the causal weight certainly cannot be placed on Germany's parliamentary system for its egalitarian efforts, it certainly stands out as a potential contributor. In the case dynamics analyzed below, I focus almost exclusively on the presidential cases. Germany serves only as a counterexample for the ways that US and Argentine presidentialism arguably diminish the likelihood of redistributive policy to reduce income inequality.

The President of the USA is the hero or villain, depending on your perspective, of all accounts of major redistributive policy in that nation. Broad redistributive policy initiatives, such as Civil War pensions, the New Deal, the Great Society, and the Affordable Care Act (ACA, also called Obamacare), are all indelibly linked to the president that championed them, not the Congress that passed them. Similarly, retrenchment is typically attributed to presidents, including Reagan and Bush's tax cuts, and Clinton's welfare reform. Although the president's only formal legislative power is the veto, clearly he plays an important role in redistributive policy, whether through budget proposals, through using the bully pulpit to press policy initiatives, or through convincing party members to form a supportive legislative coalition.

Similarly, Argentina's presidents are at the center of developments in their welfare state. Juan Perón, in particular, championed the most significant developments in redistributive policy to this day. The comparison of the USA and Argentina, however, highlights the very different legislative–executive bargaining dynamics on these matters. National policy change in Argentina happens through presidential bargaining with provincial governors either directly or through their legislative agents, with national transfers to grease the wheels. The Argentine president's much greater legislative powers, however, gives her the upper hand in these negotiations. While US bargaining over redistribution also maintains a territorial element, it occurs between a president with largely reactive powers and district-oriented legislators with static ambition. These legislators have variable incentives to work with co-partisan presidents, and prefer to be compensated in pork.

From an institutional perspective, however, the US and Argentine presidents may be just as important for redistributive policy based on what they do not do as what they do. In this regard, these nations' presidentialism fails to motivate strong, cohesive parties in the ways that the fusion of origin and survival does in parliamentary systems. The institutional effects appear particularly cogent in the Argentina case because they have electoral rules that should incentivize cohesion. Germany stands as an opposing case, in which parliamentarism encourages party cohesion despite other institutions (e.g., federalism, territorial bicameralism, partial SMD elections in the Bundesrat) that might otherwise weaken the ideological and organization strength of its parties.

In the following case studies, I will trace the institutional incentives and the roles of legislators and presidents on major redistributive reform efforts in Argentina and the USA. In the USA, I focus on efforts to expand health care insurance under Presidents Clinton and Obama. In Argentina, I examine retrenchment policies under the president of a leftist party, Carlos Menem. Even policies to pull back the welfare state were dominated by dynamics of pork, vetoes, and divided majority coalitions in presidential Argentina. The much stronger powers of the president in the Argentine case show how he got his way despite serious challenges both within and outside his party. Unfortunately, I cannot capture the potential hidden effects of presidentialism that loom large in both the USA and Argentina—i.e., the redistributive reform that was never initiated in anticipation of legislative defeat or presidential veto.

Presidents and Pork

Presidential systems may encourage geographically targeted government allocation in order to form policy coalitions at the national level (Cox and McCubbins 2001). Although the office of the presidency provides the most powerful politician with a national focus, the dynamics of election targeting and legislative targeting also incentivize the provision of geographically-targeted benefits

(Cox 2009). To win the presidency, incumbent presidents and strategic partisans in the legislature may target resources at specific districts to sway their votes for the president or co-partisan legislators. The territorialized US presidential and legislative elections provide a clear example of these dynamics. Geographically targeted distribution is also an efficient means of coalition building to pass specific legislation in separation of powers systems, as shown in the Argentine case. In instances of major redistributive reform in the USA and Argentina, we see patterns of presidents buying support to form a majority coalition.

Election Targeting

In a general sense, presidential elections in the USA and Argentina should encourage national programmatic policies and encourage nationalization of the party system. In the first case, to appeal to voters throughout the nation, parties have incentives to offer programmatic goods at the national level that appeal to their particular socio-demographic constituency (Gibson 1997). US presidential elections provide incentives for parties to nationalize by coordinating across state boundaries (Cox 1997). Because the presidency is the most important political office in the nation, and because there are clear benefits to coordinating across districts, US parties quickly formed to compete for this office after the nation's founding (Aldrich 1995). Strong presidential coattails during election years also encourage cooperation between co-partisans and presidential candidates before and during election cycles (Campbell 1991; Samuels 2002). The presidency thus contributes to party coordination in the USA, including for passage of redistributive reform. The runoff system in Argentina somewhat undermines these dynamics, but the importance of the president for policymaking incentivizes party cooperation at least during concurrent elections (Jones and Mainwaring 2003).

At the same time, presidential elections can incentivize targeted geographic spending to capture swing states in the USA (Bartels 1985; Shaw 1999). The US Electoral College decides the presidency through a system of electors at the state level. Electors are apportioned to states based on the number of seats in Congress and are chosen by state-specific methods, typically popular election. In all states but two, the winner of the popular election in the state takes all electoral votes for that state.[17] States are given electoral votes equal to the size of their legislative (House and Senate) delegation. Many states have a larger proportion of voters for one particular party, meaning they are "safe" states for that party's candidate. With its plurality rules and state-based contests, the Electoral College territorializes the election and provides incentives for candidates to target specific states with attention, appropriations, and policy promises (Kriner and Reeves 2014; Strömberg 2008; Shaw 1999). By building the vote count on Senate representation, the Electoral College also replicates to some extent the territorial malapportionment of the legislature (Grofman et al. 1997).

Until 1994, presidential elections in Argentina were also conducted using an electoral college structured along provincial lines. Similar to the USA, the design of Argentina's electoral college overrepresented less populated regions.

Peripheral provinces held 30 percent of the population but controlled 50 percent of electoral votes prior to the reform (Gibson and Calvo 2000). In the Argentine case, governors were crucial actors in the selection of party candidates for the presidential ticket. The power of the governors to choose the president has been somewhat diminished by direct elections and by the runoff system, but they retain substantial influence within the parties.

In the case of territorialized presidential contests, which are relatively rare in comparative perspective, it is more efficient for parties to target particular constituencies with their attention and their strategic distributions. Broad national distributions will likely mobilize core constituents, but for territorialized contests it matters where voters show up, not just how many show up. It should be more effective and cheaper for parties to mobilize or persuade voters in specific states rather than blanketing the whole nation with broad policies if the goal is to cross the majority threshold in particular states (Bartels 1985). Despite limitations on presidential budget powers in the USA, scholars have found evidence that presidents influence federal allocations for their own tactical electoral and partisan purposes. Larcinese et al. (2006) show that the president is very influential in the distribution of federal funds to states, and that presidents disproportionately send resources to states that were loyal in the previous election. For their part, voters appear to reward presidents for the share of federal spending that their district receives (Kriner and Reeves 2012).

Pork is also easier to manipulate for purposes of presidential elections than are party programs. Even heterogeneous parties must maintain some consistency in their party platforms in order to be useful brand names for voters (Woon and Pope 2008). Changes in parties' positions toward redistribution, even for relatively fluid parties like those in the USA, are slow moving (Dixit and Londregan 1996). Pork can more quickly adapt to the strategic needs of candidates. Dixit and Londregan (1996) provide the example of the "super collider" scientific project in (solidly Republican) Texas that lost federal funding when Bill Clinton took office, while Livermore Labs' fusion project in (swing state) California was funded. Clinton faced much greater barriers to changing national redistributive policy (as discussed for health care below) than he did to changing a geographically targeted allocation. Importantly, Arnold (1980) notes that "most decisions about geographic allocation are bureaucratic decisions" which means that cabinet members appointed by the president have significant control over pork as well (p. 8).

Legislative Targeting

Geographically targeted spending is not only useful for winning elections but also for convincing politicians already in office to support a president's policies. While legislators in the USA and Argentina have some reasons (e.g., ideological similarity, presidential coattails) to support their president, on any individual bill they might have reason to defect. Party coordination is not always in the self-interest of legislators in presidential systems. Heterogeneity in regional preferences for redistributive policy, for example, may pull even co-partisans away from the president on any given bill. For the president to have the necessary votes to pass controversial legislation, he will need to work with his co-partisans in the legislature to form a majority coalition. This may require side payments to legislators that advance the legislation through committee (Cox 2009) as well as to pivotal legislators or to those whose provinces stand to lose from cooperation. The form these side payments take depends on the career incentives of legislators. Presidents (and co-partisan majority leaders) in the USA use "tactical redistribution" or pork to entice members to support change to status quo policies (Dixit and Londregan 1996). Presidents in Argentina strategically use transfers to provinces as carrots and sticks to induce cooperation between governors and their legislators regarding policy change (Eaton 2001a). Legislating on fiscal and taxation matters in particular is highly contested by provincial governors, and presidents have a low success rate on these bills (Saiegh 2004).

Both US and Argentine federal spending show evidence of presidential coalition building. In the USA, more federal outlays appear to go to those states with presidential co-partisan national legislators and governors (Larcinese et al. 2006). In the US case, it is difficult to assess whether this pork is most useful in electing co-partisans or convincing incumbents to vote with them. The evidence seems to be stronger that pork has electoral rather than legislative effects (Strautmann and Wojnilower 2015). In Argentina, however, the effect of transfers appears to be strongest in the legislative rather than electoral realm. Many governors do not face competitive races, so presidents would have difficulty in trying to dramatically affect gubernatorial contests through targeted transfers.[18] Transfers serve to keep governors in office and dissuade potential competitors, however (Gervasoni 2010). Because party cooperation works through governors, they may need to be rewarded for their participation in the president's coalition.[19] National policymaking brings to the fore territorial differentiation in interests, and also increases targeted transfers to build redistributive coalitions despite those differences.

Argentina's federal allocation of resources reflects executive–legislative coalition bargaining dynamics. Giraudy (2007) shows that allocation of federal emergency employment programs mirrors legislative bargaining dynamics, as less populated (overrepresented) provinces and provinces with co-partisan governors received high levels of allocations. In addition, provinces with governors and legislators from provincial parties and provincial blocs of the president get the highest proportion of central transfers (Bambaci et al. 2002). The ability of presidents to exercise discretion in transfers has varied over time (Eaton 2001b). Tactical redistribution is also not employed for the exclusive advancement of redistributive policy, of course. Carlos Menem strategically doled out national transfers to provinces in order to pass neo-liberal reforms that scaled back many redistributive policies.

Electoral and legislative coalition building in the US and Argentine presidential systems encourage geographic distribution of resources as the most efficient currency. These goods may have redistributive properties, but they are not national redistributive social programs, the kinds that are typically cited for reducing income inequality. In Germany, on the other hand, gathering a national majority to form and maintain a governing coalition does not require the assent of particular voters in particular regions.

Presidents and the Veto

Presidential systems provide more opportunities for redistributive reform to be derailed by opposition groups. Rightist presidents have the opportunity to veto the legislative proposals of leftist parties. Rightist legislators can table redistributive proposals favored by leftist presidents. Thus, redistributive reform is less likely in systems where power is shared across several institutions than where power is concentrated in the executive branch (Immergut 1992; Bonoli 2001). Importantly, the legislative outcomes in presidential systems also reflect anticipated vetoes. For policy change to occur, legislative parties propose policies that presidents prefer to the status quo. In this regard, redistributive policies that emerge from presidential systems are expected to be relatively moderate (Tsebelis 1995).

The challenge to demonstrating that presidential systems matter because they limit the range of policy reform is difficult because both the institutional counterfactual (how would policy have progressed if the system were parliamentary?) and the latent demand for reform (what reforms would have been initiated if the system were parliamentary?) are unknowable (Przeworksi 2004). It is possible, for example, that presidential vetoes or the legislature's rejection of presidential prerogatives is simply a more public airing of dynamics that occur within more secretive parliamentary parties. Because all of the institutions, and the actors within them, in the USA and Argentina are "presidentialized" it is impossible to know how they would behave in a different system (Samuels 2002). In the absence of a true test of the institutional effects of presidentialism, I focus on executive–legislative bargaining in cases in which a "window of opportunity" (leftist unified government) appeared for redistributive reform in the USA and in Argentina (Kingdon and Thurber 1984).

Changing the Distributive Status Quo in the USA

For the USA, I compare the effects of separation of powers on two similar legislative initiatives—Clinton's (1993) Health Security Act (HSA) and Barack Obama's (2010) Affordable Care Act (ACA)—both of which were considered under unified Democratic (leftist) control. The HSA was never brought to a vote by the Congress; the second was passed with substantial moderation to appease right-leaning elements of the Democratic party (White 2011; Hacker 2010). In both cases, separation of power made the president's reform agenda more complicated and compromised to get through the veto power of legislators with different territorial mandates than the president.

As can be seen, the first evidence that veto actors in the US presidential systems powerfully protect the status quo is the very long road to health care reform (Oberlander 2003; Steinmo and Watts 1995; Marmor and Oberlander 2010). Despite calls for universal health care access throughout the twentieth century, reform was deadlocked until 2010 (Hacker 2010; Steinmo and Watts 1995).[20] Bill Clinton's campaign platform highlighted his health care reform ideas, and when he won he appeared to have a clear mandate to press this policy through Congress. Clinton developed the content of the HSA in the White House, and asked his co-partisans to pass it in the House of Representatives and the Senate. These efforts quickly met the resistance of Democratic Party leaders and rank-and-file members in both houses of Congress, as well as with opposition Republicans. As the battle over health care in DC waged on, citizen support for health care reform declined and it was eventually dropped by the Clinton administration. The failure to work with Congress to develop the legislation to appease their heterogeneous and district-specific interests is one of the primary reasons that the HSA is thought to have floundered (Hacker 2010).

With the ACA, Obama "produced general guidelines and left the concrete task of negotiating and writing provisions to Congress, particularly the standing committees and the leadership of both houses" (Beaussier 2012, p. 755). The resulting legislation took a turn to the right to appease pivotal moderate Democrats (White 2011). In comparison to the experience under Clinton, congressional Democrats remained united throughout negotiations despite clear ideological differences within (Brown 2011; Hacker 2010). Negotiation within the Democratic Party in particular led Democrats to give up many of the more leftist and more nationalized options for reform.[21] Among the differences between the HSA and the ACA is that the latter was more federalized, allowing for variation in generosity across states, and limiting the effectiveness of insurance risk-sharing with a larger, national pool.[22] Importantly, given the great difficulty of advancing redistributive reform in the separation of powers system, this compromise served to "illustrate a shared feeling within the Democratic health care community that their absolute priority was to pass something, even if this meant reforming the reform afterward" (Beaussier 2012, p. 756). Having the status quo policy be a redistributive policy was important because veto powers are not very useful for eliminating existing policy. The status quo, even if redistributive, is difficult to change in presidential systems.

Territorial politics were also very important to the legislative dynamics in the House versus the Senate. The House, with greater party discipline, quickly passed a more leftist version of the ACA that included a "public option" to buy insurance directly from the national government and strong requirements that employers provide insurance or pay for the insurance employees buy on the insurance exchanges. Importantly, the House bill offered a national exchange, rather than state-based exchanges with the involvement of state governments. This bill was roughly in line with the preferences of the median of the Democratic Party (Hacker 2010). Due to the Senate filibuster and the considerable overrepresentation of states that were "more rural, more Republican, and whiter," the Senate bill shifted significantly to the right to accommodate the 60 senators needed to pass the bill (ibid., p. 868). Importantly, the Senate changed the form of the health care system to a decentralized, state-based system that both allowed Senators to better control the allocation of resources to their own state, and for the states to tailor the reform to their particular circumstances.

The ACA that was ultimately signed into law in 2010 was very similar in content to the bill that Republicans championed in opposition to Clinton's 1993 HSA (ibid; Beaussier 2012). It also closely resembled, particularly in its focus on private insurance, the Massachusetts law advanced by a Republican Governor of that state and eventual Republican presidential candidate Mitt Romney. Presidentialism contributed to this (relatively) rightist outcome because it placed territorial actors, with preferences that were arguably different from the national majority, at the center of the reform effort. The possibility of a Senate veto, a Senate filibuster, and the very limited ability of the president to press forward the legislation against the preferences of the majority of his party significantly scaled back the reform effort.

Changing the Distributive Status Quo in Argentina

In Argentina, I explore a series of reforms with very different redistributive implications from those of the heath reforms in the USA—Menem's reduction in labor protections in the 1990s. Similar to the two cases introduced above, these reforms were passed under a unified leftist majority. However, Menem enacted a broad set of reforms that were unequivocally rightist and scaled back some of the existing redistributive policies (Stokes 2001).

The importance of this example for the role of territorial politics and regional disparity in limiting redistributive reform is not in the nature of the reform in Argentina, which was welfare state retrenchment, but rather for how a president with strong legislative powers and a majority in the legislature nonetheless faced considerable roadblocks to reform. On the face of it, this is entirely expected—a president trying to pass legislation that hurt labor and the working classes would obviously face serious opposition by the leftist plurality in the legislature. What is important about Menem's strategy is how he took advantage of regional disparity and the structure of territorial representation to advance this legislation (Gibson and Calvo 2000). More specifically, Menem directed resources to the least populated provinces that are overrepresented in the legislature to convince their governors to support his reform in the legislature (Gibson 1997; Levitsky 2003).[23] He also targeted provinces with large populations of relatively poor voters in which governors could effectively use patronage to drum up electoral support for the Peronists despite retrenchment (Calvo and Murillo 2004).

Carlos Menem was elected in 1989 on a traditional Peronist (leftist-populist) platform to protect the interests of labor and the poorer classes against the objectives of domestic and global business interests (Stokes 2001). The 1989 elections also brought a plurality of Peronist seats to the Chamber of Deputies and a majority in the Senate.[24] 1989 was a period of severe economic crisis in Argentina—the inflation rate spiked to over 5,000 percent during that year—and outgoing president Raúl Alfonsín chose to turn over the presidency to Menem five months early. The crisis conditions changed the policy space within which Menem could work. Once in office, Menem reversed his electoral promises and instead initiated a sweeping neo-liberal program that consisted of the privatization of state industries, scaled back labor protections, the decentralization of health and education programs, among many other reforms.[25]

The road to retrenchment for Menem required a mixed strategy of traditional legislative process, decree, and intergovernmental agreements. Despite the common characterization that Menem acted unilaterally to change Argentina's economic foundations, Llanos (2002) and others have thoroughly demonstrated that many of these policies went through the formal legislative process, were made with powers delegated by congress, or were directly negotiated with provincial governors.[26] Many of Menem's policies failed in the legislature due, in large part, to conflicts within his own party. Divergence in provincial interests was particularly clear in the Senate, where bills stalled despite the large Peronist majority and quorum (Bavastro 2001, p. 39).

Importantly, the relative powers of the president and the legislature in Argentina are reversed from those in the USA. The Argentine Congress acts more as a reactive, blunt veto and the president a proactive agenda-setter (Eaton 2001a).[27] Menem could set his legislative agenda by introducing bills and building a coalition of support with targeted resources to supportive provincial delegations (Bambaci et al. 2002). For example, although Menem shrunk the national public sector along neoliberal lines, the provincial public sector notably expanded during this period. Calvo and Murillo (2004) and Gibson and Calvo (2000) show that this is evidence of presidential coalition building, whereby Menem provided discretionary resources to governors that they used for patronage in the provinces in exchange for legislative support for his controversial measures. Tommasi (2005) shows that a group of provincial parties (either the provincial bloc of the Peronist party or small province-based parties) were pivotal in the negotiations, and they received disproportionate central transfers in compensation for support of Menem's policies. Saiegh (2004) shows that vote buying by presidents is necessary to offset the constituency interests of Argentine legislators dependent on provincial governors.[28]

The examples of the USA and Argentina show the tremendous challenge that presidents face in enacting major redistributive reform (either expansion or retrenchment). These cases also demonstrate the crucial role of territorial actors with territorial interests that made these reforms difficult to pass. In contrast, the expectation in parliamentary systems such as Germany is that redistributive policy should be both easier to pass and easier to withdraw. Indeed, Germany was an early adopter of the welfare state (much of which preceded democracy) and was among the first to pull back reforms in the era of retrenchment (Manow 2005). Institutional veto points and territorial interests play a much more minor role in the case of executive–legislative bargaining in the German parliament. Adaptations to structural changes in the economy and global economic tides, and partisanship, much better explain the timing and motivation for reform in the German case (Allan and Scruggs 2004; Swank 2002).

Presidents and the Majority Coalition

The theoretical effects of presidentialism on the ability of the majority coalition to advance redistributive policy are not straightforward. On the one hand, the president as head of his party can set the agenda on redistributive policy. Presidential elections encourage party coordination (organizational and to some extent ideological) across districts. These incentives may aid the coordination of a strong leftist party to press redistribution at the national level despite societal and territorial heterogeneity. Certainly we see the leftist chancellors of Germany and leftist presidents in Argentina and the USA championing redistributive policy.

At the same time, the institutional effects of presidentialism do not encourage party coordination or discipline to the degree that parliamentarism does (Bowler et al. 1999). Leftist coalitions are also less likely to gain office, all else equal, in presidential systems (Becher 2012). Even leftist Argentine and US presidents with majority leftist coalitions in the legislature face an uphill battle to pass redistributive reform measures. In many cases, even under the best circumstances, presidents fail to pass their redistributive programs, such as Clinton's HSA. Without the threat of dissolution, legislators in presidential systems have fewer incentives to cooperate to pass redistributive programs and much greater leverage to demand compensation for that cooperation.

In this section, I discuss the effect of separation of origin and survival of the executive and legislative branches on leftist party coordination for redistributive reform in the USA and Argentina. Separate origin limits the cohesion of parties in the US case, as legislators with districts opposed to redistributive legislation have good reason to defy the president. In Argentina, although party discipline is high, legislators understand that their political fate is firmly rooted in the province. When provincial needs diverge from the policy agenda of the president, Argentine politicians not uncommonly defect to form a separate party or faction to represent their interests (Lupu 2014).

Separate Origin

Perhaps most importantly, separation of origin creates the possibility of divided government in which one party holds the presidency and another party holds the legislative majority. In multiparty presidential systems, such as Argentina, presidents are specifically unlikely to have a co-partisan majority in the legislature (Mainwaring 1993). If unified government is crucial for redistributive reform, then it should be less likely in presidential systems because leftists are less likely to capture the needed veto points (Becher 2012). In a parliamentary government, unified origin essentially guarantees that if a leftist party or coalition gains the government, it will have the support of the legislature. Yet even if the left does gain enough seats in a presidential system, separation of purpose (based on differences in territorial and ideological constituencies) may nonetheless limit those reforms. Health care reform in the USA again provides an example.

For the left to have the power to press through redistributive reform, they need to hold sufficient seats and they need to be unified as a party. In the ACA reform in the USA described above, both of these conditions were deemed crucial. A Democratic president, a Democratic House, and a Democratic Senate, and a unified Democratic party interested in reform provided the (relatively rare) window of opportunity for reform that was nonetheless highly contested and never certain to succeed (Hacker 2010; Beaussier 2012). Even if a leftist majority captures the needed veto points, this group may not have the cohesion to pass redistributive reforms because individual members in the leftist coalition are not willing to compromise their ideological positions.

Separation of origin of the executive and legislative branches divides the majority leftist coalition along territorial lines in the USA and Argentina. In both country cases, parties understand that capturing the presidency is critical for policy influence and that legislators can be pulled into office on the president's coattails. In the USA and Argentina the parties are "presidentialized" to focus their electoral chances around winning the highest office. At the same time, to win legislative office, individual members in the USA tailor appeals to their districts (which may be opposed to the president's platform) and governors in Argentina put their provinces first.

Presidential coattails certainly incentivize cooperation in the US case because co-partisan legislators are to some extent held responsible for voters' assessment of the president. In concurrent elections, this typically works in the favor of the winning presidential candidate or incumbent. Voters with a positive assessment of the presidential candidate (or a negative assessment of the opposition) are more likely to vote for his party throughout the ballot. The Democratic waves that brought in Clinton and Obama and both houses of Congress characterize these dynamics. When a party wins unified government, this is typically interpreted as a mandate for reform. In the cases of both of these presidents, each interpreted this mandate to include health care reform.

However, coattails do not fully link the fates of co-partisans. Theodore Marmor emphasizes the challenges for presidential systems in comparison to parliamentary systems in his account of the 1960s Medicare legislative process:

> The 1961 Congress strikingly illustrated a key difference between the legislative politics of America and those of a cabinet–parliamentary system like that of England. Party, executive, and legislative leadership in the United States is not, as in England, in the same hands, and the platform on which a president rides into office need not reflect the aims of many of his fellow partisans whose assistance is crucial in the committee and floor stage of the legislative process. Kennedy's prospects for changing the votes of the crucial Ways and Means Democrats hinged on the House Democratic leadership: the speaker, the party whip, the floor leader, and relevant committee Chairman, Mills.
>
> (1970, p. 36)

The coattails of the president are not sufficient to ensure that co-partisans with considerable institutional autonomy follow the lead of the executive.

Particularly in non-concurrent elections, the perceptions of the president can specifically work against co-partisan legislators. Whether it is because voters are unhappy with the president or because legislators (including co-partisans) believe that supporting the president will work against their reelection, the party of the president typically loses seats in midterm elections (Erikson 1988). Certainly Democrats lost seats and failed to win open seats (seats with no incumbent running) in the 1994 and 2014 midterms elections, in part because voters were unhappy with the performance of Clinton and Obama on health care reform (Campbell 1997; Heath Affairs 2014).[29, 30]

Coattails also unite parties to some extent in Argentina. Despite his controversial program, Argentina's Carlos Menem was reelected in the first round in 1995 and the Peronists gained a majority of seats in the legislature. The majority of concurrent gubernatorial and mayoral elections also went to the Peronists.[31] The specific presidential election rules in Argentina, however, dilute the coattail effect. The president is chosen in a two-round runoff system. If a candidate wins 45 percent of the vote in the first round (or 40 percent with a 10 point differential from the second highest vote earner), she is ruled the victor. If nobody wins in the first round, a second round between the top two candidates is conducted. This encourages intraparty competition and a higher number of competitors in the first round (Jones 1999; Pérez-Liñán 2006). Like with primary contests in the USA, the first round reveals the heterogeneity of interests and policy preferences within the party. Even in elections that are concurrent with a presidential race in Argentina, co-partisans may not have clear coattails to follow. When Menem ran against fellow Peronist Nestór Kirchner in 2003, for example, that party was presenting two very different platforms at the same time. This limited the extent to which voters could assess what voting for Peronist legislators would mean for the eventual policy outcomes in the legislature.

While presidential elections are thought to encourage party nationalization, the specific institutions of presidential candidate selection in the USA and Argentina work against ideological cohesion within parties. In the USA, presidential candidates are chosen according to staggered primary contests at the state level. The timing and sequencing of presidential primaries encourage candidates to focus specific attention on the needs of particular states (those early in the selection cycle) (Mayer and Busch 2003). Because candidates are competing against co-partisans, they emphasize the differences within the party on important matters of policy. Legislators in the USA are also chosen in (typically partisan) primaries in their district. Primary contests tend to focus on district-specific issues and bring out a smaller subset of voters (Brady et al. 2007). Legislative primaries encourage autonomy from the parties that have relatively little control over which candidate gains the party label. In both countries, primaries weaken partisan platform coherence.

Separate Survival

Even in the case that leftist majorities capture unified government in presidential systems, separation of survival provides leeway for legislators to break from their president or party on important policy reforms. In parliamentary systems, if members of the party break with the coalition on a vote, the result can be dissolution of the legislature and a call for new elections. The threat of dissolution keeps coalitions in line because they are uncertain they will be in government after the new elections (Becher 2012). Without so dire a threat, presidents find it harder to motivate co-partisans to support controversial reforms.

The failed health care reform under Clinton again provides an example of the limits to party cohesion in presidential systems with territorial heterogeneity. Democrats in the House, most notably Jim Cooper of Tennessee, joined with Republicans to offer a rival plan to Clinton's HSA. The outlines of this reform bill better fit the more conservative constituencies of a subset of Democrats. This break in the party line certainly did not bring down either Clinton or Cooper, both of whom were reelected. In fact, if electoral outcomes following the ACA are indicative, legislators can be punished for following the president. Most of the eight defeats of Senators that voted for the ACA were in conservative states, including Louisiana, Alaska, both Senators from Arkansas, and North Carolina. Being tied to Obama and the ACA was cited as a main reason for their defeats (USA Today "On Politics" December 8, 2014).[32]

Separation of survival has different implications in the USA and Argentina. For US legislators with relatively lax party discipline, defying the president can simply mean voting against him. In Argentina, where legislative discipline is high, breaking with the president may necessitate breaking away from the party. This indeed happens frequently in Argentina, and happened specifically in response to Menem's retrenchment policies discussed above. A group of progressive dissidents broke away from the Peronists to form FrePaSo (Front for Country in Solidarity) and later the Alianza party in opposition to Menem (Hunter 2010). Importantly, many of those dissidents were from places that were particularly burned by the neoliberal reforms—especially the metropolitan provinces with strong labor organizations (Gibson and Calvo 2000). FrePaSo-Alianza ran second to Menem in the 1995 elections and won the presidency with Fernando de la Rúa in 2000. Alianza dissolved after the economic and political crisis of 2001 and most politicians rejoined the Peronists within the Kirchner Front for Victory faction.

The difference between breaking from the president in the USA and Argentina highlights how electoral rules interact with presidentialism to influence party cohesion. While closed-list PR motivates strong party discipline in Argentina, it is difficult to assess because defections from the party are common (especially to form provincial parties or federalist branches of the national parties). Rather than consistently voting against the party, they are more likely to leave the party (Lupu 2014). In the USA, individual legislators can defect from the president's majority with lower consequence for their political careers. In fact, defection may help some co-partisan politicians keep their jobs despite unpopular presidents. In both cases, despite their differences, constituency pressures within presidential systems limit the discipline of individual members to their party's agenda in the long run.

Separate survival thus weakens party discipline because members do not depend on executive success to stay in office. To overcome the conformity costs of sacrificing the interests of politicians' particular constituents in their own districts, presidents and their parties need to have forceful carrots and sticks to induce compliance. These tools exist to some degree in all presidential systems, but the common vote defections in the USA and the frequent party defections in Argentina show that these tools have their limits. Controversial redistributive reform is less likely under these circumstances because co-partisans have incentives to vote their districts above their president.

Conclusion

Separate origin and survival limit the incentives of parties in presidential systems to dilute territorial interests from within their ranks. Instead, electoral and legislative coalition-building motivates territorial distribution of resources to encourage co-partisans to support the president's program. Even many legislators within leftist parties must be convinced not to veto redistributive legislation from their own president because their regions' voters oppose it. Overall, leftist parties are challenged to hold together their coalition to support redistributive legislation because local electoral incentives and the autonomy that comes from separate elections limit the scope of agreement.

The US case demonstrates that leftists have a difficult time winning a unified majority at the national level in order to overcome conservative vetoes of redistributive reform. Even when the left does so, such as in the 1992–94 Clinton period, within-party differences motivated at least in part by district-specific factors can limit their cohesion and the possibility for change in the redistributive status quo. Territorial heterogeneity and the weakness of parties in presidential systems show that, even when redistributive change is possible, as with the ACA, it may require targeted compensation to key districts and federalization of the program in order to pass.

Argentina's retrenchment under Menem revealed that targeted distribution, in the form of national transfers, were also crucial for changing the redistributive status quo. Menem used these resources to cobble together a supportive coalition built in particular on the votes of the peripheral provinces that are overrepresented in both houses of Congress. To overcome vetoes of these reforms, Menem used decree authority to sidestep the legislature, stacked the Supreme Court in his favor, and even changed the rules of presidential reelection to maintain policy continuity. These drastic measures would not have been necessary in a disciplined party system such as Germany.

In the conclusion chapter that follows, I provide a recap of the mechanisms that I argue link institutions to territorial politics and away from redistribution. I suggest implications of these arguments for the politics of inequality, both among individuals and regions. Finally, I map the road ahead for the study of institutions, regional inequality, and government efforts to equilibrate income.

Notes

1 Overall, the policy effects of executive selection are understudied (Gerring et al. 2009).
2 On varieties of presidentialism, including hybrid systems, see Shugart and Carey (1992).
3 Coattails link their origin and survival, but this is not a constitutional mechanism. Coattails are discussed in detail below. Impeachment and censure are constitutional mechanisms by which the legislature can judge the actions of the executive in some systems. Neither tool, however, allows the legislature to unilaterally dismiss the president. On impeachment in Latin America, see Pérez-Liñán (2007).
4 On variation in discipline among parliamentary systems, see Sieber (2006) and Depauw and Martin (2009).
5 The Keystone Pipeline became a major electoral issue in the 2014 races. Senator Landrieu faced a runoff to retain her Senate seat, which she ultimately lost, to Republican House member Bill Cassidy. Landrieu tried to improve her chances in the runoff by introducing a bill to approve the pipeline in the Senate. The majority Democrats would not bring the legislation to a vote. Cassidy advanced similar legislation in the House that was passed by the Republican majority.
6 Mainwaring and Shugart (1997) argue that most presidential systems appear to compensate for weak legislative or executive powers with strength in the other. The strong policymaking tools, including decree power, available to many Latin American presidents may be an endogenous response to weak and fragmented legislatures (Shugart 1999).
7 I am not directly addressing the diversity in presidential election set ups, including two-round runoffs in this section. For the purposes of this discussion, I am grouping plurality contests and the second round of run-off presidential systems for their effect on swing targeting. The differences are addressed directly in the case comparisons of Argentina and the USA.
8 In this regard Cox and McCubbins specifically contradict the predictions of Persson et al. (1997) and Persson and Tabellini (2003). Cox and McCubbins anticipate higher rents and fiscal deficits under presidentialism, whereas Persson and his colleagues expect these to be higher under parliamentarism.
9 This is not to suggest that we never observe cross-party voting in parliamentary systems. Crowe (1980) and Norton (1987) show this is not infrequent in Great Britain, for example.
10 This raises the concern of whether institutions can activate or suppress social cleavages. For a discussion of this, see Amorim Neto and Cox (1997).
11 For a description of executive budget powers in Latin America, see Alesina et al. (1999).
12 These coordination problems should also plague the right, of course, but the left is often interested in changing policy. The right typically benefits from the (non-distributive) status quo in presidential systems.
13 Holding constant bicameralism, discussed in Chapter 4, for these purposes.
14 Brancati (2008) shows that regional parties compete more effectively at the national level during non-concurrent elections in presidential systems.
15 In this case, the president and the president's policies could be unpopular nationally or in that legislator's region.
16 Recognizing that the actual incidence of dissolution even in failed majority votes is variable across parliamentary systems (Brown et al. 1986).
17 The District of Columbia has representation in the Electoral College but not in the House of Representatives. Maine and Nebraska choose electors by House districts and two state-wide electors, with winner-take-all contests within the districts. These states can have split electoral votes if the winner varies across House districts.
18 Transfers are certainly crucial to governors' elections (Remmer and Wibbels 2000). However, a large percentage of transfers are automatic (Bonvecchi and Lodola 2011),

and transfers are useful to discourage rivals from contesting the election in the first place (Gervasoni 2010).

19 The degree of party cooperation is always relative. While presidents must work harder in Argentina to build support than must chancellors in Germany, they have an easier time than in the highly fragmented Brazil (Dillinger and Webb 1999).

20 The 1960s saw reform in health care access for the elderly and poor through Medicare and Medicaid, respectively. During that period and back to the New Deal era, however, politicians and interests groups were calling for universal access (Beaussier 2012).

21 Also reflective of differences in partisan dynamics in presidential systems, several Democrats in the House of Representatives voted against the bill to preserve their reputation back home.

22 For a more detailed comparison of the content of the two bills, see Hacker (2010) and Beaussier (2012).

23 Menem's reforms also entailed decentralization and the cooperation of governors to administer those reforms in the provinces. Menem was generally successful in passing *national* retrenchment legislation with the support of governors. Reforms within the provinces were decidedly more mixed (Eaton 2001b; Rogers 2013).

24 The size of Menem's delegation fluctuated because of Peronist defections due to Menem's neoliberal policies (i.e., the Grupo de Ocho) and due to his support from non-Peronist parties that did not see themselves as subject to party discipline (Jones 1997).

25 For a detailed treatment of these reforms, see Acuña (1994), Stokes (2001), and Levitsky (2003).

26 Menem certainly used decree power liberally. Some of his tax reforms and changes in wage and labor policy were introduced by "need and urgency decrees" (Rubio and Goretti 1998). Many of those decrees were delegated to him by the Congress (Jones 1997). Use of decree power itself, however, points to challenges with changing the status quo in separation of powers systems.

27 The most common mechanism to oppose a bill is to breach quorum procedures (Molinelli 1991).

28 As further evidence that even presidential systems with powerful executives face challenges to change the policy status quo, Menem successfully increased the size of the Argentine Supreme Court in 1993 from five to nine and appointed Peronist supporters for the additional seats. This move was quite similar to Roosevelt's 1937 effort in the USA to increase the size of the Supreme Court so that he could appoint judges sympathetic to New Deal policies.

29 Campbell (1997) finds strong evidence that Clinton's major loss in 1994 was mostly driven by "realignment" of the Republican Party to capture ideologically aligned voters in the South.

30 http://healthaffairs.org/blog/2014/11/07/health-care-policy-after-the-mid-term-elections/.

31 Importantly, Menem was able to run for reelection only because he negotiated a constitutional reform with the previous president Alfonsín of the Radical party.

32 Of the 60 Senators that voted for the ACA, 30 were out of office by 2015. Eight were defeated in reelection campaigns, the remainder retired, resigned, or passed away. http://onpolitics.usatoday.com/2014/12/08/democrats-senate-obamacare-landrieu/.

References

Acuña, Carlos H. "Politics and Economics in the Argentina of the Nineties (or, Why the Future No Longer Is What It Used to Be)." in *Democracy, Markets, and Structural Reform in Latin America: Argentina, Bolivia, Brazil, Chile, and Mexico*, edited by William Smith, Carlos Acuña, and Eduardo Gamarra. Lynne Reinner Press, Boulder CO (1994): 31–73.

Albouy, David. “Partisan Representation in Congress and the Geographic Distribution of Federal Funds.” *Review of Economics and Statistics* 95, no. 1 (2013): 127–41.

Aldrich, John Herbert. *Why Parties?: The Origin and Transformation of Party Politics in America*. Cambridge University Press, 1995.

Alesina, Alberto, Ricardo Hausmann, Rudolf Hommes, and Ernesto Stein. “Budget Institutions and Fiscal Performance in Latin America.” *Journal of Development Economics* 59, no. 2 (1999): 253–73.

Allan, James P, and Lyle Scruggs. “Political Partisanship and Welfare State Reform in Advanced Industrial Societies.” *American Journal of Political Science* 48, no. 3 (2004): 496–512.

Alston, Lee J., and Bernardo Mueller. “Pork for Policy: Executive and Legislative Exchange in Brazil.” *Journal of Law, Economics, and Organization* 22, no. 1 (2006): 87–114.

Amorim Neto, Octavio, and Gary W. Cox. “Electoral Institutions, Cleavage Structures, and the Number of Parties.” *American Journal of Political Science* 41 (1997): 149–74.

Arnold, R. Douglas. *Congress and the Bureaucracy: A Theory of Influence*: Yale University Press, New Haven CT, 1980.

Austen-Smith, David, and Jeffrey Banks. “Elections, Coalitions, and Legislative Outcomes.” *The American Political Science Review* 82, no. 2 (1988): 405–22.

Baldez, Lisa, and John M. Carey. “Presidential Agenda Control and Spending Policy: Lessons from General Pinochet’s Constitution.” *American Journal of Political Science* 43, no. 1 (1999): 29–55.

Bambaci, Juliana, Tamara Saront, and Mariano Tommasi. “The Political Economy of Economic Reforms in Argentina.” *The Journal of Policy Reform* 5, no. 2 (2002): 75–88.

Bartels, Larry M. “Resource Allocation in a Presidential Campaign.” *The Journal of Politics* 47, no. 3 (1985): 928–36.

Bartels, Larry M. “Uninformed Votes: Information Effects in Presidential Elections.” *American Journal of Political Science* 40, no. 1 (1996): 194–230.

Bavastro, Roberto. *The Dynamics of Latin American Presidentialism: Government and Opposition in Argentina: 1983–1995*, dissertation, Oxford University (2001).

Beaussier, Anne-Laure. “The Patient Protection and Affordable Care Act: The Victory of Unorthodox Lawmaking.” *Journal of Health Politics, Policy and Law* 37, no. 5 (2012): 741–78.

Becher, Michael. *Presidentialism, Parliamentarism, and Redistribution*. Paper presented at the General Conference of the European Political Science Association, Berlin, Germany, 2012.

Becher, Michael, and Flemming Juul Christiansen. “Dissolution Threats and Legislative Bargaining.” *American Journal of Political Science* 55, no. 4 (2014). DOI: 10.1111/ajps.12146.

Beck, Paul Allen. *Party Politics in America*. Addison Wesley Publishing Company, New York, 1997.

Berry, Christopher R., Barry C. Burden, and William G. Howell. “The President and the Distribution of Federal Spending.” *American Political Science Review* 104, no. 4 (2010): 783–99.

Bonoli, Giuliano. “Political Institutions, Veto Points, and the Process of Welfare State Adaptation.” in Paul Pierson, *The New Politics of the Welfare State*, Oxford University Press (2001): 238–64.

Bonvecchi, Alejandro, and Germán Lodola. “The Dual Logic of Intergovernmental Transfers: Presidents, Governors, and the Politics of Coalition-Building in Argentina.” *Publius: The Journal of Federalism* 41, no. 2 (2011): 179–206.

Bowler, Shaun, David M. Farrell, and Richard S. Katz. *Party Discipline and Parliamentary Government*. The Ohio State University Press, Columbus OH, 1999.

Brady, David W., Hahrie Han, and Jeremy C. Pope. "Primary Elections and Candidate Ideology: Out of Step with the Primary Electorate?" *Legislative Studies Quarterly* 32, no. 1 (2007): 79–105.

Brancati, Dawn. "The Origins and Strengths of Regional Parties." *British Journal of Political Science* 38, no. 1 (2008): 135–59.

Brown, Lawrence D. "The Elements of Surprise: How Health Reform Happened." *Journal of Health Politics, Policy and Law* 36, no. 3 (2011): 419–27.

Browne, Eric C., John P. Frendreis, and Dennis W. Gleiber. "The Process of Cabinet Dissolution: An Exponential Model of Duration and Stability in Western Democracies." *American Journal of Political Science* 30 (1986): 628–50.

Calvo, Ernesto, and Maria Victoria Murillo. "Who Delivers? Partisan Clients in the Argentine Electoral Market." *American Journal of Political Science* 48, no. 4 (2004): 742–57.

Cameron, Charles M. "Studying the Polarized Presidency." *Presidential Studies Quarterly* 32, no. 4 (2002): 647–63.

Campbell, James E. "The Presidential Surge and Its Midterm Decline in Congressional Elections, 1868–1988." *The Journal of Politics* 53, no. 2 (1991): 477–87.

Campbell, James E. "The Presidential Pulse and the 1994 Midterm Congressional Election." *The Journal of Politics* 59, no. 3 (1997): 830–57.

Cheibub, José Antonio. "Minority Governments, Deadlock Situations, and the Survival of Presidential Democracies." *Comparative Political Studies* 35, no. 3 (2002): 284–312.

Cheibub, José Antonio. "Presidentialism, Electoral Identifiability, and Budget Balances in Democratic Systems." *American Political Science Review* 100, no. 3 (2006): 353–68.

Claggett, William, William Flanigan, and Nancy Zingale. "Nationalization of the American Electorate." *American Political Science Review* 78, no. 1 (1984): 77–91.

Cox, Gary W. *The Efficient Secret: The Cabinet and the Development of Political Parties in Victorian England*. Cambridge University Press, 1987.

Cox, Gary W. *Making Votes Count: Strategic Coordination in the World's Electoral Systems*. Cambridge University Press, 1997.

Cox, Gary, and Mathew McCubbins. "The Institutional Determinants of Economic Policy Outcomes." in *Presidents, Parliaments, and Policy*, edited by Stefan Haggard and Mathew McCubbins. Cambridge University Press, New York (2001): 64–104.

Cox, Gary W. "Swing Voters, Core Voters, and Distributive Politics." in *Political Representation*, edited by Ian Shapiro, Susan Stokes, Elisabeth Jean Wood and Alexander Kirschner, Cambridge University Press, 2009: 342–357.

Crisp, Brian F., Santiago Olivella, and Joshua D. Potter. "Party-System Nationalization and the Scope of Public Policy the Importance of Cross-District Constituency Similarity." *Comparative Political Studies* 46, no. 4 (2013): 431–56.

Crowe, Edward W. "Cross-Voting in the British House of Commons: 1945–1974." *The Journal of Politics* 42, no. 2 (1980): 487–510.

Depauw, Sam, and Shane Martin. "Legislative Party Discipline and Cohesion in Comparative Perspective." In *Intra-party Politics and Coalition Governments*, edited by Daniela Gianneti and Kenneth Benoit, Routledge Press (2009): 103–20.

Diermeier, Daniel, and Timothy J. Feddersen. "Cohesion in Legislatures and the Vote of Confidence Procedure." *American Political Science Review* 92, no. 3 (1998): 611–21.

Dillinger, William R., and Steven Benjamin Webb. *Fiscal Management in Federal Democracies: Argentina and Brazil*. Vol. 2121: World Bank Publications, 1999.

Dixit, Avinash, and John Londregan. "The Determinants of Success of Special Interests in Redistributive Politics." *Journal of Politics* 58 (1996): 1132–55.

Eaton, Kent. "The Logic of Congressional Delegation: Explaining Argentine Economic Reform." *Latin American Research Review* 36, no. 2 (2001a): 97–117.

Eaton, Kent. "Political Obstacles to Decentralization: Evidence from Argentina and the Philippines." *Development and Change* 32, no. 1 (2001b): 101–27.

Epstein, Leon D. *Political parties in the American Mold*. University of Wisconsin Press, Madison WI, 1989.

Erikson, Robert S. "The Puzzle of Midterm Loss." *The Journal of Politics* 50, no. 4 (1988): 1011–29.

Gerring, John, Strom C. Thacker, and Carola Moreno. "Are Parliamentary Systems Better?" *Comparative Political Studies* 42, no. 3 (2009): 327–59.

Gervasoni, Carlos. "A Rentier Theory of Subnational Regimes." *World Politics* 62, no. 2 (2010): 302–40.

Gibson, Edward L. "The Populist Road to Market Reform: Policy and Electoral Coalitions in Mexico and Argentina." *World Politics* 49, no. 3 (1997): 339–70.

Gibson, Edward L., and Ernesto Calvo. "Federalism and Low-Maintenance Constituencies: Territorial Dimensions of Economic Reform in Argentina." *Studies in Comparative International Development* 35, no. 3 (2000): 32–55.

Giraudy, Agustina. "The Distributive Politics of Emergency Employment Programs in Argentina (1993–2002)." *Latin American Research Review* 42, no. 2 (2007): 33–55.

Glass, David P. "Evaluating Presidential Candidates: Who Focuses on Their Personal Attributes?" *Public Opinion Quarterly* 49, no. 4 (1985): 517–34.

Grofman, Bernard, Thomas Brunell, and Janet Campagna. "Distinguishing between the Effects of Swing Ratio and Bias on Outcomes in the US Electoral College, 1900–1992." *Electoral Studies* 16, no. 4 (1997): 471–87.

Hacker, Jacob S. "The Road to Somewhere: Why Health Reform Happened." *Perspectives on Politics* 8, no. 3 (2010): 861–76.

Haggard, Stephan, and Matthew D. McCubbins. *Presidents, Parliaments, and Policy*. Cambridge University Press, 2001.

Hallerberg, Mark, and Patrik Marier. "Executive Authority, the Personal Vote, and Budget Discipline in Latin American and Caribbean Countries." *American Journal of Political Science* 48, no. 3 (2004): 571–87.

Hicken, Allen, and Heather Stoll. "Presidents and Parties: How Presidential Elections Shape Coordination in Legislative Elections." *Comparative Political Studies* 44, no. 7 (2011): 854–83.

Howell, William G., Saul P. Jackman, and Jon C. Rogowski. *The Wartime President: Executive Influence and the Nationalizing Politics of Threat*. University of Chicago Press, 2013.

Huber, Evelyne, Charles Ragin, and John D. Stephens. "Social Democracy, Christian Democracy, Constitutional Structure, and the Welfare State." *American Journal of Sociology* 99, no. 3 (1993): 711–49.

Hunter, Wendy. *The Transformation of the Workers' Party in Brazil, 1989–2009*. Cambridge University Press, 2010.

Hutchcroft, Paul D. "Centralization and Decentralization in Administration and Politics: Assessing Territorial Dimensions of Authority and Power." *Governance* 14, no. 1 (2001): 23–53.

Immergut, Ellen M. *Health Politics: Interests and Institutions in Western Europe*. Cambridge University Press Archive, 1992.

Jones, Mark P. "Evaluating Argentina's Presidential Democracy: 1983–1995." *Presidentialism and Democracy in Latin America*, edited by Scott Mainwaring and Matthew Shugart. Cambridge University Press, 1997: 259–99.

Jones, Mark P. "Electoral Laws and the Effective Number of Candidates in Presidential Elections." *The Journal of Politics* 61, no. 1 (1999): 171–84.

Jones, Mark P., and Scott Mainwaring. "The Nationalization of Parties and Party Systems: an Empirical Measure and an Application to the Americas." *Party Politics* 9, no. 2 (2003): 139–66.

Kiewiet, D. Roderick, and Mathew D. McCubbins. "Presidential Influence on Congressional Appropriations Decisions." *American Journal of Political Science* 32, no. 3 (1988): 713–36.

Kingdon, John W., and James A. Thurber. *Agendas, Alternatives, and Public Policies*. Vol. 45: Little, Brown and Co, Boston, 1984.

Kriner, Douglas L., and Andrew Reeves. "The Influence of Federal Spending on Presidential Elections." *American Political Science Review* 106, no. 2 (2012): 348–66.

Kriner, Douglas, and Andrew Reeves. "The Electoral College and Presidential Particularism." *Boston University Law Review* 94 (2014): 741.

Kriner, Douglas L., and Andrew Reeves. "Presidential Particularism and Divide-the-Dollar Politics." *American Political Science Review* 109, no. 1 (2015).

Larcinese, Valentino, Leonzio Rizzo, and Cecilia Testa. "Allocating the US Federal Budget to the States: The Impact of the President." *Journal of Politics* 68, no. 2 (2006): 447–56.

Levitsky, Steven. "From Labor Politics to Machine Politics: The Transformation of Party-Union Linkages in Argentine Peronism, 1983–1999." *Latin American Research Review* 38, no. 3 (2003): 3–36.

Levitt, Steven D., and James M. Snyder Jr. "Political Parties and the Distribution of Federal Outlays." *American Journal of Political Science* 39, no. 4 (1995): 958–80.

Linz, Juan J. "The Perils of Presidentialism." *Journal of Democracy* 1, no. 1 (1990): 51–69.

Lijphart, Arend. *Patterns of Democracy: Government Forms and Performance in Thirty-Six Countries*. Yale University Press, New Haven CT, 1999.

Lizzeri, Alessandro, and Nicola Persico. "The Provision of Public Goods under Alternative Electoral Incentives." *American Economic Review* 91, no. 1 (2001): 225–39.

Llanos, Mariana. *Privatization and Democracy in Argentina: An Analysis of President-Congress Relations*. Palgrave, London, 2002.

Lupu, Noam. "Brand Dilution and the Breakdown of Political Parties in Latin America." *World Politics* 66, no. 4 (2014): 561–602.

Mainwaring, Scott. "Presidentialism, Multipartism, and Democracy the Difficult Combination." *Comparative Political Studies* 26, no. 2 (1993): 198–228.

Mainwaring, Scott, and Matthew Soberg Shugart. *Presidentialism and Democracy in Latin America*. Cambridge University Press, 1997.

Manow, Philip. "Germany: Cooperative Federalism and the Overgrazing of the Fiscal Commons." in *Federalism and the Welfare State*, edited by Herbert Obinger, Stephan Leibfried, and Frances Castles. Cambridge University Press (2005): 222–62.

Marmor, Theodore R. *The Politics of Medicare*. Transaction Publishers, New Brunswick NJ, 1970.

Marmor, Theodore R., and Jonathan Oberlander. "The Health Bill Explained at Last." *New York Review of Books* (2010): 1–9.

Mayer, William G., and Andrew Busch. *The Front-Loading Problem in Presidential Nominations*. Brookings Institution Press, Washington DC, 2003.

McCarty, Nolan M. "Presidential Pork: Executive Veto Power and Distributive Politics." *American Political Science Review* 94, no. 1 (2000): 117–29.

Molinelli, N. Guillermo. *Presidentes Y Congresos En Argentina: Mitos Y Realidades.* Grupo Editor Latinoamericano, 1991.

Muller, Edward N. "Democracy, Economic Development, and Income Inequality." *American Sociological Review* 53 (1988): 50–68.

Norton, Philip. "Dissent in the British House of Commons: Rejoinder to Franklin, Baxter, Jordan." *Legislative Studies Quarterly* 12 (1987): 143–52.

Nzelibe, Jide. "The Fable of the Nationalist President and Parochial Congress." *UCLA Law Review* 53 (2006).

Oberlander, Jonathan. *The Political Life of Medicare.* University of Chicago Press, 2003.

Oxhorn, Philip. "Social Inequality, Civil Society and the Limits of Citizenship in Latin America." in *What Justice? Whose Justice? Fighting for Fairness in Latin America,* edited by Susan Eckstein and Timothy Wickham-Crowley. University of California Press, Berkeley CA (2003): 35–63.

Pérez-Liñán, Aníbal. "Evaluating Presidential Runoff Elections." *Electoral Studies* 25, no. 1 (2006): 129–46.

Pérez-Liñán, Aníbal. *Presidential Impeachment and the New Political Instability in Latin America.* Cambridge University Press, 2007.

Persson, Torsten, and Guido Tabellini. "The Size and Scope of Government:: Comparative Politics with Rational Politicians." *European Economic Review* 43, no. 4 (1999): 699–735.

Persson, Torsten, and Guido Enrico Tabellini. *The Economic Effects of Constitutions.* MIT Press, 2003.

Persson, Torsten, Gerard Roland, and Guido Tabellini. "Separation of Powers and Political Accountability." *The Quarterly Journal of Economics* 112, no. 4 (1997): 1163–202.

Persson, Torsten, Gerard Roland, and Guido Tabellini. "Comparative Politics and Public Finance." *Journal of Political Economy* 108, no. 6 (2000): 1121–61.

Przeworski, Adam. "Institutions Matter?" *Government and Opposition* 39, no. 4 (2004): 527–40.

Rae, Douglas W. "The Consequences of Electoral Laws." Yale University Press, New haven CT, 1971.

Remmer, Karen, and Erik Wibbels. "The Subnational Politics of Economic Adjustment Provincial Politics and Fiscal Performance in Argentina." *Comparative Political Studies* 33, no. 4 (2000): 419–51.

Rickard, Stephanie J. "Electoral Systems, Voters' Interests and Geographic Dispersion." *British Journal of Political Science* 42, no. 4 (2012): 855–77.

Rodden, Jonathan, and Erik Wibbels. "Dual Accountability and the Nationalization of Party Competition: Evidence from Four Federations." *Party Politics* 17, no. 5 (2011): 629–53.

Rogers, Melissa Ziegler. "National Leverage: Partisan Constraints on Reform in Sub-National Bureaucracies." *Revista Sul-Americana de Ciência Política* 1, no. 1 (2013): 112–37.

Rogers, Melissa, and Dong-wook Lee. *Electoral Geography, Inequality, and Representation.* Manuscript, Claremont Graduate University CA, 2015.

Rubio, Delia Ferreira, and Matteo Goretti. "When the President Governs Alone." in *Executive Decree Authority,* edited by Matthew Shugart and John Carey. Cambridge University Press (1998): 33–61.

Saiegh, Sebastián. "The 'Sub-National'connection: Legislative Coalitions, Cross-Voting and Policymaking in Argentina." in *The Argentine Crisis at the Turn of the Millennium: Causes, Consequences, and Explanations,* edited by Flavia Fiorucci and Marcus Klein. Aksant Academic Publishers, Amsterdam (2004).

Saiegh, Sebastián M. *Ruling by Statute: How Uncertainty and Vote Buying Shape Law-making*. Cambridge University Press, 2011.

Samuels, David J. "Presidentialized Parties the Separation of Powers and Party Organization and Behavior." *Comparative Political Studies* 35, no. 4 (2002): 461–83.

Samuels, David. "Presidentialism and Accountability for the Economy in Comparative Perspective." *American Political Science Review* 98, no. 3 (2004): 425–36.

Shaw, Daron R. "The Methods Behind the Madness: Presidential Electoral College Strategies, 1988–1996." *The Journal of Politics* 61, no. 4 (1999): 893–913.

Shugart, Matthew Soberg, and John M. Carey. *Presidents and Assemblies: Constitutional Design and Electoral Dynamics*. Cambridge University Press, 1992.

Shugart, Matthew Soberg. "The Electoral Cycle and Institutional Sources of Divided Presidential Government." *American Political Science Review* 89, no. 2 (1995): 327–43.

Shugart, Matthew Soberg. "Presidentialism, Parliamentarism, and the Provision of Collective Goods in Less-Developed Countries." *Constitutional Political Economy* 10, no. 1 (1999): 53–88.

Sieberer, Ulrich. "Party Unity in Parliamentary Democracies: A Comparative Analysis." *The Journal of Legislative Studies* 12, no. 2 (2006): 150–78.

Solt, Frederick. 2014. *The Standardized World Income Inequality Database*. Working paper. SWIID Version 5.0, October 2014.

Steinmo, Sven, and Jon Watts. "It's the Institutions, Stupid! Why Comprehensive National Health Insurance Always Fails in America." *Journal of Health Politics, Policy and Law* 20, no. 2 (1995): 329–72.

Stokes, Susan C. *Mandates and Democracy: Neoliberalism by Surprise in Latin America*. Cambridge University Press, 2001.

Stratmann, Thomas, and Joshua Wojnilower. *Presidential Particularism*. Manuscript, George Washington University (2015).

Strøm, Kaare. "Delegation and Accountability in Parliamentary Democracies." *European Journal of Political Research* 37, no. 3 (2000): 261–90.

Strömberg, David. "How the Electoral College Influences Campaigns and Policy: The Probability of Being Florida." *The American Economic Review* 98, no. 3 (2008): 769–807.

Swank, Duane. *Global Capital, Political Institutions, and Policy Change in Developed Welfare States*. Cambridge University Press, 2002.

Tommasi, Mariano. "Crisis, Political Institutions and Policy Reform." Hoover Institute, Stanford CT, 2005.

Tsebelis, George. "Conditional Agenda-Setting and Decision-Making inside the European Parliament." *The Journal of Legislative Studies* 1, no. 1 (1995): 65–93.

Tsebelis, George. "Veto Players and Institutional Analysis." *Governance* 13, no. 4 (2002): 441–74.

Weldon, Jeffrey. "The Political Sources of Presidencialismo in Mexico." in *Presidentialism and Democracy in Latin America*, edited by Scott Mainwaring and Matthew Shugart. Cambridge University Press (1997): 225–58.

White, Joseph. "Muddling through the Muddled Middle." *Journal of Health Politics Policy and Law* 36, no. 3 (2011): 443.

Wood, B. Dan. *The Myth of Presidential Representation*. Cambridge University Press, 2009.

Woon, Jonathan, and Jeremy C. Pope. "Made in Congress? Testing the Electoral Implications of Party Ideological Brand Names." *The Journal of Politics* 70, no. 3 (2008): 823–36.

7 Inequality and Territorial Politics

Summary and Implications

Summary of the Argument

At a fundamental level, redistribution is an outcome of a process of bargaining among politicians. Of course, structural economic concerns affect the choice set of those politicians. However, nations under similar economic circumstances have made wildly different policy choices. This divergence is in large part explained by differences in politics.

I have argued that politicians make different distributive choices because their political distributive logics are distinct. This logic is fundamentally shaped by institutional design. Under certain institutions, politicians have stronger reasons to deliver resources home. In others they are also appealing to a subset of the population, but their constituency is not so rooted in geography. Given these basic constituency ties, log-rolling to create national policy will be varied. In territorial systems, the logs are parceled out according to districts. In centripetal systems, the logs are parceled out to broad social groups regardless of location. These dynamics are reinforced by the greater difficulty in changing the status quo and forming a coherent majority coalition for reform in those fragmented, territorial systems.

At a base level, then, territorial institutions may reduce the salience of and broad demand for national level redistributive efforts. Even while people recognize growing inequality, as they certainly have in the USA and Argentina in recent decades, this latent societal concern with inequality does not translate easily into transformative change. Thus the USA might have lower redistribution than that of Germany not because Americans have a unique culture or radically different views toward government's role in economic opportunity and access, but because their coalition-building dynamics are different. Leftist US politicians may praise the distributive logic of social insurance systems in European social democracies while at the same time recognizing that pork is what gets them reelected. Leftist ideologues in Argentina must check their ideology at the door as well, and act as good agents of their provincial principals by bringing transfers home. In both the USA and Argentina, the designs of federalism, territorial electoral rules, and presidentialism all reinforce this logic.

Related to this, I have argued that territorial institutions fragment power and place vetoes in the hands of territorial actors. The status quo bias of federalism and presidentialism due to multiple constitutional veto actors, in particular, has been frequently recognized as contributing to lower redistributive effort. Territorial electoral rules have been recognized primarily for their ideological fragmentation of parties and thus their limiting of the extent to which parties will agree to change the (non-redistributive) status quo. I suggest territorial politics provide an important explanation for why constitutional and partisan veto actors' preferences diverge. Representing the interests of regions provides an added distributive complexity to conflict on the left–right dimension.

I have also argued that interregional differences in income and economic structure are important sources of divergence in preferences among territorial actors. The provinces of Argentina vary in the extreme in their economic productivity. The policy interests of the Buenos Aires region, while by no means unified, are certainly dramatically different than the policy interests of rural Formosa or La Rioja. This is one reason why the vetoes in territorial systems are activated—the actors have different preferences—and redistributive reform is thus less likely. Moreover, where policy compromise may not be possible on policy grounds alone, regional transfers and pork offer bargaining chips to agreement.

Territorial institutions also fragment the latent national coalition that would benefit from redistributive reform, both organizationally and ideologically. According to Gerring et al. (2005), territorial institutions increase the coordination problems that inhibit national policymaking. Federalism provides an obvious example. In federal systems, groups pressing for redistribution must organize across sub-national governments with different policy environments and must coordinate to influence national policy. This is certainly a logistical challenge. Perhaps more importantly, territorial institutions also increase social choice problems in establishing what people prefer to the status quo. Territorial institutions inform different incentives among different groups and this is crucially shaped by interregional differences in wealth. Again, in federal systems, poor groups in rich regions may be better off pursuing policy change at the sub-national level. Poor groups in poor regions need the rich regions to chip in to a national program. These federal political divides fragment the ideological solidarity of the redistributive coalition (Beramendi 2012).

Implications

The discussion above has broad implications for the political economy of inequality. First, it points to more reasons why some nations devote little effort toward redistribution. If we understand the logic of politicians, it is not so surprising that certain societies devote considerable efforts to distribution and logrolling at the national level but this has little effect on the interpersonal income distribution. Pork and regional transfers satisfy one political logic and redistributive tax and expenditure systems satisfy a different one.

Accordingly, this analysis suggests that territorial politics may stand in the way of class-based politics. Clearly the distributive concerns between rich and poor, and lower and upper classes, exist in territorial systems such as the USA and Argentina. However, these conflicts do not "fit" well into these nations' political institutions. Concerns with disparities in interregional resources are much more central to the logics of these systems. And, broadly speaking, these nations' systems do a lot to equilibrate the access to resources across regions. These regional transfers and pork may not even the playing field or result in regional convergence, but they spread resources across the nation that might otherwise be concentrated in just a few places.

Related to this, the discussions in the book have suggested that most research on inequality and redistribution too readily assumes that interpersonal inequality is the dominant cleavage in society. I would agree that class politics are important in every nation. However, territorial interests are also important in many nations, and these interests are reinforced by certain political institutions. By failing to focus on the territorial cleavages and the territorial logic to political distribution, we may fail to see an important reason why inequality is so little addressed in some nations.

Research on the politics of inequality has generally left aside the debate on the territorial incentives of political institutions. In broad terms, I suggest that institutions orient competition either around territorial politics or around socio-economic politics on the basis of class or some other identity. This is an important matter for distributive issues of all kinds, including those that reach across groups with different incomes. It is also important for the formation of coalitions at the national level, including those formed within the party system.

If this assessment is right, then scholars should be looking more at the territorial incentives of institutions, and at territorial distributive conflicts, for their effects on redistributive policy (Beramendi et al. 2015). Importantly, however, this assessment also strongly suggests that we should examine the origin of territorial institutions to see if these institutions were designed precisely to manage conflicts over distribution and redistribution.

Unanswered Questions

The broad scope and limited empirical analysis of the book left open many questions for future research. Some of the propositions discussed here will be difficult to test empirically because of a fundamental concern about the endogeneity of institutions. If federalism, localized electoral systems, and presidentialism are chosen precisely to limit redistribution, statistical analysis showing the relationship between the two would not offer much insight. In this very early assessment of the territorial effects on redistribution, I preferred to focus on the theoretical development and the plausibility of the argument.

This book is an early step in identifying additional mechanisms whereby territorial political institutions are associated with lower redistributive effort. The two most prominent mechanisms to explain this outcome—veto players and majority fragmentation—tell part but not all of the story. An important component is evaluating how politicians influence the nature of government distribution in their interest. If territorially targeted resources better fit the logic of political systems, then it is not surprising that some systems emphasize these resources above centralized redistributive policies.

It is important to emphasize that this is a nascent effort to identify alternative reasons for the common empirical finding that certain institutions that I identify as territorial are associated with lower redistribution. I have not demonstrated an empirical strategy that can isolate the particular mechanisms under focus here in relation to redistribution. Instead, I have drawn out theoretical reasons why politicians have incentives to focus on distributive issues other than national level income redistribution, and have provided country case examples. I have also demonstrated that these institutions are not just associated with lower spending overall but are also strongly associated with territorial distributions, whether through spending categories associated with pork or interregional transfers. To put variables for federalism, territorial electoral systems, and presidentialism into a regression analysis to predict redistribution would replicate the efforts of many others and would tell us little about why these systems have this effect.

My approach to this book has also been motivated by a fundamental concern with endogeneity. That is, the political institutions of focus here are selected precisely because they emphasize the interests of territories over the nation and because they fragment power. If founding politicians are concerned about over-centralization or the power of the citizen majority more generally, they might reasonably choose these institutions to avoid an interventionist national government. From this perspective, territorial institutions may be chosen because of existing concerns with inequality and a desire to avoid redistribution (Aghion et al. 2004; Boix 1999). Alternatively, and perhaps observationally equivalent, territorial institutions are designed because of existing territorial heterogeneity of preferences that imply lack of agreement on shared resources (Beramendi 2012). Centripetal institutions are likely selected according to a different distributive logic.

If the institutionally determined locus of political bargaining, whether on territories or social groups, is endogenous to initial distributive conditions then standard econometric approaches will offer little satisfying causal analysis. To show that territorial institutions redistribute less and that centripetal institutions redistribute more may simply show that these societies face different problems with different solutions, and that the institutions are a mere formalization of these dynamics.

Given the concern with endogeneity, one might argue it is of little value to discuss ways these institutions are less compatible with redistributive effort. I disagree with this view because to understand whether institutions were chosen based on distributive conflicts, we first need to know exactly how and whether they are linked to distributive outcomes. This entails a thorough examination of the institutional logic behind why politicians would vigorously pursue redistribution in some systems and not so vigorously in others.

If the territorial cleavage matters to politics, a next step should be to examine the foundations of interregional differences and how they inform political power in a nation. Related research on endogenous institutions has shown the importance of economic geography both to the design of political institutions and, ultimately, income inequality (Sokoloff and Engerman 2000; Sokoloff and Zolt 2005). Like most research on income inequality, the focus has tended to be on how economic geography can lead to inequality among people and how this influences the design of political institutions. However, economic geography surely relates even more directly to the spatial distribution of income in a nation (Beramendi and Rogers 2015). Both types of inequality (interpersonal and inter-regional) may be very important to the distribution of power, and the design of political institutions.

An important implication of this research is: if territorial institutions limit efforts to redistribute income, has this been a purposeful choice of institutional designers and adopters? Do constitutional designers understand that linking politicians to their home may limit the possibility for transformative national policy change? Certainly, it is plausible that designers of federal systems kept regional inequality in mind when drawing up the powers and rights of different governments, both in the policymaking and fiscal realms (Bolton and Roland 1997; Beramendi 2012). It is less clear whether institutional designers sought the fragmenting effects of localizing electoral rules and presidentialism. At the same time, these institutional choices reflected entrenched interests and have in many cases "locked in" regional and interpersonal inequalities over time. An historical approach could illuminate whether regional inequality was a motivator in the design of some systems (the USA is suggested as an example in Beramendi and Wibbels 2010) while interpersonal inequality weighed more heavily on the minds of others.

Extensions

The theoretical links between territorial politics and redistribution offer several fruitful avenues for future research. I offer just a few in this section that come easily to mind.

The discussion in the book left many questions about how parties deal with inequality unaddressed. In many political systems, the salience of inequality is unquestioned. Parties on the left see reducing income inequality as their primary policy goal, although their views on how this should be accomplished may differ. Parties on the right consider redistribution as inimical to other important economic goals, such as economic growth, innovation, and entrepreneurship.

Conflict over regional distributions of income is less commonly a structuring cleavage within the party system. However, many obvious examples show issues of regional representation can be central. Belgium, Spain, and the United Kingdom, to name a few, feature parties that represent the economic interests of regions, in part through expressing preferences about their national governments' redistributive policies. Regional parties of this type are also present in the cases of Argentina and Germany.

Preferences for interpersonal redistribution are typically the structuring ideological cleavage upon which parties form. Thus parties tend to be internally homogenous on preferences for redistribution. National parties, moreover, draw representation from all over a nation. Of course, all national parties tend to have regional variation in their levels of support but tend to draw significant support from all parts. Within the party are representatives from places with quite different needs and preferences from those of the nation as a whole. Thus, parties typically bargain for changes in the distributive system across party lines. Changes that impact the regional distribution of income, however, should divide even disciplined ideologically cohesive parties. This creates a very different bargaining scenario between parties than within them (Bawn and Rosenbluth 2006).

Regionalism within the party system is also an important dynamic of relevance here. All else equal, we can broadly expect that regional parties compete more effectively under territorialized institutions, especially federalism (Brancati 2008). While regional parties certainly bring into focus the distributive claims of particular regions, they may also take regional concerns from an internal party distributive concern, as I discussed above, into one that is debated across parties. Whether regional dynamics are within parties or across them is important if for no other reason than the fact that mechanisms of party discipline work best within national parties to encourage policy change at the national level (Gerring et al. 2005).

Territorial constituencies may also shed light on a vexing question in the research on the political economy of inequality—if veto players are crucial to blocking redistribution, why do coalition parliamentary governments redistribute more than single party parliamentary governments (Crepaz and Moser 2004; Milesi-Feretti et al. 2002)? One possible answer is that coalitions are more likely to represent the median voter (Powell and Vanberg 2000). Crepaz and Moser suggest this requires a distinction between competitive veto points and collective veto points. Competitive, typically constitutional, veto points pit actors against each other. Parties in a coalition, however, are collective veto actors with heterogeneous interests that nonetheless share an interest in retaining government control. To keep government together, they are willing to spend more to accommodate the interests of all parties in the coalition.

Territorial politics offers another logic for this same phenomenon. In most systems with coalition governments, institutional setups have diluted the incentives to deliver territorial goods. PR and parliamentarism, as discussed throughout the book, encourage party homogenization, including by leftist parties on issues of redistribution (Becher 2012). Electoral rules that favor bipartism, on the other hand, such as SMDs, give single parties great authority but also result in heterogeneous internal coalitions. Moreover, they provide impetus to target localities, which undermines enthusiasm for bargaining via centralized redistributive reform. Although the eventual outcome may be the same, i.e., that majoritarian electoral rules hinder the chances of leftist parties, the reasons why are somewhat different than those described in, for example, Iversen and Soskice's (2006) class-based analysis.

Research on political institutions frequently recognizes that no institution operates in isolation. For example, federalism, localizing electoral rules, and presidentialism can all encourage territorialism within a party system, whereas unitarism, party-centric electoral rules, and parliamentarism can all dilute territorialism. It is impossible to know, however, to what extent the individual institutions territorialize the parties or offset the territorial effects of other institutions. Canada provides a reasonable example—does federalism or plurality elections encourage the territorialism in their party system? To what extent does parliamentarism offset those effects?

An interesting research idea by Franzese and Nooruddin (2004) laid the groundwork for some of this thinking. They argue that we should think about political systems according to the concept of the "effective number of constituencies." In territorial systems, the number of constituencies, as structured by electoral districts, presidential election districts, and federal districts, all boost the number of constituencies that play a role in national decision making. Highly centralized or centripetal systems, on the other hand, come close to having one effective constituency, the nation. This concept might form the base for a more coherent idea and measure of the effects of territorial institutions on national politics.

The theoretical development of the book is primarily focused on political institutions and how they highlight territorial distribution and territorial income cleavages. Although I discuss the importance of interregional inequality in comparative context and how it may influence the allocation of government spending, the topic is relatively underexplored in this analysis. In related research, I examine the direct effects of interregional inequality and how these disparities are exacerbated or diffused by political institutions (Lee and Rogers 2015). Importantly, we take an econometric approach in this research and make special efforts to address endogeneity. In this research, we find that, independent of institutions, higher interregional inequality is associated with lower government spending and redistribution. We suggest that regions that do not benefit from government spending use their constitutional power to block or limit government intervention.

Interregional inequality may shape the operation of territorial institutions in very important ways. One way suggested above is that interregional inequality increases conflict in the political system and makes agreement on spending and other policies less likely. This has implications for redistribution, but also for democratic stability more broadly (Rogers 2015). Another way interregional inequality may matter is if it creates conditions favorable for clientelism. Dixit and Londregan (1996) and Calvo and Murillo (2004), among others, have argued that poor individuals and poor regions should be more easily "bought" in patronage relations. If high interregional inequality implies that there are poor regions that are more easily bought, then it may encourage political clientelism. This idea is plausible in the case of Argentina, as suggested in the case discussions in Chapters 4, 5, and 6. Clientelism is certainly an important component of the interregional bargaining and intergovernmental transfers that has not been widely researched.

Territorial politics and interregional inequality may also be relevant to the broader debate on democracy and redistribution. Important recent research in the Romer-Meltzer-Richard tradition argues that the decision to democratize depends in large part on the distribution of income in society (Acemoglu and Robinson 2006; Boix 2003). Elites will only democratize if they can feel confident their wealth will not be expropriated and citizens will only accept democracy under the conditions that they gain income from the deal.[1] With these political economy of inequality explanations of democratization, again, the national interpersonal inequality emphasis is the focus. "Elites" are divorced from territory— the rich are national representatives.

However, I would argue that territorial politics is central to democracy and the effort of elites to limit contestation in several ways. For example, Albertus and Menaldo (2014) and Menaldo (2011) argue that autocrats and anti-democratic elites put in place restrictions to democracy that limit the scope of the state and its capacity to redistribute. The institutions that they point to as democracy-constraining are precisely those that favor the territorial principle—bicameralism and malapportionment. In related work, Beramendi and Rogers (2015) argue that interregional inequality structures competition among elites. If the economic endowments are highly concentrated in one region, elites are more likely to collude to create barriers to democratic competition and thus limit the scope and capacity of the state to redistribute. If regional endowments are more dispersed, however, elites must compete for influence in national politics and democratic competition is a useful mechanism to institutionalize this competition.

At a broad level, territorial politics is relevant to redistributive politics. Future research can bring this relationship further into the spotlight.

Note

1 For a critique of this argument, see Haggard and Kaufman (2012).

References

Acemoglu, Daron, and James A. Robinson. *Economic Origins of Dictatorship and Democracy*. Cambridge University Press, 2006.

Aghion, Philippe, Alberto Alesina, and Francesco Trebbi. "Endogenous Political Institutions." *The Quarterly Journal of Economics* 119, no. 2 (2004): 565–611.

Albertus, Michael, and Victor Menaldo. "Gaming Democracy: Elite Dominance During Transition and the Prospects for Redistribution." *British Journal of Political Science* 44, no. 3 (2014): 575–603.

Bawn, Kathleen, and Frances Rosenbluth. "Short Versus Long Coalitions: Electoral Accountability and the Size of the Public Sector." *American Journal of Political Science* 50, no. 2 (2006): 251–65.

Becher, Michael. *Presidentialism, Parliamentarism, and Redistribution*. Paper presented at the General Conference of the European Political Science Association, Berlin, Germany, 2012.

Beramendi, Pablo. *The Political Geography of Inequality: Regions and Redistribution*. Cambridge University Press, 2012.

Beramendi, Pablo, and Melissa Rogers. *Geography, Inequality, and Capacity*. Paper presented at the workshop on Conflict and Inequality, ETH Zurich, April 16–18, 2015.

Beramendi, Pablo, and Erik Wibbels. *Foundational Bargains: Distributive Conflicts and Representation in Federations*. Paper presented at the Meeting of the American Political Science Association, Washington, 2010.

Beramendi, Pablo, Melissa Rogers, and Alberto Diaz-Cayeros. *Barriers to the Left Turn: Distributive Tensions in Developing Federations*. Duke University, Claremont Graduate University, Stanford University, 2015.

Boix, Carles. "Setting the Rules of the Game: The Choice of Electoral Systems in Advanced Democracies." *American Political Science Review* 93, no. 3 (1999): 609–24.

Boix, Carles. *Democracy and Redistribution.* Cambridge University Press, 2003.

Bolton, Patrick, and Gerard Roland. "The Breakup of Nations: A Political Economy Analysis." *The Quarterly Journal of Economics* 112, no. 4 (1997): 1057–90.

Brancati, Dawn. "The Origins and Strengths of Regional Parties." *British Journal of Political Science* 38, no. 1 (2008): 135–59.

Calvo, Ernesto, and Maria Victoria Murillo. "Who Delivers? Partisan Clients in the Argentine Electoral Market." *American Journal of Political Science* 48, no. 4 (2004): 742–57.

Crepaz, Markus, and Ann Moser. "The Impact of Collective and Competitive Veto Points on Public Expenditures in the Global Age." *Comparative Political Studies* 37, no. 3 (2004): 259–85.

Dixit, Avinash, and John Londregan. "The Determinants of Success of Special Interests in Redistributive Politics." *Journal of Politics* 58, no. 4 (1996): 1132–55.

Franzese, Robert J., and Irfan Nooruddin. *The Effective Constituency in (Re) Distributive Politics: Alternative Bases of Democratic Representation, Geographic Versus Partisan.* Manuscript, Social Science Research Network (2004).

Gerring, John, Strom C. Thacker, and Carola Moreno. "Centripetal Democratic Governance: A Theory and Global Inquiry." *American Political Science Review* 99, no. 4 (2005): 567–81.

Haggard, Stephan, and Robert R. Kaufman. "Inequality and Regime Change: Democratic Transitions and the Stability of Democratic Rule." *American Political Science Review* 106, no. 3 (2012): 495–516.

Iversen, Torben, and David Soskice. "Electoral Institutions and the Politics of Coalitions: Why Some Democracies Redistribute More Than Others." *American Political Science Review* 100, no. 2 (2006): 165–81.

Lee, Dong-wook, and Melissa Rogers. *Comparing Inequalities: Regional and Interpersonal Income Disparity, Institutions, and Government Spending.* Manuscript, Claremont Graduate University CA, 2015.

Menaldo, Victor A. "Democracy, Elite-Bias and Redistribution in Latin America." *Available at SSRN 1820866* (2011).

Milesi-Ferretti, Gian Maria, Roberto Perotti, and Massimo Rostagno. "Electoral Systems and Public Spending." *The Quarterly Journal of Economics* 117, no. 2 (2002): 609–57.

Powell Jr., G., Bingham and Georg S. Vanberg. "Election Laws, Disproportionality and Median Correspondence: Implications for Two Visions of Democracy." *British Journal of Political Science* 30, no. 3 (2000): 383–411.

Rogers, Melissa. "Inequality and Democratic Representation in Latin America: Regional and Interpersonal Effects on Government Spending." in *The Quality of Democracy in Latin America Today*, edited by Joe Fowacker and Delores Treviso. Lynne Reinner, Boulder CO, (2015).

Sokoloff, Kenneth L., and Stanley L. Engerman. "History Lessons: Institutions, Factors Endowments, and Paths of Development in the New World." *The Journal of Economic Perspectives* 14, no. 3 (2000): 217–32.

Sokoloff, Kenneth L., and Eric M. Zolt. "Inequality and Taxation: Evidence from the Americas on How Inequality May Influence Tax Institutions." *Tax Law Review* 59, no. 2 (2005).

Index

For Product Safety Concerns and Information please contact our EU
representative GPSR@taylorandfrancis.com
Taylor & Francis Verlag GmbH, Kaufingerstraße 24, 80331 München, Germany

www.ingramcontent.com/pod-product-compliance
Ingram Content Group UK Ltd.
Pitfield, Milton Keynes, MK11 3LW, UK
UKHW021959180926
475701UK00003B/106

* 9 7 8 1 0 3 2 2 4 2 6 6 8 *